Japanese in Action

D0862392

Chinese In Action

"

Japanese
in Action

An Unorthodox Approach
to the Spoken Language
and the People Who Speak It

by JACK SEWARD

Revised Edition

WEATHERHILL
New York • Tokyo

First published, 1968 (Japan), 1969 (U.S.)
Fourth paperback printing, 1981
Second edition, 1983
Fifth printing, 1990

Published by Weatherhill, Inc., New York, with editorial offices at
Tanko-Weatherhill, Inc., 8–3 Nibancho, Chiyoda-ku, Tokyo 102,
Japan. Protected by copyright under terms of the International
Copyright Union; all rights reserved. Printed and first published in
Japan.

LCC Card No. 68-55570   *ISBN 0-8348-0033-0*

Contents

for Mother

Introduction

I have written this book both for students of the Japanese language and for others having a general interest in Japan and its people.

For the latter, I have included a considerable number of narrative incidents—some humorous and others not—that should offer an insight into the character and fundamental attitudes of the Japanese people, as well as of certain of those many foreigners who have worked—and played —in Japan since the end of World War II in September, 1945.

For students of the language I have offered advice about: 1) how to study the Japanese language, 2) how to derive enjoyment from these studies, and 3) how to utilize what they learn. In this teaching aspect, the book does not pretend to be a language text in the usual sense. It contains few grammatical rules. Its pages are not crammed with elementary vocabulary listings like "white," "red," and "black"; "book," "desk," and "pen." I hope I have managed to avoid such inane example sentences as "Mary is a girl," "Mary likes puppies," "I hate puppies," etc. For the likes of these you will have to search elsewhere.

Most teachers of the Japanese language are themselves Japanese and, as Japanese, have never had the experience of approaching this language from the viewpoint of adult Westerners. For this reason, their instruction often omits certain background explanations without which Japanese is an even harder language to come to grips with. In all the formal instruction I received, I never came across most of the explanations of which I speak. They came to me slowly—a piece here, a hint there—over the years. For the student, I have tried to include most of them in this book.

The example words and sentences herein may lean a bit heavily in the direction of harsh language, frank talk, and the night life of Japan, but if so, it is because standard textbooks shun these topics. For reasons more fully explained later, the student will find around him an abundance of instruction in elegant, polite Japanese—but very little of the comparatively rough, everyday speech of Mr. Average Japanese. I will

1

try to fill that gap, and the student should bear in mind that not everything herein will be suitable for use at the emperor's garden party.

I have occasionally used in my examples an old-fashioned word (like *mikudari-han,* "a letter of divorce") or a literary expression not commonly used in everyday speech, but I have tried to make notations to that effect where appropriate. To those who might question why these were included at all, I can only say that such words sometimes have a marvelous flavor and that Japanese would be a poorer language without them. (In the language school at the University of Michigan, one of my classmates chanced upon the word *kuko* in the dictionary and delighted all of us with its meaning: "the Duke of Argyll's tea tree." What a strange and wonderful language this Japanese must be, we thought, to have a special word to describe one particular tree belonging to the Duke of Argyll. It was with distinct disappointment that I learned years later that *kuko* is really a species of tea tree that was named after the duke.)

I have divided this book into three sections or stages, for beginning, intermediate, and advanced students. It may be well, however, for both intermediate and advanced students to begin with the first stage. There are very few people so advanced that they will not profit from the first several chapters as well.

Within each chapter, I have tried to arrange all example words and sentences roughly in ascending order of difficulty. There are a few exceptions, but in general you will find that the first words or sentences in any list are in more frequent use than those that follow.

I may be accused of a certain levity in some of what I have to say. This I will not deny. Humor is a good hammer to drive nails home with, and I have never found that humor and learning are absolute incompatibles. In fact, had my publisher's soberer judgment not prevailed, I should have liked to have called this book *Japanese in Twenty-five Hard Years.* Perhaps some critics might have pointed to such a title as a weather vane of my facetiousness, but at least it would have registered my protest against all those books and language courses that offer to teach the student Japanese by various shortcuts in jigstep time— *Simple Japanese, Japanese in Twenty Lessons, Japanese in Six Weeks,* and even *Instant Japanese!* The present title, however, also serves to make a point that I feel strongly—that in the final analysis a language can only be learned by using it and living it. Perhaps my own experiences with Japanese in action will be of help to others.

Since this book deals with conversational Japanese, I have only used *kanji* (the ideographs or written characters) where they are needed to illustrate a point. Japanese words and sentences are italicized except for place—and personal—names not in the body of example sentences.

I have used the Hepburn system of romanization throughout. Defenders of the National or Kunrei system say that it, being based on the phonemic theory, is more systematic, but to me it is an abomination. The only realistic test is in usage, and the unsuspecting visitor to Japan who tells a taxi driver that he wants to go to Sinbasi (Shimbashi, according to Hepburn) will probably end up somewhere else. This National system also teaches such spellings as *dai-iti* for *dai-ichi* (number one). During the Occupation, most occupants of the Dai-Iti Hotel called their billet the "Die-Itty," and this led on to "Die Itty-Bitty" and finally to "Die Itty-Bitty at a Time Hotel."

For those readers unfamiliar with Japan and the Japanese, I here add a few brief explanations and definitions that may provide enough background to ease them into more technical matters in the body of the book.

Japanese is generally believed to belong to the Ural-Altaic family of languages and is now in what is called the agglutinative stage of its development. Spoken Japanese is in no way similar to any of the dialects of Chinese and was a functioning language long before the first known contacts of any significance with China. What the Japanese did borrow from the Chinese, however, was a large number of the ideographs or *kanji,* which word itself means "Chinese writing." The Japanese had the spoken words but no way to write them, so they took over the *kanji,* giving them their version of the Chinese pronunciation as well as their own pronunciation of the word of the same meaning. For example, the word for man in Japanese was *hito* and in Chinese *jen,* written with the character 人. So the Japanese adopted the same character, giving it both their pronunciation of *hito* and, in compound words, that of *jin,* their approximation of the Chinese word. But, however pronounced, the character always represented the object we call "man."

In addition, the Japanese have developed for use in writing what are called *kana,* characters that are usually simpler than the *kanji* and are used for their sound alone, like our alphabet. There are two of these *kana* syllabaries of forty-eight characters each. One is called *hiragana,* written in the cursive style, and it is the one you will meet most often. The other is called *katakana,* written in block style, and learned after *hiragana* in school by Japanese children. Words and names of foreign origin are written in *katakana.* Whereas the *kanji* are used to represent the basic words of a sentence, e.g., "I," "you," "go," "come," "town," "buy," and so forth, the *kana* are used as postpositions, verb inflectives, and auxiliaries, e.g., "to," "from," "did," "will," and those words like *wa, ga,* and *wo* that indicate whether a noun is the subject or the object of the action of the verb in a sentence.

Before the close of World War II, most Japanese newspapers stocked over five thousand *kanji* in type, and literary scholars might know as many as twenty thousand ideographs, which are made up of at least one element called the radical and, in most cases, one or more nonradical elements. Thus a character may consist of only a single radical of one brush stroke, such as — for *ichi* or "one," or of a radical of sixteen strokes plus nonradical elements bringing the total stroke count up to forty-eight strokes, such as 龘 for *dō* or "dragons moving."

As the name "ideograph" suggests, *kanji* were originally pictures for ideas or things. Imagine a rough picture of a mountain, like this ∧, with a moon rising behind it 夕, and finally a circle representing a man's mouth 夕; then over the years, for ease in writing with a brush, the circles became squares 夕, and eventually half the mountain was cut away to give a character still in use today 名. The meaning? If the moon is coming up, it is evening—and dark. And why else should a man open his mouth in the evening but to identify himself in the dark and speak his name? Thus 名 is the *kanji* for *na* or "name."

The radicals (usually the upper or left element) of which a *kanji* is composed often suggest the meaning of the character. For example, 木 is the radical for tree or wood and the many characters in which it appears are often trees or objects made of wood, such as 橋 for *hashi* or "bridge," 樸 for *kohada* or "bark," 樟 for *kusu(noki)* or "camphor tree," 橇 for *sori* or "sled," 根 for *ne* or "root," 檜 for *hinoki* or "Japanese cypress," and 椿 for *tsubaki* or "camellia."

Two or more radicals may combine to suggest the meaning of the *kanji,* e.g., 魚 is the character for "fish" and 葉 is that for "leaf." In combination, part of the second character is dropped, and we have 鰈, the *kanji* for *karei* or "flounder," the fish that is flat and is shaped like a leaf.

Unfortunately, whatever they may have looked like in their initial pictorial condition, many *kanji* today look like nothing more than a mass of strokes written without apparent rhyme or reason and have to be memorized by sheer rote.

In the SCAP-inspired postwar language reform, the Ministry of Education selected 1,850 of the most frequently used *kanji* and directed that only these be taught to children in school, together with, of course, the *kana* syllabaries. It also recommended that all publications limit themselves to using these so-called *Tōyō kanji*. There are now 2,111 characters which are known as *jōyō kanji*.

The formal written language prior to this reform was a formidable beast indeed, and it differed from the prevailing spoken language chiefly in the postpositions, verb endings, and auxiliaries. Today's written language is much closer to spoken Japanese.

The speech of educated persons living in Tōkyō has been taken as *hyōjungo* or standard Japanese in contrast to the several distinct dialects of certain other parts of Japan. The written language is the same everywhere in Japan, and *hyōjungo* is understood throughout Japan, but a native of Tōkyō could have difficulty understanding the speech of the inhabitants of, for example, the prefectures of Kagoshima, Aomori, and Fukuoka.

Although it is not essential to an understanding of this book, the reader could enhance the benefits from both books by reading one of the briefer histories of Japan in conjunction with it. We generally consider 1868 as the beginning of the modern era in Japan, that being the date of the Meiji Restoration, when more power was restored to the emperor after the downfall of the last of the Tokugawa shoguns.

References to "the war" and "postwar" should all be taken to mean World War II, which to me will always be *the* war, although I was also involved in the troubles in Korea. The "Occupation" was that armed occupation of Japan which began in September of 1945, when Colonel Charles Tench and Major Faubion Bowers (another graduate of the Japanese language school at Michigan) led the party off the first of the C-47s landing at Atsugi airbase a few miles west of Yokohama, and ended with the signing of the peace treaty in 1952. U.S. military forces are now stationed at such bases in Japan as Sasebo, Yokosuka, Iwakuni, Chitose, and Misawa under the provisions of the so-called Security Treaty.

During the Occupation, however, our troops and military administrators were in every city. Tōkyō itself looked like a huge U.S. army base: ninety-nine out of a hundred cars on the streets were O.D. in color and most of the intact buildings in the Marunouchi district in the heart of Tōkyō were either offices or billets for our personnel. MP's in the white helmets that earned them the nickname of *shiro-nabe* (white pots) directed traffic—with the assistance of Japanese policemen—cruised the streets in jeeps, and wielded much resented authority over all of us,

Japanese, American, and British alike. General Douglas MacArthur used the former U.S. Embassy as his residence and commuted daily to his office in the Dai-Ichi Life Insurance Building, near the intersection of Hibiya-dōri and Harumi-dōri (avenues) and overlooking the Imperial Palace grounds. That the Japanese people were not insensitive to MacArthur's (they translated his rank of general of the army as *gensui*) position of superiority (both physical and abstract) over that of their emperor was reflected in their nickname for MacArthur: *Heso Gensui* or "General Navel." (The word *chin* in Japanese has two meanings: 1) it is used by the emperor as "I," and 2) it can mean the male reproductive organ. MacArthur was above the emperor just as the *heso* [navel] is above the *chin*.)

Geographically, Japan comprises the four main islands of Honshū, Hokkaidō, Kyūshū, and Shikoku, which are divided into forty-six administrative subdivisions: forty-two *ken* or rural prefectures, two *fu* or municipal prefectures, one *dō* or regional prefecture, and one *to* or the metropolitan prefecture of Tōkyō. This mountainous chain of islands, about 1,300 miles long in contrast to 140 miles at its widest point, has a population of over one hundred and twenty million—a population that is steadily migrating to such urban centers as Tōkyō (with over twelve million people), Ōsaka, Kyōto, Yokohama, Kōbe, and Fukuoka.

Japan can also be divided into "natural regions," e.g., Kyūshū, Shikoku, Chūgoku, Kansai (or Kinki), Hokuriku, Chūbu, Kantō, Tōhoku, and Hokkaidō. Of these, the names Kantō and Kansai are heard especially often. Literally, Kantō means "east of the barrier" and Kansai means "west of the barrier," the barrier being one of many set up early in the Tokugawa period to control internal travel. Now Kantō is used to mean the region around Tōkyō, including all or parts of the prefectures of Chiba, Kanagawa, Shizuoka, Yamanashi, Saitama, Tōkyō, and Ibaraki, whereas Kansai is used to mean the region around Ōsaka, Kōbe, and Kyōto, including all or parts of the prefectures of Wakayama, Nara, Ōsaka, Hyōgo, Kyōto, Mie, Fukui, and Shiga.

Stage One: Elementary

CHAPTER 1

The Devil's Language

Language Frustration

When a missionary reported to Rome many years ago that the Japanese language must have been devised by the Devil to hinder the preaching of the Gospel to the heathen of Japan, this man of God was only giving vent to the intense frustration that has been felt by many other foreign students of this language. And whether or not we agree today that it was the work of Satan, the Japanese language is nevertheless so difficult that the number of Westerners who know it well is pitifully small.

In one of the six Japanese language schools that I attended, the students used the expression *"kanji* head" to identify a nervous condition apparently arising from too intense study of the language and its many complicated ideographs. Belief in this ailment was later fortified by the attempted suicide of one of our classmates and the successful suicides of two others, for reasons never satisfactorily explained.

This language frustration is a very real thing, and I have witnessed many examples of it. One of the more recent took place one day in the dining room of the Imperial Hotel, where I had been invited to have lunch with two Americans from my home office who had just arrived in Japan for a visit. They had asked another American, who was in Japan to establish his company's multi-million-dollar joint-venture company, to join us. When I arrived a few minutes late, these three were already seated at a table in the dining room and deep in conversation. I was briefly introduced to the third American (whose true identity I shall cloak with the name "Tom") as being with the same company as the first two men. Tom mistakenly assumed that I too had just arrived with the others and was, like them, a complete newcomer to Japan.

Tom, we soon learned, had been sent to Japan six months before to initiate his company's new and very important manufacturing venture, not because he had any knowledge of this country but because he had been successful in getting a similar venture started in Europe. He was a vice-president of the parent company, about fifty years old, and generally

9

regarded as a "success." Shortly after coming to Japan, he had begun taking lessons in Japanese. He was a voluble talker and was now lecturing us on business conditions in Japan, the mentality of Japanese business-men, certain wondrous Japanese customs, and how to make out in a Japanese nightclub. One of the men from my company tried twice to break in on Tom's torrent of advice to tell him that I too was stationed in Japan, perhaps to save Tom from later possible embarrassment, but Tom had no intention of relinquishing the reins of conversation even for a minute.

At this point, a Japanese acquaintance of Tom's happened to pass our table and said hello to him. Tom answered, apparently in Japanese. The man, not comprehending, stopped and raised his eyebrows in polite inquiry. Tom repeated his remark and then, seeing that he still was not getting through, said it a third time. With this, an impasse was reached, and the Japanese man walked away with a dubious look on his face. But if this encounter bothered Tom, he did not let it show, and he re-sumed his lecture to us on things Japanese.

When, at length, one of my friends finished his luncheon plate, Tom signaled our waiter, whose accent identified him as a native of Ōsaka, and said something that sounded to me like *"Sarah toddy grand nuh sigh."*

This meant no more to me than it did to our waiter from Ōsaka, who continued to stand there nervously displaying a polite smile of mild in-terrogation.

Again Tom said, *"Sarah toddy grand nuh sigh."*

When the waiter still did not respond properly, Tom flashed a quick, apologetic smile at us as if to say you know how waiters are, and, raising his voice two decibels, tried again, *"Sarah toddy grand nuh sigh!"*

The Ōsaka waiter now began to look around uneasily, perhaps in search of a handy escape route, but made no motion to comply with Tom's order—whatever it was.

Tom now realized that he stood in active danger of being made to appear a fool and was growing desperate. He rose to his feet and in a querulous voice demanded, *"Sarah toddy grand nuh sigh! Sarah toddy grand nuh sigh,* damn it!"

The headwaiter hurried over and tried to calm Tom, who was by now nearing the frothing stage, but this only served to further exacerbate him. A hush had fallen over the entire dining room of the Imperial, where all the diners were closely watching our little tragicomic play.

Perhaps because my ear is better attuned to the mistakes we foreigners make in Japanese, I at last understood, before the waiter, what Tom was trying to say, i.e., *Sara totte goran nasai* (Please take the plate away), and was just on the point of telling the waiter in Japanese what it was that Tom wanted him to do when Tom, lowering his voice to a somewhat pleading note, said one final time, *"Sarah toddy grand nuh sigh,* please?"

Still seeing no understanding in the faces of the waiters, Tom sat down in defeat and, picking up the empty plate, handed it silently to our waiter from Ōsaka.

Now dubious smiles of partial understanding lit up their faces. By this time I had also finished my lunch and, hoping to take advantage of the commotion around us, I said in a low voice to the Ōsaka waiter, *"Summahen ga kore mo sagete kuremahen ka?"* ("Would you take this away, too, please?")

Thinking to ease the tenseness of the moment, I had deliberately said this in the Ōsaka dialect, but the headwaiter heard it, too, and then he and the Ōsaka waiter smiled in relief and began chattering away at me in Japanese, asking if I was born in Ōsaka and what language it was that Tom had been speaking and so forth.

Tom fixed me with a steely glance and then finished his lunch in sullen silence. Later, when we all parted in the hotel lobby, he pointedly ignored me and left with only a curt goodbye to my two friends.

One night about three weeks later, I happened to see Tom and his wife seated two tables from mine in the Copacabana Club in Tōkyō. At the close of the evening, when many tables were getting their checks and the witching—and bitching—hour approached, I heard the sounds of an altercation from Tom's direction. Looking over, I saw him again on his feet and shouting something apparently unintelligible to the waiter standing before him. In his left hand he held a pocket-size dictionary at which he was vigorously pointing with his right forefinger. In a moment, he angrily shoved the dictionary in his pocket and stalked out, leaving his wife to pay the check.

It was not too long after that scene in the Copa that someone told me that Tom and his wife had returned to the U.S. because of certain "trouble" he had had here. I am reasonably confident that Tom's "trouble" was simply language frustration. The reason he was not understood by the waiter that day at the Imperial was his atrocious pronunciation. (See comments on this topic in Chapter 3, "Pronounce It Right.") If so, Tom shouldn't feel too bad. The Japanese language has bested better men. In fact, it can even be confusing to the Japanese themselves.

In 1949, when I was the telecommunications censorship officer for western Honshū and Shikoku, one of my telegram examiners, himself a well-educated Japanese, found in the traffic we reviewed a copy of a telegram (the original had been transmitted earlier in the day) that read: *Sentōki wo sugu okure. Okure* is the imperative form of the verb *okuru* (to send), *sugu* means immediately, and the only meanings given in the dictionary for *sentōki* are fighter plane and battle flag. The examiner, therefore, translated the telegram as: Send fighter plane (or battle flag?) immediately.

He rushed the telegram and its translation to my desk in the Ōsaka Telegraph Office, where I checked the sender and addressee boxes and found that the telegram had been sent from an Ōsaka address to a company in Wakayama City, south of Ōsaka.

Something did not quite make sense, and I was suspicious. First of all, who—no matter how fanatical—would be fool enough to send such a message in open text? How would anyone get a fighter plane into the city of Ōsaka, occupied as it was by the U.S. 25th Infantry Division? Or, if *sentōki* meant battle flag, why should such an object, in those postwar days, be important enough to justify a telegram? (Since all internal Japanese-language telegrams are written in *katakana,* the *kanji,* which would have solved the puzzle, were not available to us.)

I was sorely tempted to toss the telegram into the wastebasket, but I finally decided against taking that responsibility on myself, so I sent copies of the telegram with its translation by special messengers to the Counterintelligence Corps and to the provost marshal of the division. Soon jeeps filled with armed men were screeching to a halt in front of the Ōsaka address from which the telegram had been sent and speeding over dusty roads south toward Wakayama.

The explanation, when we finally received it, was both simple and embarrassing. The Ōsaka sender, a small trading company, had telegraphed the Wakayama addressee, a maker of porcelain, to ship them immediately one thousand pieces of a particular kind of porcelain ware that the trading company always ordered. In speech, "one thousand pieces of porcelain" would be expressed as *issenko no tōki* but, for the sake of economic brevity in the telegram, the sender had written only *sentōki* (thousand porcelain). This was readily understood by the porcelain maker in Wakayama but not by the Japanese telegram examiner in my office—or by me.

How Long Should It Take?

Beginning students often want to know how difficult Japanese is and how long it will take to learn. According to the U.S. Department of State's Foreign Service Institute, it should take 1,320 hours of study of Japanese to reach the same level in speech that can be attained in 240 hours of Spanish (or Vietnamese) study—five and a half times as long. Note, however, that this estimate says "to reach the same level." It does *not* say "to become fluent in," which is another matter entirely.

If you studied one hour daily, five days a week, it would take more than five years to reach the level the Foreign Service Institute has in mind, whatever it is. On the other hand, if you studied eight hours daily, five days a week, the time required to reach that same degree of competence would be only eight months.

To cite the example with which I am most familiar, I began the study of Japanese thirty-nine years ago at the University of Oklahoma and continued it subsequently at the Universities of Michigan and of Hawaii as well as in two Army language schools (not including the one under the auspices of the University of Michigan). It was at Michigan where, under pressure of the wartime emergency, we took at least six—and often eight or more—hours of instruction a day, including Saturdays. In addition, we studied individually in the latrines after "lights-out" and even while marching in formation—reviewing our *kanji* cards—from class to class on the Michigan campus. We were receiving more hours of instruction in one month than a student in one of today's peacetime colleges would receive in about one year and a half.

With that foundation I went on to study at other schools, but it was not until I had lived in Japan for a number of years that I began to feel any significant degree of confidence in my ability in written and spoken Japanese (which I continue to study even today, knowing I will never become as proficient as I would like to be).

This is not, however, to suggest that it will take you thirty-nine years —or any major portion of thirty-nine years—to arrive at the stage in Japanese where you can derive significant benefit and enjoyment from your ability. That should come much more quickly, but not, I'm afraid, as quickly as one language school in Tōkyō promises. This school has advertised that they will give their students a rough time of it for three weeks, but they assure us that their graduates will emerge speaking another language. One is tempted to ask: Just what language will that be—and how will they be speaking it? If they emerge from the school speaking

Japanese no better than friend Tom in the above anecdote did after six months of study—and if they do not continue to study and learn—then they too may very well have to face frustrations as vexing as those that drove Tom out of Japan, firmly believing, no doubt, that Japanese *is* the Devil's language, after all.

CHAPTER 2

How to Study Japanese

Start Now

Each student of Japanese should tailor his program of study—its length, content, intensity, method, and direction—to suit his own career, planned length of stay in Japan, personal likes and dislikes, available time, and leisure activities. You must be the one to decide how much Japanese you want to learn and how much time you can devote to study each day and each week. The advice, cautions, and comments in this chapter must, therefore, be general in nature, although they are, I believe, of a rather broad applicability.

Although the length of time that you will study Japanese is up to you, I believe it is pertinent to remark that *kōin ya no gotoshi* or "time flies" (lit., light and shadow are like an arrow) and that you may find yourself spending more time in Japan than you dreamed possible in the beginning. Many foreigners have come to this country intending to stay only one or two years but have remained for five or ten or even more. And, if you are going to study Japanese at all, you would do better to begin your studies right away. The longer you put it off, the harder it seems to be to start, until one morning you awaken and find yourself to be one of the weirdest of creatures—a foreigner who has been in Japan physically for months or years but has always been on the outside mentally, getting only an occasional glimpse of what really goes on within.

Do not make the common mistake of hoping that Japanese will just "sort of come to you," as foreign languages sometimes come to the heroes of storybooks. It will not. It will require much time and effort.

Start studying as soon as possible and suspect that you may stay in Japan longer than you had at first planned.

Whether or Not to Learn Kanji

One of the most important decisions you will have to make is whether

15

or not to learn *kanji*. These ideographs represent one of those situations in which you should go all the way—or not start at all. A knowledge of one hundred or five hundred *kanji* will not do you much good because almost any newspaper, magazine, or novel in Japanese that you attempt to read will contain most of the 2,111 *kanji* in common use.

One objection to the study of *kanji* is the amount of time required. But, despite this, *kanji* are worth learning. In Japanese speech, one is not infrequently exposed to *jukugo* (compound words) that he has never heard but will understand if—but only if—he knows *kanji*. Suppose, for example, that you go to Ōsaka (which means "great slope") and meet a friend there and he asks you, *"Itsu raihan nasaimashita ka?"* (When did you come to Ōsaka?). Supposing too that you had never heard the word *raihan* but, because you know *kanji*, you know that *rai* is one reading for the character which means "to come" and *han* is one reading for the character meaning "slope." Given the context, and if the compound is not too far out, you can readily understand his question. The example is not farfetched. Sometimes the Japanese even make up their own *jukugo* on the spur of the moment, and plays on words (and on *kanji*) are a prime source of humor, such as it is, in Japan.

In further illustration of the value of *kanji*, suppose you are asked to learn the romanized form *yōchō-taru* and its meanings of winding or meandering. Because there is no visual connection between the word and its meaning, memorization is not easy for you. But if you approached this same word by the *kanji* road, you would learn that *yō* means "sheep" and *chō* means "entrails." Winding back and forth like the entrails of a sheep. Which approach is the more vivid? Which makes a deeper impression on the memory?

Knowing *kanji* is somewhat comparable to knowing all the root languages of English—Latin, Greek, German, etc.—and using that knowledge to understand otherwise unfamiliar words in English. But few of us know the root languages that well, and it is evident that such knowledge is not essential to the efficient and enjoyable use of our language. In Japanese, however, the relationship between the root and the fruit is much closer. When the average Japanese stops to think about a word, the *kanji* appears on his mental blackboard. When a question about a word arises in conversation, the common reaction is to reach for pencil and paper and write the *kanji*.

After you reach a certain stage, *kanji* knowledge makes further progress in the spoken language faster and easier. Suppose, for example, that you learn the *kanji* for *to* or *wataru*, (to cross) as well as the *kanji* for America *(Bei)*, Europe *(Ō)*, England *(Ei)*, and France *(Futsu)*. Later you happen to discover the word *tobei*, meaning "to cross over the ocean to America" or "to go to America" and written with the above *to* and *bei*. Now, by easy extension, you can add three more words to your vocabulary: *to-ō* (going to Europe), *toei* (going to England), and *tofutsu* (going to France).

If you plan to be in Japan more than two or three years and if you are serious about acquiring something more than merely a superficial knowledge of the language, you should begin the study of kanji *and undertake to learn all of the 2,111 standard characters and their more often used compounds.*

Study Materials

The selection of good textbooks and dictionaries is very important. The spoken-language textbook we used in school is *Modern Conversational Japanese,* written by Joseph K. Yamagiwa and published by McGraw-Hill in 1942. I have not, however, seen it in bookstores in recent years. *Japanese in a Nutshell* by Takeshi Hattori and Wakako Yokō is a good elementary text with much detailed and valuable advice on intonation and accentuation. *Essential Japanese* by Samuel E. Martin is also very good and goes deeper into the language. I was impressed by the detailed explanation of pronunciation at the beginning of this text. It is so detailed and thorough, however, that it may frighten the beginner away. I would suggest that you read that portion once or twice without becoming too entangled with all the precise distinctions of accent and stress, then review it often as you progress in your studies.

I must, however, object to a portion of *Easy Japanese,* a smaller book by the same Samuel E. Martin, although I understand what he is trying to do. Throughout the first twenty-three lessons of this book, the author teaches the student Japanese sentences and phrases from which many of the proper *teniwoha* (postpositional particles) are omitted. I grant that this makes the job of learning (and teaching) easier, but how does the student who uses such sentences and phrases sound? Suppose we reverse the situation and have a Japanese businessman, Mr. Kemmochi, go to New York. There he studies a simplified form of English, from which many prepositions and auxiliary verbs have been omitted. One day he meets an American friend, Mr. Brown, on the street:

BROWN: Hello, Mr. Kemmochi. How are you?

KEMMOCHI: I fine, Mr. Brown. How you?

BROWN: I fine, too—no, no, I mean I *am* fine, too.

KEMMOCHI: You go town?

BROWN: Yes, I go-uh, I *am* going to town, dammit! Would you like to go along with me?

KEMMOCHI: No. Thank you. I busy. I go meet bar girl.

So saying, Sitting Bull Kemmochi rides off into the badlands west of Broadway.

For many years Mr. and Mrs. Vaccari (he is Italian and she Japanese) have been working industriously to ensure that there is no shortage of textbooks on both written and spoken Japanese. Their work has been prodigious and, despite some mistakes in English as well as in Japanese, I would be more kindly disposed toward their efforts were it not for circumstances—arising from one of their books—that earned me the nickname of Apple Man in a bar in Fukuoka.

It was in early 1943, I think, when I began to use a Vaccari textbook. This may have been changed later, but in the edition I had the word *ringo* (apple) with its *kanji* (林檎) was given in the first or second lesson. Nothing being written to the contrary, I assumed that this writing was in common use and I bent efforts to learn it. (As you can see, it is not a simple one.) It was, in fact, the first really difficult *kanji* combination I learned and, although I did not see it elsewhere in my studies, I came to cherish it and I believed it would one day perform yeoman service for me in Japan.

Shortly after the war, I was sent to Fukuoka, and before long I had found for myself a congenial cabaret with about three dozen hostesses and a five-piece band. Now the time had come, I felt, to display my wares. On the first night in this cabaret, W. Haven Dizer and I sat at a table with four hungry, thirsty hostesses. Between rounds of drinks, I kept ordering snacks, hoping that apples would be served. (Stranger foods do appear, believe me, on the tables of Japanese cabarets.) Late in the evening, no apples having appeared, I was growing desperate. Just then, Dizer happened to ask the prettiest of the four if she would have dinner with him the next night. Here, at last, was my chance! In a ringing voice, I broke in: *"Shokuji de omoidashimashita ga ringo tte dō kaku ndesu ka, ne?"* (Speaking of dinner reminds me: how do you write [the *kanji* for] apple?).

During subsequent weeks and frequent visits to this cabaret, which was only a short distance down the street from the *ryokan* (inn) we had requisitioned, I believe I managed to ask almost all of the girls working there if they knew the *kanji* for *ringo*. All answers were negative. I, of course, knew, and I had been waiting to dazzle them with my brilliance when someone asked me if I knew—but no one had. Now, however, I was beginning to worry that no one at all would ever even have seen the *kanji,* which would make the whole thing rather meaningless.

In the meantime, as I learned later, the girls had begun to call me, among themselves, *Ringo no Otoko* (Apple Man) and to regard my strange interest in apples as possibly erotic. One of the girls, better educated than the others, had heard the story of Adam, Eve, and the apple in the Garden of Eden, and when they all heard her tell this, it deepened their suspicions.

About that time, *Ringo no Uta* (The Apple Song) was one of the two most popular songs in Japan. (The other was *You Are My Sunshine,* by the future governor of Louisiana.) One night, just as I was making my daily entrance into the cabaret, the band struck up with the strains of *Ringo no Uta:*

Akai ringo ni	Touching your lips
Kuchibiru yosete	To a red apple
Damatte mite iru	The blue sky watches
Aoi sora	In silence above.

A hostess had put them up to it. And from then on, whenever I entered, the band stopped whatever else it was playing (I spent a lot of money there) and began beating out *Ringo no Uta.* The hostesses now called me *Ringo no Otoko* to my face, and apples were served with my drinks in place of peanuts or *sembei* (an odious rice cracker). At last, I was driven to seek out another cabaret where no one knew me—and where I tried to drown all memory of the *kanji* for *ringo* in Calvados brandy.

The many excellent *Nihongo Notes* by Osamu and Nobuko Mizutani are deserving of my warm recommendation. These books offer detailed explanations of when and when not to use many everyday expressions in Japanese. Too many of us foreigners use *sayōnara,* for example, in the same situation in which we would say "goodbye" in English, not having learned that in Japan close friends and members of the same family say *sayōnara* to each other only rarely.

In language school we used Arthur Rose-Innes's *Beginners' Dictionary of Chinese-Japanese Characters,* which may have been a pioneer work in its field. In 1962, however, *The Modern Reader's Japanese-English Character Dictionary* by Andrew N. Nelson was published and it is a much more comprehensive and up-to-date work.

For *rōmaji* (romanized Japanese words), I use *Kenkyūsha's New English-Japanese Dictionary* and *Kenkyūsha's New Japanese-English Dictionary.* The former gives English words in alphabetical order, but the Japanese definitions and explanations are in *kanji* and *kana.* The latter gives Japanese words in *rōmaji* in alphabetical order with the meanings in English. The example sentences, however, are written in *kanji* and *kana* with English translations. *Kenkyūsha's New Japanese-English Dictionary* is an exceedingly valuable book. It is hard to find words to praise it sufficiently. The example sentences are carefully selected to give the student an insight into various kinds of speech and writing. When you can read *kanji,* you should use this dictionary as a source of pattern sentences. (The publishers of such reference works would do beginning students a great favor by giving the *rōmaji* readings of the *kanji-kana* sentences as well.)

Mistakes in this dictionary are notable by their absence. One of the few I have found is where "a loving ambassador" is given as the meaning of *idō-taishi* when it should be "a roving ambassador." But I find that I rather like the idea of a loving ambassador. Some years ago in Tōkyō, the press reported the romantic activities of the ambassador from an unnamed country. His *modus operandi* was to approach parties of teenage country girls who were sightseeing in Tōkyō and offer, through their teacher or chaperon, to buy them refreshments. While having tea or ice cream, he would casually mention his address and, in parting, invite them to come to see him when they next visited the capital.

Evidently some did—singly or in pairs. And the "loving ambassador" laid lustful hands on them. Being a student of depravity, I was eager to read further startling revelations (especially the name of his country), and I followed both the Japanese- and English-language newspapers closely for more than a week, but a curtain of silence had fallen over the affair. I still hope to someday learn his identity, however.

Although frequent reference to a dictionary is essential, it is wise to double-check the dictionary meaning of certain critical words with educated speakers of the language. While browsing through a Kenkyūsha dictionary one day many years past, I came across the phrase *keikoku no bijin,* the meanings of which are given as "a woman of matchless beauty," and "a woman whose eyes are the doom of a king." (The *kanji* mean "A beauty who can ruin a country.") I thought this was a wonderful expression for use in my courtships so, as the Japanese would say, I engraved it on my liver *(kimo ni meijita)*. In subsequent years, I made good (or at least frequent) use of *keikoku no bijin*. Recently, however, while flipping through the pages of Nelson's dictionary, I found the same expression. Nelson, however, in addition to "a peerless beauty," lists the meaning of "prostitute." Upon shuddering reflection, I now remember that many of those girls did smile in a rather sickly way when I gazed deep into their eyes and stoutly declared that nothing would ever budge me from my opinion that they were magnificent, unsurpassable *keikoku no bijin*.

Rare are the books on Japanese that seem to be bereft of redeeming merit, but sadly there are a few, among which are some written by Roy Andrew Miller. As a writer, Mr. Miller has a style that is both obscure and overgenerous in its use of criticism, while in his position as a teacher of and expert on Japanese, he appears to be rather misinformed concerning the qualifications of others in the field.

One more note about dictionaries. For pocket-size volumes, I have found Sanscidō's English-Japanese and Japanese-English dictionaries very serviceable.

Select good textbooks and dictionaries. In the case of kanji *dictionaries, spend enough time in the beginning to learn how to use them correctly. It will save time otherwise lost in fumbling later.*

Vocabulary Cards

Vocabulary cards (for both *rōmaji* and *kanji*) are extremely helpful aids. I still use them, frequently adding and discarding. The 3″ × 5″ index card, cut into four equal parts, provides a handy size.

In language school in Ann Arbor during the war, many of us reviewed our *kanji* while marching between classes. We would glance at the back side of the card, which gave the reading and meaning, and then practice writing the *kanji* itself in the air with our forefingers, before looking at the front side of the card. The fact that we were studying Japanese was classified information, and we were not supposed to explain to the curious why we were making such odd motions in the air while marching about the campus. This gave rise to hard-to-live-with rumors that we were all certifiable, and many citizens of Ann Arbor began to move to the other side of the street when they saw us coming.

The Japanese, however, are accustomed to this finger-writing in the air, so you can practice your *kanji* all you want while walking the streets of Japan.

Make vocabulary cards for all new words, pattern sentences, and kanji. *Review them often. Always carry a pack with you for study while riding in trains and cars, while waiting for your date to appear at Yūraku-chō station, etc.*

Literary Classics

When you have mastered enough *kanji* to work your way, albeit slowly, through short stories and novels in Japanese, you should try reading those books *(taiyaku-bon)* that carry the original English on one page and the Japanese translation on the facing page. These are editions for Japanese students and include many of the classics of English literature. For example, I can see on my bookshelf *The Tempest, The Rubaiyat, Moon and Sixpence, The Summing Up, Confessions of an English Opium-Eater, Virginibus Puerisque, Autobiography of Benjamin Franklin, The Sire de Maletroit's Door,* and others in such editions. Also helpful is the sixteen-volume *taiyaku-bon* set of modern Japanese literature published by Hara Shobō.

Read the Japanese page first and refer to the English side only when you do not understand or when you want to review the whole page or chapter to confirm your understanding. The major advantage to this method of study is that it will save you many tedious hours of tracking to earth elusive meanings.

Another adventitious advantage (to me, anyway) was the renewed (or first-time) acquaintance with many English literary masterpieces. These were not forced-draft scannings for school study assignments but painstaking, word-by-word ingestions, first in a foreign language and then in the original English. I did not really begin to appreciate William Shakespeare or Erskine Caldwell until I read some of their works in Japanese.

Build a library of these inexpensive literary classics and begin to read them for profit and pleasure as soon as you are able.

Practice

Teashi no tsuita jibiki is a walking dictionary (lit., a dictionary with hands and feet)—and one of these is a fine way to combine study with pleasure. Their usefulness, however, comes not from their serviceability as a substitute for a dictionary but from their charming (we hope) presence, which should inspire us to frequent attempts at communication. Not only will they listen sympathetically to our faltering Japanese, but they will also, if asked, correct our syntax, pronunciation, and choice of words.

One caution: be careful not to let excessively feminine (or, if you are female, excessively masculine) expressions taint your speech.

By all means, get yourself a living dictionary—if your spouse doesn't object. Bear in mind, however, that this is only an accessory to—not a substitute for—other forms of study.

Assistance from Japanese Friends

The average Japanese speaks better Japanese than you or I do. At least, his accent and fluency are superior. You or I might eventually learn more words or *kanji* than he knows but, because we began our studies of *Nihongo* as adult foreigners, we will never quite have the all-round grasp of his native tongue that he has—which is only as it should be. Nevertheless, it behooves you not to look upon all Japanese as authorities on their own language. After all, you would not, I trust, consult a New York City taxi driver about the meaning of words like sesquipedalian and pseudocyesis.

You may not be concerned with how to say sesquipedalian and pseudocyesis in Japanese (for the curious: *nagai kotoba wo tsukaitagaru* and *sōzōninshin*) for some time yet (if ever), but the principle is unchanged. It is often easier to ask whatever Japanese happens to be handy for definitions and explanations, but it is also dangerous. His English may not be adequate to encompass the full explanation needed. Or he may be so eager to assist the foreign guest that he steps slightly beyond the bounds of his own certain knowledge to seek a likely sounding meaning or etymology to please your ears. Or he may be tempted to teach you pidgin Japanese, thinking that it is all you want to learn or that it is easier for you than standard Japanese.

Make friends with erudite and voluble Japanese. Save your harder questions for them.

Maximum Exposure

Don't be shy or hesitant in speaking Japanese for fear of making mistakes. Speak forth when you have the opportunity and create such opportunities. Urge your Japanese friends to correct your speech. Associate with the Japanese. Do not fall into the habit of spending most of your leisure hours in the American Club, the Press Club, or other foreign islands in the sea of Japanese culture. Walk the streets often and observe your environment keenly. Adopt the habit of reading a Japanese periodical, even if you have to read it with painful slowness and can only finish part of it. Don't stop to look up everything you are not sure of. Get the general meaning and read on. The more times you see and comprehend a *kanji,* the more completely it becomes your property. Reading speed will increase with the amount of reading you do. Try to think in Japanese; this will not come to you quickly, but when it does, you will know that you have come a long way in your studies. As an aid to start thinking in Japanese, imagine a pending meeting with a Japanese friend. Rehearse in your mind what you want to say to him and guess what he will say in reply. Then, visualize yourself relating the details of this meeting to another Japanese later.

Movies are a good study aid. If you have time for the cinema, see a Japanese movie. If possible, get a copy of the scenario beforehand and study it. (Three Japanese magazines which carry scenarios are *Kinema Jumpō, Eiga Geijutsu,* and *Shinario.*) If you go to see a foreign movie, try to read the Japanese subtitles before they disappear from the screen. Of course, this won't leave much time for enjoying the movie itself, so you might want to sit through it a second time.

In short, expose yourself to the Japanese language in every way feasible.

Specifics

You should strive to learn Japanese through pattern sentences. Suppose you want to say in Japanese, "I don't know why, but she is prejudiced against French men." The unwary student, translating almost word for word, might say, *"Watakushi wa naze ka shirimasen ga kanojo wa Furansujin no otoko ni taishite henken wo motte imasu.''* This sentence is grammatically correct and it is quite understandable to a Japanese but it is not the way a Japanese would have said it. He would have preferred something like, *"Kanojo wa dō shita koto ka Furansujin no otoko wo ke-girai shite imasu.''* (*Ke-girai* means, literally, "to hate to the hairs.") Since this is the more natural expression, you should memorize the pattern and, by substituting other words for "she," "French," and "men," you can have on call a wide variety of naturally expressed sentences, even including such as, *"Uchi no ōmu wa dō shita koto ka Taiwan no shumokuzame wo ke-girai shite imasu"* (I don't know why, but our parrot is prejudiced against the hammerhead sharks of Taiwan).

Learn by memorizing pattern sentences.

Living in Japanese-style rooms, eating typical Japanese food, riding the subways and buses instead of taxis and private cars, tuning in the Japanese radio stations instead of the U.S. Armed Forces Far East Network, and associating mostly with Japanese who don't speak any English are of inestimable value in learning the Japanese language and gaining a deep understanding of the country. To me, this is painfully obvious. And yet, the average American who undertakes to study Japanese does not follow such advice to any significant extent. His desire for comfort and pleasure evidently outweighs his desire to master Japanese.

As far as practicable, live in the Japanese style and manner.

Jiiai-go (lit., GI language) is what the Japanese call the few words of broken Japanese that they like to believe typify the American GI in Japan. Such a sweeping condemnation is obviously unfair, but it is undeniable that many GI's (as well as other foreigners) tend to overuse, misuse, and mispronounce certain Japanese and quasi-Japanese words, e.g., *daijōbu* (all right), *tonde mo nai* (preposterous) *tonde mo happun* (it could never happen), *mama-san* (usually the female manager of a bar), *papa-san* (any hapless, older man who happens to be standing around), *haba-haba* (quickly, from a Papuan word), *sukoshi* (a little), *takusan* (a lot), *sukebei* (horny, suggestive, raunchy), and others.

Of the foregoing examples, *daijōbu, tonde mo nai, takusan,* and *sukoshi* are perfectly good words (when properly used) and are heard often in everyday speech. It is dubious that you could avoid then entirely. Nevertheless, frequent usage of such words by any foreigner puts him in danger of being lumped into the same category with the rough-and-ready frequenters of GI bars. (No offense intended. I was there, too.)

Avoid—or strictly limit—the use of Americanized Japanese words.

Devise ways to check and correct your pronunciation periodically.

If your use of a word in Japanese puzzles anyone, check with a Japanese friend to see if it is being mispronounced. Habits of malpronunciation are difficult to correct once they have become encrusted and locked in with age. If you are beginning the study of Japanese as an adult, your pronunciation will probably never be perfect. You will always be in need of some corrective adjustments.

Always be conscious of pronunciation and constantly strive for improvement.

Pronounce It Right

Women, Vegetables, and Embarrassing Vowel Sounds

For the serious student of Japanese, this is the most important chapter in this book. I cannot urge the student too strongly to bear in mind its message—that is, to be constantly aware of pronunciation, and to continually strive for improvement.

Correct pronunciation of Japanese should be comparatively easy, which is not the same, however, as saying that reasonable proficiency can be achieved in a few days or weeks. In Japanese, there is nothing comparable, luckily, to the dread five-pitch tonal system of Chinese. The five vowels in Japanese have only one pronunciation each, whereas there are twenty-nine ways to pronounce the five English vowels. With the possible exception of *tsu* and *r,* Japanese has no very difficult sounds for the beginner to master.

And yet incorrect—almost laughable—mispronunciation is the most common serious failing I have noticed among Western students of this language. Since many of these same students have demonstrated laudable ability in other languages as well as in other aspects of Japanese itself, I can only infer that their teachers failed to sufficiently emphasize correct pronunciation.

While I was attending the Japanese language school at the University of Michigan, Dr. Shohara—a fine scholar and a dedicated teacher—patiently drilled a group of us in correct pronunciation three evenings a week, for months. We were made to repeat words and phrases endlessly, it seemed, until we were sick of pronunciation, weary of Japanese, and disenchanted with our school. We left each drill session threatening to deliberately fail the next comprehensive examination in order to be expelled and shipped off to front-line duty with the infantry—a threat, I should add, which no one put into execution. I doubt that any of us ever satisfied Dr. Shohara, she being a scholar of phonetics and a perfectionist to boot. But some of us continued to go back to her drill sessions, which were not compulsory, time and again because even then we realized that pronunciation might be the most important part of our language training.

Most of the students, however, attended Dr. Shohara's drills only occasionally or not at all, and among the latter were two men who completed the language course and who have spent many of the intervening years in Japan. Both read Japanese well; they can write their *kanji* with tolerable proficiency; their comprehension of the spoken word is excellent. Yet when they begin to speak Japanese, puzzled looks of incomprehension come over the faces of their Japanese listeners, who—until they become accustomed to their individual defects in pronunciation—do well to understand half of what is said.

One of the two, for example, has persisted all these years in saying *o-na* (vegetables) for *onna* (woman) and *jōsei* (situation) for *josei* (female). Once he spent a weekend alone in an isolated inn on the west coast of the Izu Peninsula. Back in Tōkyō, he urged me to visit the same inn, saying that the service was excellent, the cuisine unusual, and the scenery magnificent. I had an opportunity to follow his advice not too long after that, and, while there, I casually asked the manager if he remembered my friend. The tall American? Yes. Growing bald? "Yes, indeed, I remember him well," the manager replied. "A very kind gentleman. He was quite concerned about the welfare of the farmers around here. All weekend he kept asking us about the *vegetable situation.*"

This same friend—let's call him Peter—has, in recent years, become closely associated in business with a Mr. Sakamoto, a wealthy Japanese entrepreneur, and often serves as Sakamoto's U.S.-market adviser.

One Saturday afternoon Peter and I were waiting in Sakamoto's private office for him to arrive. We had sent his secretary out to fetch us some beer (it was, after all, Saturday afternoon) and, while she was gone, an eight-member delegation from Sakamoto's home prefecture came calling. There being no one else around, Peter took charge and—in his interesting Japanese—told the delegation: *"Sakamoto-san wa mō jiki ni kimasu ga watakushi ni nani ka dekiru koto ga areba osshatte kudasai. Watakushi wa Sakamoto-san no kōmon desu kara..."* (Mr. Sakamoto will be here soon, but please tell me if there is anything I can do for you. You see, I am Mr. Sakamoto's anus ...).

Never have I seen anything convulse a group of Japanese the way Peter's bland statement did that afternoon. Usually the Japanese quality of restraint prevents laughter from getting out of control—but not that day. The delegation members were already tittering from the unaccustomed experience of being greeted by a tall, blue-eyed foreigner speaking slightly odd Japanese, and, coming on top of that, Peter's solemn statement of the anatomical position he occupied in relation to Sakamoto-san shattered their control asunder. They whooped, they yelled, they howled, they did everything but roll on the floor.

What Peter had meant to say, of course, was not *kōmon* (anus) but *komon* (adviser)

Two other classmates of mine were driving toward Kumamoto one summer day when dusk overtook them. They stopped near an innocent bystander and told him they wanted to find an inn. At first, the bystander did not appear to understand what they said, so they kept repeating the word for inn.

After several minutes of this, he shook his head dubiously, told them to wait, and disappeared down a side street. After what seemed an interminable wait, the man came walking out of the darkness and handed them a plate piled high with a kind of Japanese candy made of bean-paste.

This candy is called *yōkan,* while the word for inn is *ryokan.*

To me, it seems a phenomenon of perverse stupidity to spend hundreds, perhaps thousands, of hours mastering the grammar, ideographs, and vocabulary of Japanese, only to spoil the finished product—and to seriously hamper the utility of it all—by coating it with the ugly, harmful paint of mispronunciation.

That said, let us go on to look at what constitutes correct pronunciation. First, the five vowels:

a	as in f*a*ther
i	as in macaron*i*
u	as in Z*u*lu or h*u*la
e	as in *e*xtra or m*e*t
o	as in s*o*lo

As we use the word "facetious" as a mnemonic to remember the order of the English vowels, so can you use "Hail, UNESCO!" to remember their order in Japanese.

I am assuming that the student-reader of this book is either now in Japan or has the assistance of native speakers of Japanese (in person, on records, or on tapes) or has spent enough time in Japan in the past to have his ears attuned to the sound of spoken Japanese. Otherwise, to begin the study of the spoken language cold, so to speak, in a place where no Japanese is spoken could be folly, as far as the acquisition of correct pronunciation is concerned. I will not, therefore, set down rules to cover all the fine points of pronunciation but will offer instead general advice that, if followed, will give the student most of what he needs to get started on his way toward the goal of correct pronunciation The rest can and should be obtained through careful mimicry of educated native speakers.

Let me add the obvious: that tape recorders are most useful in this context. Record your teacher's words as well as your own. Compare them. Try to speak smoothly and avoid the up-and-down inflection typical of our speech in English.

A Guide to Good Pronunciation

Here, then, to help you keep your vegetables and women straight, are thirteen suggestions for good pronunciation:

1. The distinction between long and short vowels is vital in Japanese, as illustrated above by my ex-classmate who still occasionally forgets and announces himself to be the anus of a certain Mr. Sakamoto. Long vowels are denoted by a dash or macron over the vowel itself, as in *kūki* (air), or by repetition of the vowel, as in *kuu* (to eat). Dictionaries and texts for the study of Japanese should always make this distinction clear. Other English writing about Japan often does not, which is one reason for the puzzled looks on the faces of Japanese to whom new arrivals from the West try to speak about well-known places and things in Japan.

The student should always take pains to determine which vowels are long and which are short. In Japanese, long vowels are called *chō-on* (lit., long sounds) and short vowels are called *tan-on*. Since this difference between long and short vowels does not appear to come easily to most Westerners, you should exaggerate the length of the *chō-on* in the beginning, giving them even more than twice the duration of the short vowels. A natural shortening of the sounds to approximately the correct length will follow as you become able to speak faster.

2. Double consonants are frequent in Japanese—and are frequently mispronounced by Westerners. The root of the trouble appears to be that we fail to treat the consonants as separate syllables.

For instance, take the word *otte* (pursuer). The beginner is tempted to pronounce this word as if it contained only two syllables, i.e., *o* and *te*. What then comes forth sounds more like "your hand" or "honorable hand" *(o-te)* than "pursuer." When you learn the *kana* syllabary, however, you can see that *otte* is written with the three *kana* symobls ォ *(o)*, ッ *(tsu)*, and テ *(te)*, which may make it easier to remember to treat the additional consonant as a separate syllable. Done correctly, there is a slight pause after the first *t* (written *tsu*) in *otte,* after which the final syllable *te* is released in a small explosion of breath. This same breath explosion can also be heard in pronouncing the double consonants *kk,* as in *makka* (bright red), and *pp,* as in *jippi shuppan* (vanity publishing).

Similar care should be taken with all the double consonants in Japanese, as in these words: *bummei* (civilization), *suppai* (sour), *kakke* (beriberi), *kekkon* (marriage), *zatto* (roughly), *sonnō* (reverence for the emperor), and *kissaten* (coffee shop).

3. Accent in Japanese is a matter of higher or lower musical pitch, of which there are three degrees—low, mid, and high, Where the pitch will fall is entirely unpredictable, and so rules—even general ones—are impossible. To worsen matters, in Kansai and in parts of Kyūshū and Shikoku the pitch is the opposite of what we hear in standard Japanese *(hyōjungo)* around Tōkyō. What saves the day, however, is that the degree of variance in pitch is so small that the beginner is even advised to voice all Japanese words, with the exceptions of the devocalized *i* and *u* noted below, with a steady evenness of pitch. You should, in fact, extend this monotony of pitch to entire sentences, taking care to use little of the rising interrogative inflection of English in the spoken Japanese question mark, *ka.* Sooner or later, depending on the sharpness of your ear, you will come to be able to distinguish and mimic the existing minor variations in pitch, and, in the meantime, almost nothing will have been lost. Pitch will be the least of your problems in learning Japanese.

Someone may point out the three *hashi* (bridge, chopsticks, and edge) to you and caution that you cannot distinguish among the three without proper pitch. Pay such woe-criers no heed. No one is going to rush at you on a dark night shouting *"Hashi!"* and then run on, leaving you to wonder if you should reach for your trusty chopsticks, sharpen the edge of your samurai sword, or spring for the bridge.

Context will save the day—or the night. The Japanese guest in your dining room who asks for *hashi* will have little use for edges and none for bridges.

4. The initial *g* in Japanese is hard, as in goal, with the exception of the postposition *ga,* which is soft. Here are some examples: *gorotsuki* (ruffian), *gesubatta koto wo iu* (to talk vulgarly), *gumpō-kaigi* (court-martial). Within a word, *g* is closer to the *ng* in ring, as in *eiga* (movie), *kagaku* (science or chemistry), *mago* (grandchild), *fushigi* (strange, wonderful, unaccountable), and *hokorashige ni* (proudly).

G, whether initial or medial, is softer (like the *ng* in hanger) in northern Japan and harder (as in go) in southern Japan.

5. There is a tired old story about an American midget who enters a Tōkyō snack bar and says to the Japanese waiter: "Hey, *boi-san! Haba-haba!* Gimme some flied lice, huh?" The waiter studies the midget coolly for a moment and then replies: "That's fried rice, you lidiculous lunt!"

But, in the first place, the Japanese could not have really been guilty of this alleged lallation because, although they can't pronounce our *r* perfectly, they can't pronounce our *l,* either. And, in the second place, our version of their *r* is no better than their version of ours.

The Japanese *r* is undeniably a difficult sound for beginners, as well as for some others who should have mastered it years ago. Our difficulty with this *r* identifies our Japanese speech as foreign more quickly and more indisputably than any other single mispronunciation; that—and the inflectional rise and fall we Americans arbitrarily assign, it seems, to our sentences in other languages. The Japanese spoken by one of our recent ambassadors to Japan was, although quite fluent, immediately marked as foreign by his somewhat harsh pronunciation of *r.*

To a layman like myself, the Japanese *r* sounds like a blending, in equal parts, of the *l, d,* and *r* of English. To a scholar of phonetics, it is a single-tap *r* with the tip of the tongue hitting briefly against the ridge behind the upper teeth and immediately descending. Try saying the English name Eddy, pronouncing the *dd* only very briefly and touching the tip of the tongue to the ridge behind the upper teeth only very lightly. This should give you a close approximation of the Japanese word *eri,* meaning collar.

Once you know how to say the *r,* you should practice it by repeating a Japanese word or sentence filled with *r*'s after a native speaker of the language. You might start with *Rippa na hōrōsha no rireki* (a splendid tramp's personal history) and progress to *Sono rippa na rappa ga urare-mashita ka?* (Has that fine bugle been sold?). Finally, polish your *r*'s by repeating an old Kyūshū mouth-filling tongue twister that was confected more for its sound than meaning:

> *Den derareru nara*
> *Dete kuru batten*
> *Den derarenken denken konken*
> *Konkorarenken korarera*
> *Renkenkon.**

---

*Roughly translated, this Kumamoto dialectal confection says: If I could've gone out, / I would've gone out, / But since I can't get out, / I'm staying in. / And as I can't get out, / I don't go out.

6. The Japanese *i* and *u* are often weak, sometimes almost lost between any pair of the following consonants or consonant combinations: *ch, f, h, k, p, s, sh, ts,* and *t.* Pronounce them as shown in these examples: *kusa* (grass) as if it were *k'sa, shita* (tongue or below) as if it were *sh'ta, kita* (north) as if it were *k'ta,* and *shichi* (seven) as if it were *sh'chi.*

According to the foregoing rule, both *shuten* (main point) and *shiten* (branch office) would become *sh'ten* and would be indistinguishable. Notice, however, that the rule says "sometimes almost lost." Almost— but not quite. A good memory aid is to picture them like this: SHu-TEN and SHiTEN.

7. Special attention should be accorded to the single consonant *n,* which has a nasal sound and which should be given the force of a whole syllable. The unwary student might be tempted to pronounce *San-in* (that part of southwestern Honshū facing the Japan Sea) as if it were two syllables, i.e., *San* and *in.* It is, instead, four—and this is easier to understand when one sees that *San-in* is written in *kana* with four symbols (サ, ン, イ, ン), each of which should be pronounced as a separate syllable.

Before *b, m,* and *p,* this *n* is pronounced as *m.* The 1954 edition of *Kenkyūsha's New Japanese-English Dictionary* retains the *n* spelling, as in *shinbun* (newspaper), whereas the 1949 edition gives *shimbun.* In the following examples, I have chosen to follow the phonetic rendering: *amma* (massage), *jimbutsu* (person, character), *sampatsu* (haircutting).

This *n* before *ch, d, j, t, ts,* or another *n* is pronounced with the tip of the tongue behind the upper teeth. Remember to elongate it, to give it the value of a full syllable, in words like these: *kichinto* (exactly), *banji* (all things), *hannichi kanjō* (anti-Japanese feeling), *shinchiku* (new building).

Before *k* or *g,* this *n* is pronounced as if it were *ng,* as in: *anki* (memorization), *hanketsu* (verdict or decree), *benki* (bedpan), *ringetsu* (the last month of pregnancy), *kankaku* (sensation, feeling). In these examples, pronounce *hanketsu* like *ha-ng-ke-tsu, benki* like *be-ng-ki, ringetsu* like *ri-ng-nge-tsu,* and *kankaku* like *ka-ng-ka-ku.*

When it precedes *y* or *w* or any vowel, this *n* borrows a bit of the sound which follows, as in: *bunya* (field, e.g., professional, industrial, etc.), *danwa* (talk, colloquy), *shin-ō* (epicenter). Note that when *n* precedes the vowels *i* or *e,* a *y* sound (as in young) is slightly voiced, as in *shin-ei* (pro-British), which is pronounced *shin-(y)ei,* or *sen-i* (textile, fiber), which is pronounced *sen-(y)i.* When the *n* comes before *y,* as in *gyūnyū* (milk), it is pronounced like the Spanish *ñ* in *señor,* with the middle part of the tongue touching the roof of the mouth and the breath passing partly through the mouth and partly through the nose.

When the *n* is at the end of a word, it is pronounced (still with the value of a full syllable) with the tongue near but not quite touching the roof of the mouth. Examples are: *ampan* (a sweet, jam-filled bun), *bin* (bottle), and *jitaku bumben* (child delivery at home). This same pronunciation applies when *n* precedes *f, h, r, s, sh,* and *z,* as in these examples: *tansan* (carbonic acid, a brand of carbonated water), *shinsha* (new car), *manzai* (a comic stage dialogue), *shinrō* (bridegroom), *Taiwanfū* (Taiwan style), *shinri* (mentality).

8. The final *u* in *desu* (the polite verb for am, are, is) and in the polite verb-ending *masu* is muted, except in some dialectal speech, notably that of the *Kyō-onna* (the women of Kyōto). This devocalization is indicated in *rōmaji,* if at all, by a line under the *u (desu),* omission of the *u (des),* replacement of the *u* with an apostrophe *(des'),* or enclosing it in parentheses *des(u).*

9. The syllable *tsu* may give some students trouble, but, to me, it was easier than the *r.* Extend the tip of the tongue just through the nearly closed teeth and try to say the name Sue. This method will bring you tolerably close to the correct pronunciation of *tsu.* For perfection, listen carefully to and mimic native speakers.

10. Consonants prefixed to diphthongs beginning with *y,* e.g., *kya, kyo, kyu, rya, ryo, ryu, mya, myo, hya, hyo, hyu, nya, nyo,* and *nyu* may give momentary pause to the beginner. He should, however, be able to master them quickly. Let the sound of the initial consonant blend in with that of the following diphthong Since, with the single exception of *n,* there are no consonants that can be written alone in the *kana* syllabary, the initial consonants in the sounds given above cannot be written as *k, r, m, h,* or *n,* but must be written as *ki, ri, mi, hi,* or *ni.* In *kana,* the succeeding diphthong is often written below and slightly to the right of the preceding symbol, instead of directly below, to indicate that the two sounds should be blended rather than given two completely separate sound values.

One particularly nauseous violation of this simple rule is the manner in which most Americans (including those stationed in Okinawa) pronounce *Ryūkyū,* the name of the archipelago of which Okinawa is the main island. They say it as if were *Rye-you-key-you.* Then they compound the offense by adding the plural *s,* making it *Rye-you-key-youse.* I can only wonder why the Okinawan people have not, after hearing the name of their homeland so vilified, taken up their pitchforks and manned the barricades.

11. Bear in mind that the Japanese *f* is a lighter *f* than that in English. We make our *f* with the lower lip against the upper teeth, but the Japanese don't use the teeth at all. They bring the lips almost together as if about to whistle, and then blow the *f* out with a very slight puff. Practice this *f* with words like these: *fude* (writing brush), *fuyu* (winter), *futoru* (to be fat, big), *fūtō* (envelope), *futsuka-yoi* (hangover; lit., twoday drunkenness).

12. An *h* before *i* or *y* is something like the *sh* in the English "ship" and the *ch* in the German *ich*. Examples for practice are: *hidoi* (harsh, severe, unfair), *hijō ni* (extremely), *hin* (quality), *hi no kuruma* (extreme poverty), *hyō* (leopard), *hyōmen* (surface, exterior).

13. When *wo*, the postposition indicating the accusative case, follows a word ending in *n*, it is pronounced with the lips stretched slightly outward—as in the beginning of a smile—and not rounded. For example: *Sono jigyō ni hyakuman-doru no shihon wo toshi shita* (I invested a million dollars in that enterprise).

When, however, it comes after a word ending in a vowel, e.g., *hiyō wo motsu* (to bear expenses), the *w* is nearly inaudible. It is so nearly inaudible, in fact, that some textbooks give *o* for this postposition. It is, however, written with the *kana* symbol for *wo* instead of that for *o*. In school, we were taught to make a conscious effort to pronounce the *w* in *wo* in the early stage of our studies but to devaluate it later, the intention being to let only a very small trace of it remain.

CHAPTER 4

Yes and No

"Yes, I Am Not Going"

It is understandable that the English-speaking student is tempted to use the Japanese equivalents of yes and no as often as and in the same way that he uses them in English, but to yield to this temptation is to fall into one of the several pitfalls awaiting the unwary beginner.

The first difficulty with these words (*hai* for yes and *iie* for no) is that newcomers to the language are often told that they are used in a manner that is exactly the opposite of our English usage, and this, at best, is only half accurate.

If I ask Mr. Kosaka in Japanese if he is going to Yokohama, he will answer either *"Hai, ikimasu"* (Yes, I am going) or *"Iie ikimasen"* (No, I am not going). The usage in this case is similar to that in English. If, however, I had phrased my question negatively and had asked, "Mr. Kosaka, aren't you going to Yokohama?" he would have answered either *"Hai, ikimasen"* (Yes, I am not going) or *"Iie, ikimasu"* (No, I am going).

This occasions merriment among some students. But slow down for a minute and think about it. In saying, "Yes, I am not going," Mr. Kosaka is, with his first word, confirming the implied assumption that he is not going and then reconfirming that he is not going with a negative form of the verb. If he had said, "Yes, you are right in your assumption. I'm not going," perhaps there would have been no cause for confusion or laughter. Regard, therefore, his statement "Yes, I am not going" as a contraction of "Yes, you're right. I'm not going," if you find this an easier path to clarity.

A note of caution: The Japanese often use *ja arimasen ka or ja nai ka* (isn't it, aren't they, etc.) after a positive statement when calling for agreement, e.g., *Ano seiji-ka no nigō-san wa iya ni unuborete iru ja nai ka?* (That politician's mistress is awfully conceited, isn't she?). Even though this sentence ends with *ja nai ka* and its built-in negation, the statement itself is positive—and the speaker expects positive agreement. So, if you know that particular politician's mistress and if you agree that she is conceited, you should answer *Hai,* not *Iie.*

One objection to the word *iie* is that it is hard for beginning students to pronounce correctly. (After the long or double vowel *i,* the *e* is like a small explosion of breath.) Another objection is the infrequency of its use: A few Japanese use *iie* often, most of them seldom use it, and some may go through life hardly using it at all.

You may ask, how then do they express a negative answer. Instead of *iie,* Mr. Average Japanese may use *Chigaimasu* (literally, It is different). When asked "Are you Mr. Kosaka?" Mr. Tanigawa could answer *Chigaimasu* rather than *Iie.* Or Mr. A. J. could use only the negative form of the verb in the question asked him: *"Okusan ni mikudarihan wo yatta ka?"* (Did you give your wife a letter of divorce?)

"Mada yaranai" (Not yet; lit., Have not given yet.). Or he could use *Sō de wa arimasen* or *So ja nai nda* (It is not so) instead of *Iie.*

"Yes, I'm Listening"

The dangerous aspect of the word *hai* for the beginner is that it is often used to mean not affirmation or agreement but rather that one person is following attentively the speech of another. This usage is especially noticeable in telephone conversations, perhaps because the Japanese mistrust the reliability of this instrument of communication. The following dialogue is given as a cautionary example:

FIRST SPEAKER: *Tonikaku, nē . . .* = Anyway . . .
SECOND SPEAKER: *Hai.*
FIRST SPEAKER: *Karakketsu da kara, nē . . .* = I'm broke, so . . .
SECOND SPEAKER: *Hai.*
FIRST SPEAKER: *Okane wo hayaku okutte moraitai nda ga . . .* = I want you to send me some money quickly . . .
SECOND SPEAKER: *Hai.*
FIRST SPEAKER: *Itsu okutte moraeru ka?* = When can I expect it? (lit., When can I get you to send?).
SECOND SPEAKER: *Hontō ni sumanai ga ima kotchi mo okane ga nakute komatte iru* = I'm really sorry, but I'm short of funds and am in a bind myself.

In this dialogue, the second speaker obviously did not intend affirmation or agreement each time he said *Hai.* What he did mean was, "I'm listening" or "Say on, I can hear you."

Often at conferences attended by American and Japanese businessmen, I have heard chilling exchanges like this:

AMERICAN CAMERA IMPORTER (speaking through interpreter): Can you ship by the end of this month? = *Getsumatsu made ni shukka dekimasu ka?*

JAPANESE CAMERA MANUFACTURER: *Hai. Raigetsu no hatsuka goro shukka dekimasu* = Yes. We can ship about the twentieth of next month.

The American importer, knowing enough Japanese to think that he knows that *hai* means yes, smiled brightly when he heard the word *hai*, but this reaction switched to puzzlement and then irritation when the interpreter went on to explain that the shipment would be effected around the twentieth of next month. In this case, *hai* meant only "I have heard and understood your question."

Instead of saying *hai* when we would say yes in English, a Japanese often says *Sō* or *Sō da* or *Sō desu* or *Sayō desu* or *Sayō de gozaimasu,* all meaning "It is so," in ascending order of politeness. Or he would repeat the verb in the question asked him, as in this example: *"Sake no mushi ga okotte imasu ka?"* (Are you ready for a drink? lit., Is your *sake* bug acting up?). *"Okotte imasu"* (It is acting up).

The Virtue of Vagueness

A major difficulty with yes and no answers in Japan is that the Japanese are fundamentally against them. They regard vagueness as a virtue. This was stated over a hundred years ago by Abe Masahiro when he proposed to the *shōgun* what the government's attitude toward Commodore Perry and his men should be: "Our policy shall be to evade any definite answer to their request while at the same time maintaining a peaceful demeanor."

This fondness for evasion may have had its roots in the fact that all during the feudal ages a samurai could lop off the head of any commoner if he acted "otherwise than expected." Not always knowing exactly how they were expected to act—or think or answer—many came to seek refuge in verbal vagueness and evasion.

Furthermore, the Japanese felt—and still feel—that it is better to be harmonious than right, and to this end they will go to great lengths to avoid appearing to oppose anyone. I recall a time when I was working as the export sales manager of a Japanese manufacturer of cameras. It was in the spring and the company's annual outing was approaching. A committee, consisting of one member from each of the company's sections, was formed and assigned the task of ascertaining the wishes of the employees and voting on where they would all like to go to enjoy a three-day holiday during the so-called Golden Week in early May.

I chanced to be named as the representative of the Export Department and, after some discussion, I learned that the thirty-odd members of Export preferred to spend their three-day weekend in the resort of Itō, on the Izu Peninsula. (It is pertinent to remark here that the expenses of the trip were to be equally borne by the Employees' General Fund, which was supported solely by monthly deductions from our salaries, and by the company itself.)

When the committee gathered for a decision, we each expressed the view of those we represented and then voted accordingly, some for Atami, some for Nikko, some for Itō, and so forth. Before a final tabulation of the votes was made, however, the male secretary (who came as an "observer" to the meeting) of the company president spoke up and said that the president was of the opinion that we all might like to go to the town of Suwa (where the company factory was situated) and spend our weekend learning how cameras were made.

A pall of silence fell over the committee. At length, embarrassed by the telltale silence, I took the bit in my stubby teeth and quickly reviewed the earlier voting: two for Atami, one for Nikko, three for Itō, two for Hakone, etc. Itō prevailed with three votes, so I asked if there were any objections.

The president's secretary looked around at us and, in a rather embarrassed manner, said: *"Suwādo-san wa o-wakari ni naranakatta deshō ga shachō no go-iken wa Suwa desu."* (You may not have understood, Mr. Seward, but the president thinks we should go to Suwa).

Still not *really* understanding, I proposed one more vote, which, needless to say, was now in favor of going to the town of Suwa to see our factory, with only one dissenting vote—mine.

Now I began to understand the lay of the land, but I nevertheless continued to protest. *"Dōse shachō no iken ni shitagau nara naze kono iinkai wo tsukutta ndesu ka?"* (If we were going to do what the president wanted anyway, why did we bother to form this committee?).

No satisfactory answer was forthcoming.

Then the chief of the Accounting Section, who was also head of the committee, asked me to reconsider and vote affirmatively. I felt, however, that I had to be true to the wishes of the Export staff, so I persisted in my vote. The end of the working day broke up the meeting, and I went home, realizing that the majority had voted in favor of Suwa and trying to find a scintilla of satisfaction in the thought that I had voted in accordance with the preference of my constituency.

That, however, was not to be the end of the comedy. Around ten o'clock the next morning, the president's secretary sidled up to me and asked if I would not reconsider my vote. I replied, *"Nan da! Mō kimatta nja nai ka? Suwa ni iku ndeshō. Sore yori nani ga hoshii ndesu ka?"* (What! It's already decided, isn't it? We're going to Suwa, aren't we? What more do you want?).

He replied, *"Suwādo-san no shōdaku ga hoshii ndesu"* (We want your agreement).

Having escorted one of our European distributors around Tōkyō until one o'clock that morning and having consumed much beer and *sake* in the process, I was in no mood to be trifled with. I was, in fact, ready—even eager—to quit the company and the camera business entirely. In this frame of mind, I launched myself into a four-minute monologue about the fatuities of the Japanese system, ending with a ringing declaration that I would never betray the trust placed in me by my fellow workers in Export. Eventually, however, I did just that—when I learned that buses for the trip to Suwa had been reserved two weeks before the first meeting of the committee. The whole thing had been nothing more than an empty ritual. They had gone to the trouble of forming the committee and having the trip discussed in each section so that, superficially at least, we would appear to be one large happy family, all of the same mind.

So I finally voted yes, but I tried to assuage the pains in my conscience by insisting that I go by train, where I could sulk, while everyone else went by bus.

I must say that I had a good time in Suwa that weekend, but I felt that my principles had been irretrievably compromised.

CHAPTER 5

Sign Language

The Style's the Thing

The Japanese have an evident fondness for doing things in stylized fashion. At times one is tempted to suspect that form is more important to them than substance. Witness the warming-up exercises that precede a brief practice session on the golf driving range. And the complete uniform, down to spiked shoes, that is necessary before a ten-year-old boy will consider playing a few casual innings of sandlot baseball. And the *de rigueur* position for taking photographs (left foot forward, knees slightly bent) and for being photographed (stiffly erect, stern expression, proper attire, thumbs along seams of trousers, heels together).

This fondness for stylized motion (also seen in the precise, almost contortionistic posturing of the traditional dances and in movie scenes of swordplay) provided a fertile soil in which gestures (*temane;* lit., hand mimic) could develop, and their growth was given impetus by a frequent compulsion to transmit certain ideas without resort to direct speech. The many gestures in use in Japan today are the result.

This chapter lists the more common and useful *temane*. Because you are a non-Japanese, many Japanese—convinced, somewhat illogically, of the universality of sign language— will use an extraordinary number of gestures in their initial efforts to establish communication with you. For this reason alone, you should familiarize yourself thoroughly with the sign language described in this chapter. As an additive far out of proportion with the slight effort needed to learn them, the use of these gestures will give viewers the impression that you are a person of considerable and varied experience in Japan.

First, note what the fingers are called in Japanese:

oya-yubi = thumb (lit., parent finger)
hitosashi-yubi = forefinger (lit., person-pointing finger)
naka-yubi = middle finger (lit., middle finger)
kusuri-yubi = ring finger (lit., medicine finger; from the use of this finger

for applying cosmetics when they were considered a kind of medicine)
ko-yubi = little finger (lit., child finger)

Twenty-eight Signs

What follow here (with illustrative anecdotes) are twenty-eight ways in which the Japanese employ sign language:

1. A circling motion with the forefinger pointed at one's own ear or temple casts doubt on the sanity of the person being discussed. *Hidari-maki,* a word meaning "to wind counterclockwise," is used to describe a perverse or eccentric person, so the circling movement of the forefinger in this gesture should be, strictly speaking, in the same direction. Purists who make this distinction also tell us that a clockwise movement carries the meaning of vanity. My experience, however, has been that any sort of circular motion of the forefinger near the ear signifies a doubt about someone's sanity. (Caution: I advise against using this gesture in jest.)

2. A circle formed by the index finger and thumb is interpreted as a reference to money.

3. The right hand held stiffly up in front of your face with the thumb nearest your nose, the palm facing to your left, is a gesture used when passing between two persons or crossing someone's path or when about to do something considered impolite.

It is somewhat similar to the American child's gesture of dislike or defiance, but the finger does not touch the nose and it is accompanied by bowing.

I saw this gesture used one day in a dining car on a Tōkaidō express train. The dining car was nearly empty, and I was seated so that I could see two Japanese men, each eating alone at tables on opposite sides of the aisle. One was trying to eat half a broiled chicken, and it was apparent from his difficulties that he had not had much experience with a knife and fork. Then, while I was wondering why he didn't eat it with his fingers, he made a powerful thrust at the bird—which flew across the aisle and landed on the plate of the other Japanese man.

It so happened, at that precise moment, that the second Japanese man, who was aristocratic in mien and conservative in dress, was gazing out the window at the waters of Lake Hamana. An empty plate had been set before him but his lunch had not yet been served. The rattle and clatter of the train must have covered the noise of the chicken's descent because he did not turn back to the table for a minute or two.

When he did, he found half a broiled chicken before him. (The first man had not been able to get even a bite.) The *table d'hôte* menu gave us a choice that day of Lunch A (steak) and Lunch B (broiled chicken), and I guess that he too must have ordered chicken. At least he accepted the fact of the fowl's arrival with equanimity and, taking utensils in hand, prepared to do it justice.

The now red face of the first Japanese became a study in conflicting emotions. Should he retrieve his bird, order something else, or just forget all about it? When he had made up his mind, he took a deep breath, stepped across the aisle, bowed, used the above gesture, and then silently picked up the chicken gingerly and returned with it to his table, leaving the astounded second man with his knife and fork poised over empty space.

The first man now assumed an air of studied nonchalance and returned to his struggle with the chicken, while the second stared in disbelief and wonder. Then he stood up abruptly and stalked to the rear of the dining car, where he began to wave his hands in the air and talk excitedly with the waiter.

My navel was about to boil tea (*o-heso ga o-cha wo wakasu,* meaning "to be convulsed with laughter"), so I dropped a thousand-yen note by the side of my check and fled out the other end of the dining car.

4. Going through the motions of putting a cigarette to the lips conveys a desire for one.

5. The motions of striking a match and lighting a cigarette are a request for a light.

6. The right index and middle fingers slapped against the palm of the half-cupped left hand means *sushi.* You will understand why when you watch a cook prepare these morsels of fish-topped vinegared rice.

7. The right forefinger pointed at your own nose means yourself in the same way that we would indicate ourselves by pointing to our hearts.

8. The left hand cupped and held near the mouth as if holding a bowl of rice and the fingers of the right hand going through the motions of using chopsticks signify eating or food.

9. Holding up the four outspread fingers of the hand, thumb folded in, is a pejorative gesture that indicates an *eta,* one of the outcast class of Japan. (See the chapter titled "How to Be Insulting in Japanese.")

10. Women—especially older women—tend to cover their mouth when they laugh. For a man to do so would be considered affected.

11. The right index and middle fingers tapped against the lips denote a kiss.

12. To call a person to you, extend your right arm straight out, bend the wrist down, and flutter the fingers. By elevating the fingers only a couple of inches, you would have our wave of goodbye.

One day in Hakone, I was watching a Japanese girl-guide whose American tourist-charges had become separated from her by a considerable distance and saw her use this gesture to try to gather her flock of about twenty elderly, bewildered-looking souls about her. The diverse effects were amusing. Some thought that they had been abandoned by their girl-guide and began to mill about like worried sheep. Others appeared to think that this was the signal for a drink and started to straggle back toward the bar of the hotel. Still others apparently interpreted it to mean that they were now on their own and began to disperse through the town.

13. Most Japanese shrink from the bodily contact of the handshake, which is not, of course, native to Japan. A few Japanese, knowing American ways, will shake hands with you vigorously. Others, knowing the manners of continental Europe, will shake hands at every meeting. But the average Japanese will shake hands—if he does so at all—with a limp, discouraged grip. Some natural-born comedians—both Western and Japanese—try to shake hands while bowing, which is both difficult and ridiculous. You should determine to do one or the other. And if you shake hands, don't try to break the bones in the other fellow's hand.

How deeply or how often to bow depends on several factors that I will not undertake to explain here, but a simple rule of thumb is to avoid extremes. One American I know, in his early, Lafcadio Hearn-ish enthusiasm to be as completely Japanese as possible, bowed deep and often to everyone—including his maid, the children in his neighborhood, and even *suigara-hiroi* (men who pick up cigarette butts) in front of Tōkyō station. Seeing this, Japanese acquaintances began to shun him. Not long thereafter, bitter and disillusioned, he quit his job and returned to the U.S.

14. The little finger pointed straight up means girlfriend, wife, or mistress. An advantage of this finger gesture is that you can use it to refer to the woman you saw Mr. Moribe out with last night when you are afraid to hazard a guess at the exact relationship between them. If you want to know if she will be in Mr. Moribe's company again tonight, you should point your little finger toward the ceiling, like a caricature of a prim tea drinker, and say: *"Konya mo* [finger up] *irasshaimasu ka?"* (Will the lady come with you again tonight?).

15. The thumb pointed up refers to a boyfriend, husband, patron, or *oyabun* (a boss, usually of gangsters or gamblers).

16. Some Japanese use the wink as a signal of understanding or suggestion of desired intimacy, but I believe that it is a recent import from the West and I doubt its effectiveness. It has never accomplished anything for me—other than eliciting giggles.

17. A fast crossing or tapping together of the index fingers tells the viewer of strained relations or of a fight. It is an example of a gesture replacing a word that the Japanese would rather not say, as if its utterance would invest an unpleasant situation with more reality.

18. The thumb rubbed against the nose suggests a card game called *hana*. *Hana* means both nose and flower and, there being flower designs on the cards, the Japanese punningly refer to the floral card game by drawing attention to the nose.

19. A tightly clenched fist has the same meaning as the English idiom "tightfisted."

20. Put your hands to your forehead with your two index fingers pointing up and angling outward. This *temane* says that someone is jealous. Whereas in English putting horns on a head means cuckolding a husband, Japanese horns tell of jealousy. The headgear—no one would call it a hat—worn by Japanese brides is called a *tsuno-kakushi* or horn-hider. This grotesque get-up is designed to conceal the bride's horns or jealous nature, at least for the duration of the wedding ceremony. Personally, I would prefer a *tsuno-nuki* or de-horner.

21. A hooked forefinger informs us that someone's fingers have a regrettable habit of catching on to—and carting off—the possessions of others.

22. Moving the thumb back and forth is a *temane* for *pachinko*. If you have played or watched this upright pinball game, you will recognize the motion.

23. The heel of the open hand hit lightly against the head shows your dismay when you suddenly remember something that you should not have forgotten.

24. Put your hand on the top of your head. Scratch or stroke your head briefly. This tells us that you are *komatta* (in a predicament or puzzled).

25. Moving the open hand, palm facing left, back and forth before your face as if fanning a flame signifies a negative response. The Japanese use this gesture often with foreigners whose comprehension of their language is in doubt.

26. Spread the fingers of the right hand slightly, hold this hand near your face with the edge directed to the front, and move it backward and forward, jerkily, a few times. Accompany this with bows of the head or body and repetitions of such locutions as *De wa, tanomimasu kara . . .* (Well, please do what I asked...). This gesture with words comes from a supplicant about to part from someone of whom he has asked a favor. (Similar, in appearance, to gesture 3, above.)

27. Raise the right arm, bent at the elbow. Make one spasmodic motion with the hand open. This breezy gesture of greeting can be used at any time of the day or night and is often accompanied by such words as *Yō!* (Hi!), *Ōssu* (Good morning: *Ohayō gozaimasu* is first shortened to *Ohayossu* and then to *Ōssu* or *Ossu*). Accompanying it with *Ō* (Hey, is it really you?) is popular among students and factory workers, as is *Dochira e?* (Where are you going?). This familiar gesture is also used when parting, followed by such phrases as *Jā, mata* (Well, see you again).

28. Some might argue that laughter is not a gesture in the proper sense, but I list it here because the Japanese use it to convey meaning without actual speech, as, of course, we also do. In addition to the emotions we usually associate with laughter (mirth, derision, relief, scorn), the Japanese extend it further to include embarrassment, confusion, shock, and even grief. In a way, laughter can be just as much a warning signal to the Japanese as the upraised hand, palm out, is to us. Used this way, laughter may be telling you to say no more, abandon this topic, or don't delve any deeper into whatever you were talking about.

CHAPTER 6

The Civilities

"Where Are You Going?"

Although these may not be mentioned in standard textbooks, two of the most frequently used greetings in Japanese are: *Dochira e?* (Where are you going?) and *O-dekake desu ka?* (Are you going out?).

For years I was unable to fully suppress a feeling of irritation when someone I hardly knew asked me where I was going, and so, in defense, I devised and used a variety of retorts hopefully designed to abash such interrogators. Some I used are: *Yopparai ni mairimasu* (I'm going to get juiced), *Sōri-daijin to kinō no dekigoto wo sōdan shite kuru* (I'm going to discuss yesterday's events with the prime minister), *Kanai no imōto to issho ni tetsudō-ōjō wo toge ni ikimasu* (My wife's younger sister and I are going to throw ourselves in front of a train), *Makka na momohiki wo katte kimasu* (I'm going to buy a pair of bright-red long johns), *Mise-monogoya ni kimi no otōsan wo mi ni ikimasu* (I'm going to the freak show to see your father), and *Moyori no karyūkai ni mairimasu* (I'm going to the nearest "flower-and-willow-world" [red-light district]).

Although I delivered these with stern face and steely glance, I usually got no more than nervous titters in reply. Nor could I detect any subsequent diminishing in the frequency of questions about my destination.

The second greeting, *O-dekake desu ka?* conjures up memories of a slumlike Tōkyō home in which I roomed for two years. The dear lady of the house stood waiting in the *genkan* (entrance) every morning to see me off on my way to work. As I came down the stairs and approached the door—with briefcase in hand and dressed for the office, it was her unfailing custom to ask if I was going out.

For months I answered simply, *Hai, dekakemasu* (Yes, I'm going out) because, at that hour of the morning, I am always busy thinking about how to get through the day. But little by little her matutinal ritual began to intrigue me. Every morning at the same time, except Sunday, I came down the stairs, fully dressed and equipped for work, and then left the house. And every morning upon seeing me, she asked the same question:

47

O-dekake desu ka? The more I thought about it, the more I wondered if there was not a sinister design behind her question.

Then one bleak, wintry morning when I was in a particularly gruff mood, I decided that the time for the counterattack had come. My tactics went like this:

LANDLADY: *O-dekake desu ka?* = Are you going out?
SEWARD: *Chigaimasu* = No, I'm not.
LANDLADY: *Ā, sō desu ka? De wa itte irasshai* = Oh, is that so? Well, goodbye.

Thereupon I left the house as usual. The following morning we had this exchange:

LANDLADY: *O-dekake desu ka?* = Are you going out?
SEWARD: *Dekakemasen* = I'm not going out.
LANDLADY: *De wa, itte irasshai* = Well, goodbye.

And the morning after that, this is what we said to each other:

LANDLADY: *O-dekake desu ka?* = Are you going out?
SEWARD: *Kyō uchi ni orimasu* = I will stay home today.
LANDLADY: *Itte irasshai* = Goodbye.

I tried a few more times after that, but my heart was not in it. Perhaps she did not really listen to what I said—or perhaps she was making allowances, as may often have been necessary—for the caprices of a barbaric American.

Over the years the patience of the Orient finally bested me. Like Kipling, I learned that you can't change the East. Nowadays when a man I scarcely know asks me, *Dochira e?* I smile a crooked smile and say, *Chotto sokorahen made* (Just down the street a ways). He probably does not really want to know my destination, anyway. And when someone asks, *O-dekake desu ka?* I breathe deeply and, forcing what little cheer I can muster into my voice, I answer, *Hai, itte kimasu* (Yes, I'm on my way).

I might add that, according to Osamu and Nobuko Mizutani, *O-dekake desu ka?* really means "How are you? I hope you enjoy yourself."

Salutations Using the Appreciative Form

A cardinal rule to remember about salutations in Japan is that you should first thank the person you are greeting for whatever he did for you at the time of your previous meeting. The Japanese seem to be able to always remember to do this, no matter how long the interval of time. Common forms used are: *Kono mae wa arigatō gozaimashita* (Thank you for [whatever you did] the previous occasion), *Senjitsu wa dōmo sumimasen deshita* (Sorry to have troubled you the other day [or Thanks for what you did for me the other day]), and *Yūbe wa taihen go-chisōsama deshita* (Thank you for the excellent dinner last night).

Even if you were the host or the giver of the gift or the doer of the good deed, it would not be inappropriate for you to make first mention of the occasion, the idea being that you are apologizing for not having done as much as you should have. This is especially valid if your vis-à-vis is a person whose good will you value highly. In such a case, however, you should say: *Senjitsu* [or *Kono mae* or *Yūbe*] *wa dōmo shitsurei itashimashita* (I was quite rude the other day [or on the previous occasion or last night]). You may, of course, have been a paragon of politeness, but—no matter. You have to say such things if you want to play the game.

Common Civilities: Thirteen Guidelines

1. Meeting an Acquaintance

1. *Ohayo gozaimasu* = Good morning (lit., It is early). This can be used until noon but it is better to begin using *Konnichi wa* instead around ten A.M. Persons who work at night, however, can use this expression at the beginning of their working hours. *Ohayō* is the familiar contraction; *Ohayossu, Ōssu,* and *Ossu* are slangish forms used mostly by students and laborers.

2. *Konnichi wa* = Hello (lit., As for this day). Seldom used with members of one's own group.

3. *Moshi-moshi* = Hello (when speaking on the telephone). Long years of poor telephonic connections during and after World War II have instilled in many Japanese a semiconscious distrust of this instrument. Hesitation in answering gives rise to the suspicion that the line has been cut and then we hear *Moshi-moshi* over and over again, meaning "Hello!" "Are you there?" "Can you hear me?"

4. *Komban wa* = Good evening (lit., As for this evening). In general use after dark, but see caution under 2. above.

5. *Ikaga desu ka?* = How are you? (lit., How are?). Many foreigners misuse and overuse this question. In addition to the meaning given, it

can also mean, "How about it?" Let us say, for example, that you frequently have a drink with one of your co-workers at the end of the working day. On this particular day you see him approaching you in the corridor and you say, *"Ikaga desu ka?"* He will not take this to mean that you are inquiring about his health. Instead, he will assume that you mean, "How about it? Shall we have our drink?"

6. *O-genki desu ka?* = Are you in good health? This greeting is more specific than *Ikaga desu ka?* It is best used to someone you have not met for quite a while and whose health you really want to know about.

7. *Dōzo o-saki ni* = Please go ahead of me. When you meet someone in a doorway or crowded passage, you can use this phrase if you want him to precede you. It is often shortened to *Dōzo,* particularly when accompanied by a gesture. The word *Dōzo* alone, however, presents problems for foreigners who are tempted to always use it in the same way they would use "Please" in English. The Japanese use *Dōzo* more when granting than when requesting permission or a favor.

8. *Shibaraku desu (nē?)* = It has been a long time since I last met you (hasn't it?).

9. *Hisashi-buri de gozaimasu* = same as *Shibaraku desu.*

II. ENTERING A HOME OR SHOP

1. *Gomen kudasai* = Excuse me. Japanese homes are inadequately equipped for summoning people from the interior, so the custom is to slide open the door and step inside to the place where you would change your shoes for slippers. There you call out *Gomen kudasai* or the name of the person you want to see. Although *Gomen kudasai* and *Gomen nasai* are both translated as "Excuse me" or "Pardon me," the former is usually used when entering or leaving a house or to mean "Goodbye" at the end of a telephone conversation or when parting from a friend, even on the street. The latter is used more to mean "Excuse me" by family members to each other and is more favored by women.

2. *O-jama shimasu* = I am intruding. When you have been invited to enter, use this locution after you have changed your shoes for slippers and are stepping into the house. *O-jama sasete itadakimasu* (Please allow me to intrude) is a degree politer.

3. *Yō-koso* = Welcome (said by the host). An abbreviation of *Kore wa yō-koso oide kudasaimashita* (How good of you to have come).

4. *Yoku irasshaimashita* = I am glad to see you (lit., You are well come). Also said by the host.

III. As a Guest, Before Eating

1. *Itadakimasu* = I will partake, I will have some, *or* Here goes. Say this just before taking the first bite or sip.

IV. As a Guest, After Eating

1. *Go-chisōsama de gozaimashita* = It was an honorable feast. This is the fearfully worn but nonetheless correct and most often used expression. Actually, you would go farther toward persuading your host or hostess that you truly enjoyed the dinner if you said something like, *Jitsu ni oishikatta desu* (It was really delicious).

V. As a Host, Serving Guests

1. *O-kuchi ni awanai deshō ga dōzo* = You probably won't like this food, but please begin. I have a brilliant but eccentric Japanese friend who likes to respond to such offerings with: *Sore nara itadakimasen* (If that's so, then I won't have any).

2. *Nanimo gozaimasen ga go-enryo naku o-meshiagari kudasai* = We have nothing to offer you, but please partake of it freely. We hear this contradictory offer quite often.

VI. Returning Home

1. *Tadaima* = I'm home *or* I'm back (lit., Just now). The full form is *Tadaima kaerimashita* (I have just now returned). This is said upon entering the house after being out all day or at least for longer than only a brief stroll in the garden.

2. *O-kaeri-nasai* = Welcome home (lit., Please return). This is the greeting used by people who stayed at home to the one who has just come back.

VII. PARTING

1. *Sayōnara* = Goodbye (lit., If it is so *or* If it must be so). This is a proper word but Occidentals tend to overuse and mispronounce it. (See Chapter 3, "Pronounce It Right," 5.) To mean "Goodbye," the Japanese use other words and phrases at least as much as they use *Sayōnara,* which is rarely if ever used among family members, or to older persons, or to one's superiors.

2. *Mata* = See you again. Several civilities include this word, e.g., *Ja, mata* (Well, see you again), *Mata ashita* (See you again tomorrow), *Mata aimashō* (Let's meet again), and *Ja, izure mata* (Well, so long).

3. *O-genki de* (or *O-genki de itte irasshai*) = Go in good health *or* Take care of yourself. This is said to one leaving on a trip.

4. *O-yasumi-nasai* = Good night (lit., Please rest). This should be spoken to one who is on the point of retiring for the night, but it is often used when friends part at the end of an evening, although they may still face a long road home.

5. *Mata o-me ni kakarimashō* = I hope to meet you again (lit., Again I'll hang before your eyes).

VIII. EXPRESSING APPRECIATION

1. *Arigatō* = Thanks. More politely, *Arigatō gozaimasu, Arigatō gozaimashita,* or *Arigatō zonjimasu. Ari* is from the verb *aru* (to be) and *gatō* is from *gatai* or *katai* (difficult). A direct translation would be, "It is difficult to be," which succinctly expresses the Japanese reaction after receiving gifts or favors. In a sense, the Japanese dislike being the recipients of such kindnesses because it places a burden—what they call an *on*—on them. They feel obliged to reciprocate but worry that they may not be able to easily do what may be asked of them. Most Americans experience difficulty in correctly pronouncing *arigatō,* with its *r* and medial *g* and long *ō*. Until good pronunciation is mastered, such students would do well to use other words of appreciation (see 2, 4, and 5, below). Most of us use this word too often, anyway.

2. *Sumimasen.* The Japanese seem to use this word more often than *arigatō* in situations where we would say "Thank you." We can translate it either as "Thanks" or as "I'm sorry," but the literal meaning is, "This is not the finish," or "It has not ended." And, of course, this is exactly what the Japanese are saying when they express appreciation—

that this is not the end of the matter, that it will not be over until they have somehow repaid their benefactor. *Sumimasen* is used more to express thanks for unexpected or undeserved favors and is somewhat more popular with women and the young.

3. *Dō itashimashite.* This troublesome phrase (the pronunciation of which certain defectives quaintly imagine to resemble "Don't touch my moustache") can be used to mean both "You are welcome" and "Thank you." The most apt single translation is "Don't mention it." Let's say a friend compliments you on the distance you can spit. In English, if you take any pride at all in such an accomplishment, you might reply, "Thank you." In Japanese, however, it would be better not to reply, *Arigatō,* because receiving a compliment is not the kind of favor that makes one feel very "difficult to be." Rather, you should say, *Dō itashimashite,* meaning "Don't mention it" or "It's not worthy of your notice."

4. *Iroiro to dōmo* = Thank you very much for the various favors (lit., Various very much). These words could be followed by *arigatō gozaimashita* or *o-sewasama de gozaimashita* (see 5, below). Standing alone, they are well understood, especially if accompanied by bows.

5. *O-sewasama de gozaimashita* = Thank you for your help (lit., It was your honorable assistance).

6. *Sore wa, sore wa. . . .* This is short for *Sore wa kekko desu ne,* or for *Sore wa dōmo arigato gozaimashita* (That is fine *or* Thank you for that.)

7. *Sō osshararete wa haji irimasu* = Your saying that makes me blush. A bit hard to pronounce but a very classy expression.

8. *Kyōshuku desu* = I am grateful (lit., I grow small with fear, e.g., in awe of the magnitude of the favor.) Often used.

9. *Sekkaku desu ga. . . .* Thanks but (I can't go; I can't accept).

IX. ASKING PARDON; APOLOGIZING

1. *Gomen nasai* = Pardon me *or* Excuse me (lit., Please give me your honorable dismissal or forgiveness [for my offense]). (See II. ENTERING A HOME OR SHOP, 1, above.)

2. *Sumimasen* = Pardon me. (See VIII. EXPRESSING APPRECIATION, 2, above.)

3. *Shikkei* = Whereas the literal meaning of *shitsurei* is "to lose one's manners" that of *shikkei* is "to lose one's [proper] respect [for others]." In effect, both mean "I was rude" or "Please forgive my rudeness." *Shikkei* alone is rather informal—a word blurted out in the confusion of

the moment. Also, *Kore wa shikkei!* Note that *De wa, shikkei (shimasu)* and *De wa, shitsurei (shimasu)* are both used on parting and mean "Well, I must be rude and leave you now."

4. *Shitsurei shimashita* = I was rude. Also, *Tsui shitsurei itashimashita* (I was accidentally rude).

5. *O-yurushi kudasai* = Please forgive me.

6. *O-matase itashimashita* = I'm sorry to have kept you waiting.

7. *O-machidōsama deshita* = I regret making you wait. (This is used more by people engaged in serving customers.)

8. *Mōshiwake arimasen* = That was inexcusable *or* Please forgive me. Some teachers translate *mōshiwake* as "apology" and then go on to render *Mōshiwake arimasen,* which would, accordingly, mean, "I have no apology," or "I apologize." Analysis of the word *mōshiwake,* however, brings the picture into clearer focus: *mōshi* is from *mōsu,* a polite verb meaning to speak; *wake* means reason or sense. When one says *Mōshiwake arimasen,* he is saying, in effect, that he has no way of telling or explaining his (rude) action that would make sense (from the viewpoint of good manners). He has no reasonable excuse for what he did, so all that he can do is to throw himself on your mercy and beg your forgiveness, which good manners dictate will be forthcoming.

9. *Go-meiwaku wo kakemashita* = I'm sorry to have caused you trouble.

10. *Go-mendōsama de gozaimashita* = I'm sorry to have bothered you.

11. *Go-burei de gozaimashita* = I apologize for my rudeness. Whereas *shitsurei* means "loss of manners," *burei* means "no manners." To me, this locution smacks of the language of professional military men—polite but stern and somehow harsh.

12. *O-wabi itashimasu* = I apologize.

13. *O-kinodoku-sama de gozaimashita* = I'm very sorry (lit., It must have been poison to your honorable spirit). Technically, this sentence should not be included here, but I have done so because some beginners learn the translation "I am sorry" and mistakenly use this phrase when apologizing. It should, of course, be used when one is sympathizing with another's grief or disappointment.

14. *Dōmo habakari-sama de gozaimashita* = I'm sorry to have bothered you.

15. *Anata ni ayamaritai ndesu ga . . .* = I want to apologize to you for . . .

X. CALLING ATTENTION TO YOURSELF

This brings up problems that are often vexing for a foreigner living in Japan. How many hundreds of times have I been kept waiting at counters in stores for someone to sell me what I wanted! The following true incident is both illustrative and typical: The curtain rises with me standing patiently at a counter in Tōkyō's Matsuzakaya Department Store. I have been there for five minutes. Other (Japanese) customers have come and gone. Four idle salesgirls loiter behind the counter, all staring fixedly in other directions. Occasionally one whispers to another and they all begin to titter. Having coughed and cleared my thoat until hoarse, I finally say, *"O-negai itashimasu"* (Will you help me, please?).

This evokes no reaction at all. Diffidently still, I repeat my request. At last one of the girls, whose eye I have caught by nimble physical maneuvering, flushes and, with a muttered aside to her still idle co-workers, hurries off toward the rear of the store. I silently pray that her trip is connected with my presence and not merely a fortuitous call of nature. Six minutes later she returns leading an old gentleman who is still knotting his tie. She points him at me. He approaches, inhales audibly, and says, "May I herupu you, sah?"

I am devastated. She has fetched an interpreter. But I regroup my faltering forces and press forward again: *"Sumimasen. Sono hyaku-en no hankachi wo ichimai kaitakatta ndesu ga"* (Sorry to bother you. I wanted to buy one of those hundred-yen handkerchiefs).

The old gentleman is momentarily taken aback but he covers his confusion with laughter. The salesgirls—sensing comedy in the raw—begin to edge in.

"Ah, you speakku beri good Japanneezu. Ha, ha, ha. Wheah you rearn?" (For the aging interpreter to revert to Japanese at this point would cause him great loss of face.)

By now five customers have gathered to regard this eerie scene in which a Japanese is speaking English to an American and the American is speaking Japanese to the Japanese. But I too have passed the point of no return, so I say, *"Dō itashimashite. Kanda-umare no Shiba-sodachi desu"* (It's really nothing at all. I was born in Kanda and raised in Shiba).

This lie stuns the old fellow. He signals for the salesgirl to take over and, after an unsteady bow, he staggers off to his hidey-hole in the rear. I have won—but it is a Pyrrhic victory. I still don't have my handkerchief, I have lost seventeen minutes, and the girl I was on my way to meet in front of Yūraku-chō station may have become indignant and gone back home. Exit Seward, weeping. Curtain.

1. *Ano nē* = Excuse me (lit., That ... isn't it?). However, there is no really good translation. It is used as the British use, "I say there!" This form is also interlarded into conversation with the meaning of "As I was saying" or "Now listen." Sometimes *Ano* alone is used.

2. *Chotto* = Just a minute. This is rather informal and nonpolite. It is often used in calling the attention of waitresses, bartenders, and so forth.

3. *Oi* = Hey (rough).

4. *Kora* = Hey (rougher).

5. *Moshi-moshi* = Hello there. It is often used to call for service when one enters an apparently empty shop. (See also I. MEETING AN ACQUAINTANCE, 3.)

6. *O-negai shimasu* = Will you help me, please? (lit., I ask).

XI. FOR GUESTS DEPARTING

1. *O-saki ni* = Pardon me for leaving before you. This is short for *O-saki ni shitsurei shimasu* and is said to one's co-workers and supervisor when leaving the workbench or office before they do.

2. *Gomen kudasai* = Excuse me. It is said when leaving a home or when parting with an acquaintance. (See also II. ENTERING A HOME OR SHOP, 1.)

3. *Shitsurei shimasu* = I must leave now. (Compare with IX. ASKING PARDON; APOLOGIZING, 4.)

4. *O-jama shimashita* = I have intruded on you.

5. *Mata o-jama sasete itadakimasu* = I'll call on you again (lit., I'll cause you trouble again).

6. *Mō o-itoma itashimasu* = I must be going now. *Itoma* means "leave-taking."

7. *Dōmo nagai itashimashita* = I have stayed too long. *Nagai* is composed of *naga* from the adjective *nagai* (long) and *i* from the verb *iru* (to be).

8. *Dōmo nagajiri itashimashita* = I have stayed too long. *Naga* is the same as in 7, above, but *jiri* is from *shiri* (hips, buttocks).

XII. SEEING OFF GUESTS

1. *Mata dōzo* = Please come again.
2. *Mata o-ide kudasai* = Please come again.
3. *Motto go-yukkuri nasareba ii no ni* = I wish you wouldn't hurry.
4. *Mada yoroshii ja arimasen ka?* = Same as 3.

XIII. THE BOW AND BOWING

Although bowing is soundless (except for the creaking of old joints like mine), no review of the Japanese civilities that does not mention it could be tolerated. The bow *(o-jigi)* is so automatic to the Japanese that I have seen sincere men and women bowing to persons miles away—on the other end of a telephone conversation. It enhances, emphasizes, and augments many of the civilities described above. If you ever have the opportunity, observe two older women having a *kōtō-sen* in the road or in the middle of a busy sidewalk, oblivious to all around them. (*Kotō-sen* is a bowing contest and *kōtō* means hitting the head against the floor. Our word "kowtow" comes from the original Chinese. This word is not in common use in the spoken language, although the *kanji* are immediately intelligible to even twelve-year-old Japanese children.) Regard how the two women, even at the nadir of their bows, covertly eye the depth and duration of the other's obeisance. Watch how they keep trying to get in the last bow, like children playing tag. See how each bows slightly to her own right to avoid bumping the other's head. When they part at last and begin to walk away from each other, note the difficult contortions they go through to bow and look over their shoulders at the same time.

Recent statistical surveys have found that seventy percent of all Japanese men bow at a five-degree-from-vertical angle, twenty-five percent bow at an angle of fifteen degrees, and five percent at thirty degrees. In the case of women, thirty percent bow at angles of five degrees, sixty percent bow at twenty degrees, and ten percent at thirty degrees. Office girls were found to bow, on the average, once every eleven minutes, and conductors on busy trains about 2,100 times daily. But the hands-down winners of this Oriental Aching Back Contest were the girls who stand at the entrance to the escalators in department stores—they bow at least 2,500 times every day.

One day in Kamakura I happened to see a Japanese man relieving himself in a ditch by the side of the road. Just then a woman in *kimono*—evidently an acquaintance—came out of a nearby house and walked toward him. Ah, the dilemma: should he greet—or ignore—her? The struggle to decide showed clearly on his face. Once he made up his mind, however, he carried out his decision manfully. With remarkable flexibility for his age—and with remarkable self-assurance for any age, he lifted his hat with one hand and bowed from the waist toward the woman, all the while carrying on the business at hand—the *other* hand, that is.

Not long ago I received a letter from Ray Bidwell, a friend in Japan, who has experimented with some of the expressions I have suggested for use. One morning when he was leaving the Japanese house where he is rooming, the mother of the family and her grown son came to the *genkan* to see Ray on his way. When they asked his destination, he told them he was going out to buy some *makka no momohiki* (bright-red long-johns). The mother, who is a slightly hard of hearing, asked her son what Ray had said, and the son repeated the American's words verbatim. "Oh," the mother said, "he likes *red* ones?" The way of the humorist is very hard.

CHAPTER 7

Titles

Shoulder Writing

The Japanese people are as addicted to titles as they are to tea and rice. One apperceptive Japanese observer of the scene has written: *"Nihonjin wa hito no nōryoku ya seikaku ni me wo mukezu chii ya katagaki de handan suru kuse ga aru"* (The Japanese tend to judge a person more by his title and social position than by his character and actual ability).

Titles are more important than names because names alone—unless those of famous persons—give no hint as to what places in the social cosmos their owners occupy. And, to the Japanese, a person's *hombun* (his station in life, assigned by fate) is extremely important.

As a casual experiment, I once had printed a batch of *meishi* (name or business cards) that gave only my name and Tōkyō telephone number in English on one side and the Japanese equivalent on the back. At the time I was quite active around Tōkyō and must have passed out at least a dozen of these *meishi* daily. At first I was astonished, then amused, and finally intrigued by the consternation they caused. To those who asked, I explained that these *meishi* gave my name, in both English and Japanese, and told how to communicate with me. Was that not sufficient? Indeed not, they protested. A name and telephone number were far from being enough. Just what was I? What was my position, my company, my sphere of influence? The truly important data, they clamored, were not written on the card at all.

What they wanted, of course, was a title or *katagaki* (lit., writing on the shoulder). I have even met Japanese who did not know that their emperor's name is Hirohito, although this was before the publication of the Japan edition of the book by that name. This extreme example was occasioned not so much by love of nescience as by the fact that the emperor is always referred to by title, i.e., His Majesty the Emperor *(Tennō Heika* or *Kinjō Heika)*, rather than by title and name, i.e., Emperor Hirohito.

Name-Suffix Titles

The foreign student of Japan and of its language and people should learn correct forms of address and titles as early during his sojourn as possible. There is little that grates more harshly on Japanese ears than misusage of these forms. We Americans take it as a cardinal rule of social conduct that we should learn the family name of another person immediately upon meeting him, use his name frequently in our colloquy with him to demonstrate that it has been indelibly imprinted on our memory, and then advance expeditiously to the stage, if not there to begin with, where the casual use of given names is the order of the day. But the Japanese do not feel this way about it at all. They would prefer to avoid the use of names and show to whom or of whom they are speaking by titles and by polite or nonpolite forms of speech. If names are used, they should be followed, not preceded, by the correct title or form of address. The common Japanese name-suffix titles are:

san	Mr., Mrs., or Miss
sama	Mr., Mrs., or Miss (more polite)
dono	Esquire (a written form)
kun	Used instead of *san* among, to, and about boys and students and by men on close terms
chan	Used as a diminutive suffix of endearment, usually attached to the first names of children
shi	A polite form of address used in the written language

Since none of these lend themselves to exact English translation, we should examine them more carefully.

I. SAN

This is the form of address you will use most frequently. As noted in the foregoing list, it carries the meanings of Mr., Mrs., or Miss, but it is used more extensively in Japanese than these equivalents are used in English. If you had a maid named Betty Brown in Bug Tussle, Texas, you likely called her Betty, unless, perhaps, she was a much older woman or unless you preferred the endearing form, "Hey, you!" But if you have a maid in Yokohama whose name is Katō Hanako (given name last), you should call her Hanako-san. If the Hashimoto family next door to you has an eighteen-year-old son whose first name is Ryūnosuke, you should address him as Hashimoto-san or Ryūnosuke-san, the latter especially if you are much older than he or have known him for some years. If you summon the conductor on a train, you should say, *Shashō-san* (Mr. Conductor), not *Shashō* alone.

Because *san* is commonly used for Mr., Mrs., or Miss, confusion may sometimes arise about exactly whom you mean. Let us suppose that you telephone the Morimoto residence to speak to their captivating twenty-year-old daughter, whose first name you unfortunately do not know yet. A woman answers the telephone. You ask, *"Morimoto-san desu ka?"* (Is this Miss [or Mr. or Mrs.] Morimoto?). The woman answers, *"Hai, Morimoto desu"* (Yes, this is Morimoto). At this point you do not know whether you are speaking to the twenty-year-old charmer or her ogress of a mother or her cronish grandmother—or even to a servant, who would have been saying, "Yes, this is the Morimoto residence." The answering female voice trembled slightly, but you cannot be sure whether this was from old age or an evil temper or the vibrant thrill of getting a call from you. So you have little choice but to explain yourself (which may not be a wise course if the mother is like most Japanese mothers and suspects the intentions of all Americans, most Frenchmen, and even a few Englishmen), and you say, "My name is Thompson. I met Morimoto-san yesterday at the Fūten Tea Parlour. She kindly offered to serve as my girl-guide . . ." If you have not heard a disconcerting click by this time, you may soon be talking to your future truelove.

To specify that you want to speak, for example, to the Morimoto-san who is the head of the family, you can ask, *Morimoto-san no otaku desu ka? Go-shujin wa irasshaimasu ka?* (Is this the Morimoto residence? Is the "honorable important-person" there?). In the case of the wife, you could ask, *Morimoto-san no okusama wa irasshaimasu ka?* (Is the wife of Morimoto-san there?).

If you want to speak to one of the children and do not know his or her first name, you can use one of the words that indicate the sex and age-ranking of the children, such as: *chōnan* (eldest son), *jinan* (second son), *sannan* (third son), *chōjo* (oldest daughter), *jijo* (second daughter).

Geisha often call guests with whom they are *en rapport* on the *tatami* by the first syllable of their family name with the suffix *san*. Thus a Mr. Miyoshi might be addressed (preferably after a round or three of *o-sake*) as Mii-san, the initial syllable being purposely elongated. Although basically a *geisha* ploy, it has migrated to some bars and nightclubs. It is a distinctly incongruous experience to hear Mr. Hata, the stern, dignified head of a mighty *zaibatsu* corporation offhandedly called "Hā-san," but, of course, the great use of Japanese-style restaurants *(o-zashiki)* is not so much for the consumption of comestibles as it is the breaking down of formality and the establishment of familiarity. But take heed: it does not follow that because a *geisha* calls Mr. Hata "Hā-san," you can too. Don't even consider it.

If you are an American, you may be itching to cast aside all this formality. You may be chafing under the restraint of having to call your maid Miss Hanako or your office boy Mr. Tanaka. But be patient. In due course, these forms of address will come to seem quite natural. Then you may shudder at the mere thought of uttering such names without their proper name-suffix titles. I have in mind one Japanese man two years younger than I am, with whom I have associated closely for seventeen years. His name is Hori Makoto. I have always called him Hori-san; now I could never bring myself to call him Hori or Makoto or even Makoto-san.

If, of course, you are speaking in English to a Japanese who is Westernized or Americanized, then you should, I believe, follow the practices of the foreign country in which he had his experiences. Be certain, however, that the man to whom you are talking is thoroughly accustomed to our ways. It is easy to be deceived by a firm handshake and a few phrases of passably fluent English. By "accustomed," I mean that he should have resided abroad for at least several years. Having studied English for six or eight years in schools in Japan is not, in any sense, sufficient qualification.

II. SAMA

The suffix *san* is a contraction of the politer word *sama* and is heard more often. In the written language, however, *sama* is used extensively. It is always used, for example, in addressing envelopes and packages. In the spoken language, *sama* is not normally used with a person's name; *san* is the common usage. We often hear *sama,* however, in such words as *danna-sama, okusama, ojisama, obasama, okosama,* and *ojōsama* (master, wife, uncle, aunt, child, and daughter). Note that *sama* in some words may become *chama* when said to or by children, e.g., *ojichama, obachama,* etc.

III. Dono

The *kanji* for *dono* is 殿, which is also read *tono,* as in *tonosama,* meaning feudal lord. It is a derivative polite form of address used only in the written language. "Esquire" is an often used, if not quite precise, translation.

IV. Kun

The *kanji* for this title is 君; another reading of the same character is *kimi,* both a familiar word for "you" and an old word meaning "prince" or "ruler." (The town of Kisarazu in Chiba was originally called Kimisarazu, meaning "the prince will not depart"; the bride of a certain prince was drowned in the waters of the bay near there and the prince, inconsolable in his grief, mourned there so long that at length his disconcerted courtiers reported in consternation to the court that *Kimi sarazu.*)

The suffix *kun* is commonly used among male students and among boys who grew up together. In the latter instance, they may continue to use this form of address, no matter how superannuated and decrepit they become. Assuming that they are approximately equal, two men who meet for the first time in, say, their thirties may come to use the suffix-title *kun* with each other but not until some time has lapsed and they have become close friends.

The above usage of *kun* is the so-called familiar form, based on friendship and intimacy. Another usage can be called the "superior-to-inferior form," employed more to emphasize a difference in station than any feeling of closeness or affection. In this reference, teachers at precollege-level schools use *kun* with their male students, and adults in general may use *kun* in speaking with boys up to college age.

For years I was puzzled by the manner in which Japanese newspapers use *kun.* In one story, a twenty-two-year-old man would be called *kun;* in another, a seventeen-year-old boy would be called *san.* Individual newspaper interpretation varies, but it would appear that the decision of whether to use *san* or *kun* is based not only on age but also on whether or not the person is married, going to school, or working. A seventeen-year-old youth, gainfully employed and married, could be called *san;* a twenty-two-year-old man, single, and studying for an advanced college degree, could be called *kun.*

In companies, shops, and government offices, a supervisor is entitled to use *kun* with his subordinates, but, of course, this usage is unilateral. Here we have no hard-and-fast rules. Some supervisors may, from the first day they take up the duties of their new positions, begin addressing all their subordinates as *kun,* to smother in embryo any doubt about who is boss. Others may be more circumspect and wait until they are surer of their footing, until they are cognizant of the various cliques and whose sister is married to the younger brother of the company president, but in due course most of them will get around to using *kun.*

Oddly, I have heard supervisors address young office girls as *kun,* but this name-suffix title is nevertheless regarded as essentially masculine in nature.

V. CHAN

This diminutive of *san* is used as an affectionate form of address to both male and female children and is heard most often in the home, one's own neighborhood, and kindergarten. It is used with the given name only, not with the family name. It may be attached either to the given name in its full form, e.g., Tarō-chan or Jirō-chan, or to an abbreviated form of the given name. In the case of the latter, Yoshiko would be called Yot-chan, Saburō would be called Sabu-chan, and Masako would be called Masa-chan. Whether the *chan* attaches to the full given name or to an abbreviated form is generally predeterminative and not discretionary; although predetermined, it is based on common usage and euphony, and is not amenable to clear-cut rules.

The habit of addressing a person as *chan* may persist even after he or she has reached adulthood. Children who grew up together may continue to use *chan* when addressing each other even into their twenties. And it is not inconceivable that a seventy-year-old mother might call Kazuko, her fifty-year-old daughter, Kazu-chan.

Nicknames can also take *chan* as a suffix. A girl of dark complexion might be called Kuro-chan, *kuro* being the root of *kuroi,* an adjective with the meaning of "black." This would be like calling her "Blackie" in English. "Fatty" would be Bū-chan, *buta* being the word for pig and *bū-bū* being the equivalent of oink-oink. I have heard the emperor *(Tennō Heika)* referred to as Ten-chan, but this is highly irreverent (albeit basically much more affectionate than contemptuous) and should be avoided.

Analogous to *chan* is the suffix *bō,* which is attached only to the names of boys. It is used in the family and neighborhood, more by adults when speaking to boys than among boys themselves. Sometimes, however, the boy's name with the *bō* suffix will become sufficiently popular to be used by other children as well and may even adhere to the boy as he grows up. Normally, the *bō* is suffixed to the first two syllables of the given name, e.g., Kazutsugu would become Kazubō, Masaru would become Masabō, and Shin would become Shimbō.

VI. SHI

In the written language, *shi* is sometimes suffixed to family names instead of *san* to indicate men of considerable stature who may not have specific titles as *sensei* (teacher), *buchō* (department head), *kyoku-chō* (bureau chief), or what have you. It is occasionally used in the spoken language when one is speaking rather formally or (sometimes) facetiously.

Titles for Social Positions

In addition to these name-suffix titles, actual titles of position such as section chief and branch chief are used extensively. As long as there is no doubt which section chief is meant, the title alone, without the name, can suffice. Though speaking directly to a particular section chief, one can and often does use third-person forms, just as we might say in English, "When does the General wish to have his staff car sent around?" even when speaking directly to the general in question. Thus we might say in Japanese the equivalent of, "When does the *Buchō* (Section Chief) wish to call the meeting?" or "Shall I telephone the *Buchō's* wife and tell her that he is leaving on a trip?"

Sensei, meaning teacher, is perhaps the most senselessly overused title in Japanese. In addition to all true teachers, a great many other people who are merely good at something or other are honored with this title. (In Japan, I should inject, teachers are held in much higher esteem than in the United States.) Master chefs, fashion designers, senior cartoonists, political commentators, and a great host of others can be called *sensei.* I knew a twenty-eight-year-old fashion model, a high-school dropout, who was addressed as *sensei* by other models only a few years her junior. And I suspect that one would not be thought eccentric even if he were to address *pachinko* experts, champion spitters, and drag-race winners as *sensei*.

Physicians *(isha)* are always addressed as *sensei;* Dr. Doi, for instance, would be called Doi Sensei.

Attaching the suffix *san* to the word for one's occupation transforms it into a kind of title. For example, the *nikuya* (butcher) becomes Niku-ya-san (Mr. Butcher), the *untenshu* (driver) becomes Untenshu-san (Mr. Driver), and the *kangofu* (nurse) becomes Kangofu-san (Miss Nurse).

The housewife will seldom know the names of tradespeople near her, even though she may have patronized them for years. If she has to get the attention of her butcher she will call out, *"Nikuya-san"* By extension, almost everyone is entitled to one of these occupational titles and is often so called, as in these examples: *Gakusei-san* (Mr. College Student), *Haitatsuya-san* (Mr. Delivery Man), *O-hyakushō-san* (Mr. Farmer), *Funanori-san* (Mr. Sailor), *Uekiya-san* (Mr. Gardener), and *Denkiya-san* (Mr. Electrician).

It is axiomatic that no one attaches *san* to his own name or title, with the exception of children who might do so unwittingly or adults who might do so deliberately in order to posit polite usage in the mind of a very young listener.

The foreign student of Japanese is advised to use *san* almost exclusively during the first one or two years of his studies. Awareness of the nice distinctions in usage should come in time. Even then, if in doubt, use *san,* since it is better to err on the side of politeness; no one will really think less of you for using *san* when a native Japanese might have used *kun*.

Whatever you do, be certain to use one of the forms of address we have discussed. (Japanese newspapers suffix *san, kun,* or *chan*—or titles— to all names except those of criminals and, sometimes, of foreigners— which shows where we stand.) To call a person by his family name alone (e.g., *"Oi, Inukai!"*) indicates either a far greater degree of intimacy with a Japanese (of the same sex) than a foreigner who comes to Japan for the first time as an adult can normally expect to achieve—or that you are consciously being extremely rough and perhaps even bellicose in your speech. Use of the first name alone (e.g., *"Gonsuke"*) would not sound quite so rough but could be taken as even more contemptuous and, in any case, would be regarded as an aberration.

CHAPTER 8

The Reverse of the Coin

We All Make Mistakes

The comments in this chapter on the English mistakes I have seen and heard in Japan are not made for the purpose of ridiculing the persons responsible. On the contrary, I have sincere admiration for the devoted intensity—although not always for the end product of that intensity—with which the Japanese study English. (I know an elderly Japanese doctor who was invited—a year before the event—to attend a medical convention in the U.S. Having not studied or spoken English in many years, he arranged to take English lessons two evenings every week throughout the year until the convention, which was to last only three days.)

Be that as it may, I believe that the following comments deserve being made to show the student the other side of the coin. If he sees how ridiculous these English mistakes are, he should realize that he could make errors in Japanese that are equally bad, or worse. Perhaps this will inspire him to study harder to ensure that he does not make them. Furthermore, no matter how fluent he becomes in Japanese, he will always —for the reasons explained in the first part of the chapter called "How To Sound Better in Japanese Than You Are"—have to face up to the problem of "Japlish" (Japanese-English) as long as he remains in Japan. (How I detest that word, Japlish! How much better it would have been if Basil Hall Chamberlain had popularized the reverse abbreviation, i.e., "Enganese.")

The quality of the English spoken by Japanese is not nearly as high as it should be, considering the efforts devoted to English studies, but why should this be so? In addition to the obvious reason that English itself is a difficult language and harder for the Japanese to pronounce correctly than it is (or should be) for us to pronounce Japanese, there are, I think, three main reasons. First, according to an official in the Ministry of Education, only a small percentage of the Japanese teachers of English in this country have ever even traveled to an English-speaking country, much less lived in one. Second, the *kana* syllabary, in which most Japanese students at least begin to learn English, is far from being an ideal vehicle for the transportation of correct sounds from one language to another. For example, writing the word "English" in *kana* would give us this combination of sounds: *I-n-gu-ri-shi-u*. Third, the concept of "face" prevents a Japanese, once he has completed his course of training in English, from accepting or even seeking constructive criticism of his mistakes, especially if he is expected to know English in his work.

The Japanese "Face" and Their English

Several years ago, when I was in charge of the export sales section of a Japanese manufacturing company, each of the men who worked for me was assigned a block of foreign countries and given the responsibility for all communication with our distributors in those countries. Our section produced a large volume of correspondence, almost all of which was in English, and I reviewed these letters in draft form, to ensure that the messages as well as the language were correct.

When I found one day that some of these letters were being taken directly to the typing section, without crossing my desk, I called the section together and cautioned them to be sure to route all outgoing letters in draft to me before typing. I explained—and I thought that this explanation would be especially acceptable in Japan—that the company face was at stake. If I allowed, I told them, letters written in poor, often laughable English to be sent all over the world, our company would suffer. Letters in poor English could be equated with lack of export experience, incompetent personnel, or even commercial instability.

Everyone bowed, and I thought that I would have no more trouble. But the struggle was only beginning. They would do it my way for a week or two, but then they would revert to slipping the letters past me to the typists again, and I was too busy to station myself in the typing section all day to guard against uncorrected letters. So I would call another meeting and I would caution them again. (They always, of course, had their excuses: either I had not been at my desk when they brought the draft around for correction or the letter in question needed to be posted urgently or one of the typists must have picked it up by mistake.) Again our correspondence would flow correctly for a week or so until one day when I would happen to pass through the typing section and find more drafts of letters without my initials of approval on them.

This cycle of events was repeated so often that I decided to set an example by having the worst offender discharged, even though I knew that the employer-employee relationship in Japanese companies is a much more firmly cemented bond than even that of marriage itself. At every meeting of the section chiefs with the company president for five weeks thereafter, I proposed that this offender be discharged—and every time my proposal was turned down.

At length, in near desperation, I began having private talks with the typists and the people in my section. Piece by piece, I constructed the picture. The letter drafts with my red-pencil corrections on them went to the typists, who, of course, noticed particularly those drafts in need of the most extensive corrections and often mentioned these later to others in the office, saying things like: "Oh, you should see Mr. Tanaka's letters! They're just a mass of red marks when I get them." "I'll bet they're not as bad as Mr. Sumida's." "I wonder where we ever got the idea that Mr. Matsuzawa knows any English." "Why, I learned more English in kindergarten than Mr. Mori knows now!"

These reports were spreading slowly but surely throughout the company and were causing increasing discomfiture to the persons concerned. I had not been totally unaware of such a possibility from the beginning, but I thought that a few sharp words to the typists (which failed to have any discernible effect) and *aisha seishin* (spirit of devotion to one's company) would counteract this.

Here we had a clear confrontation between *aisha seishin* and *jicho* (taking care of oneself, placing one's own interests over those of others). If my subordinates would let me correct their letters, it would improve the overall tone of our worldwide correspondence, but it would also detract, to varying degrees and in the way described above, from their individual reputations as competent writers of English. In this struggle between *aisha seishin* and *jichō,* the latter was winning, hands down.

My predicament was seemingly hopeless. I had appealed to their reason and to their *aisha seishin,* I had cajoled, and I had threatened. I had tried frequently to have the worst offender discharged. All to no avail.

This combined with one or two other factors to persuade me to request a transfer to the company's branch in New York, where I had the opportunity to observe still another facet of the Japanese approach to English.

The home office in Tōkyō wrote to us in New York and gave us tentatively proposed English names of the new models (of cameras) that we were to introduce to the U.S. market that year. On the list were Minister and Lynx. I opposed these names and wrote to the home office to explain my objections. Whoever selected the name Minister obviously must have had the Japanese word *daijin* (cabinet minister) in mind, but I pointed out that most Americans would think first of a preacher when they heard the word minister.

In the case of Lynx, the person responsible probably had the sharp eyes of that animal in mind but, I continued in my letter of opposition, the average American thinks of the lynx as a sly, cruel animal. This unpleasant association would transfer itself, at least in part, to the product and our sales might fall below our expectations.

But right thinking lost this round, too. The Minister and the Lynx were marketed in the U.S. and I didn't stay around long enough to find out how they fared. (I did learn, however, that one of the senior officers of the company had suggested these two names, from the scanty fund of his English knowledge, and that no one was willing to offend him by supporting my opposition.)

English Names for Japanese Products

An American with a sound knowledge of the U.S. market and a feel for English words should be able to make a success in Japan of a business that would advise Japanese clients on the selection of English names for products, shops, bars, and so forth. There is a desperate need for such a service. It is obvious that such names should have a connection with the products or establishments in question and should somehow enhance their appeal to the consumer or customer.

Instead, however, we see only too often names like Cactus gasoline, the Cedric car (imagine a Detroit car manufacturer naming a new model Ralph or Jerry or Ernie), the Richard electric shaver, Pecker mechanical pencil, Violent blue jeans, Rony Wrinkle rubber prophylactics, Puddy (a prepared pudding mix), Creap (a powdered coffee cream), Calpis soft drink (which I somehow associate with bovine urine), Family Germ (wheat germ), and Pocari Sweat (a drink).

In fortunate contrast to such names, we are seeing, at the time of this writing, a countertide in which the pendulum is swinging in the opposite direction. Not only are these new names purely Japanese words but they also represent places and things that are heavily imbued with the history and ancient culture of Japan. Some product names I have noted are: Asuka (a place near Nara, which was the capital in the seventh century), Saga (a section of Kyōto where many old temples are located), Takao (a mountain west of Kyōto, which is crowned with an ancient shrine and is famous for its autumnal colors), Katsura (the detached palace in Kyōto), Takumi (masterly craftsmanship), Irodori (colorfulness), and Utage (an old literary word for party or banquet).

There is one Japanese whose ability at dreaming up wondrous names in English I have admired from afar for years. He was that mysterious man who named the stage shows of the Nichigeki Fourth Floor Music Hall in Tōkyō. I only wish that I had made a list of the names of those shows over the years. Three that come to mind offhand are: "Three Dervishes at a Whippenpoof Whing-Ding," "Shag and Shimmy at the Shine-town Shindig," "Titillate Me Purple in the Tulip Time." On days when all is not going right with the world, I sometimes lie around and dream of being titillated until I am purple with passion or pleasure, after which I can usually reduce my daily ration of tranquilizers by one or two pills.

Fractured English

The *Asahi Evening News,* an English-language daily published in Tōkyō, once held a contest in which they paid ¥1,000 for weird examples of Japanized English, substantiated by photographs. One photograph of the label of a medicine bottle revealed the prescribed dosage as: "Adults: 1 tablet 3 times a day until passing away." Another submission was the photograph of the front of a small store that sold blankets, quilts, and mattresses: "Sleeping Shop Tezuka." A third showed a parking sign: "Vertical Parking Only." But at last the *Asahi Evening News* got caught in its own trap. Someone sent in a photograph of an article from that newspaper, the headline of which read: "Solution to Laotian Crisis Unsolved."

Scooping from the dank tarn of my memory, here are a few examples of fractured English I have seen here and there around Japan: "Humbug Steaks," "Strawberry Crash," "Sardine Sand," "The Highest Black Tea" (from Ginza menus); "Fruits Parlour and Porcelain Jewelry," "Softly!! Matless, Pillows, Cushions" (from Ginza signs); "Dresses for Ladies and Gentlemen (chiselled in the marble facade of a clothing shop in the Ginza); "Let's Reduce Noise by Ourselves" (a traffic sign); and "Fondle Dogs" (a sign over an Ōsaka pet shop). The creator of the sign must have thought that "fondle," being longer, was a more impressive word than its synonym "pet."

A sign erected near the busy Roppongi intersection in Tōkyō ordered: "Have Many Accidents Here." One day in an idle moment and under the impulse of contrary humor, I entered the police box at the intersection and asked the policeman on duty, *"Kokorahen no doko de jiko wo okoshimashō ka?"* (Where shall I have the accident?).

"Ē? Naa-ni?" (Huh? What's that?), the cop said, blinking in surprise.

When I had repeated my question, he eyed me narrowly for a minute, then called his superior, who had been lying down in the tiny room in the rear. Again I asked my question and, because I was getting tired of saying the same thing, I explained that "Have many accidents here" is a direct command in English and that I have a very highly developed *jumpō seishin* (spirit of obedience to the law). I said that I had seen the sign several times already and that I wanted to apologize for not yet having acted in compliance with the crystal-clear orders of the authorities. (Here I bowed deeply, the second policeman bowed in return, and the first policeman stood up and began to nervously adjust his cap and tie.)

To save face, the second policeman went through the pretense of not having seen the sign itself and had me lead him to it. When we got there, he studied it gravely for a minute, nodded, and began to bark angrily at his subordinate for allowing such a stupid sign to be erected.

When that pleasing little one-act comedy was over, he turned back to me and, bowing, thanked me for cooperating with the police and said there would be no need for me to obey *this* particular sign. The next day the sign was gone.

What the writer of the sign would have said in Japanese was *Kono fukin ni jiko ōshi* (In this area accidents are frequent), and what he was trying to say in English was "Drivers have many accidents here."

The legend on one Tōkyō map reads, "Dirty Water Punishment Place." The *kanji* next to it, *Osui Shobunsho,* will indeed yield this meaning, for one of the meanings of *shobun* is punishment. There is, however, another meaning for *shobun,* that of "treatment" or "disposal," and *osui* can be translated as "sewage" instead of "dirty water." The English legend, therefore, should have been "Sewage Disposal Plant." Pitfalls of this sort await the unwary translator at nearly every step.

The truly classic example of fractured English is one that—and I shall regret this omission all my life—I did not see. I have heard about it, however, from so many eye-witnesses that I must accept it as genuine, although it is almost too good to be true. When the aging Douglas MacArthur was being boosted as a possible presidential candidate, an enthusiastic group of his Japanese well-wishers, who sometimes had difficulty distinguishing between the English *l* and *r*, arranged for a mammoth banner to be displayed in downtown Tōkyō, right at the intersection of the streets that are now called Hibiya-dōri and Harumi-dōri. The huge letters on this banner read: "We Pray for MacArthur's Erection."

Stage Two: Intermediate

CHAPTER 9

Introductions and Names

Introductions: Mechanics and Responsibilities

In Japan the mechanics of introducing one person to another are relatively easy, thanks to rigid procedures and to *meishi* (business or name cards). The person of lower rank is, of course, introduced to the person of higher rank, not in reverse order. In the somewhat farfetched introduction which follows, you—as the introducing party—first announce what you are going to do: *"Go-shōkai itashimasu"* (I will now make the introduction). Then, speaking to Mr. Aoki, but indicating Mr. Ushiyama with a gesture, you say: *"Aoki-san, kochira wa Dai-Ichi Bussan no sōji-gakari no Ushiyama-san desu"* (Mr. Aoki, this is Mr. Ushiyama, head janitor at the Dai-Ichi Trading Company). Reversing your field, you then go on with the formula, saying: *"Ushiyama-san, kono kata wa gaimudaijin no kaban-mochi no Aoki-san de gozaimasu"* (Mr. Ushiyama, this is Mr. Aoki, who carries the foreign minister's briefcase).

Messrs. Aoki and Ushiyama now bow to each other, exchange *meishi*, and utter the tried-and-true locution: *"Aoki [or Ushiyama] desu. Yoroshiku o-negai itashimasu"* (I am Aoki [or Ushiyama]. I beg you to treat me kindly in the future).

Recovering from their bows, they now fall to studying each other's *meishi* and trying to chance upon mutual acquaintances. Mr. Aoki might say something like this: *"Ā, sō desu ka? Dai-Ichi Bussan desu ka? Naruhodo. Uchi no yatsu wa daibu mae ni Dai-Ichi Bussan no yunyū-buchō no Iki to iu yatsu ni mōshon wo kaketa koto ga aru ndesu ga"* (Oh, is that so? The Dai-Ichi Trading Company? I see. Quite a while ago my wife made a pass at a fellow named Iki, the import section chief at Dai-Ichi).

In the meantime, you—the introducer—can be making explanatory comments about Messrs. Aoki and Ushiyama, such as: how long you have known them, what trustworthy friends they are, how important Mr. Ushiyama's janitorial duties are to Dai-Ichi, and so forth. At the close of whatever social event you have been attending, Ushiyama should

77

say to Aoki something like, *"O-chikazuki ni narete kōei desu"* (I'm happy to have met you).

That part of it is easy enough. The difficulty with introductions, however, is that you, as the introducing party, are accepting responsibility for the future actions of Aoki and Ushiyama involving each other. If Ushiyama runs off to Atami with Aoki's flirtatious wife, Aoki may very well demand that you correct the situation—assuming, of course, that he is displeased at all about his wife's leaving.

Whenever a Japanese is wronged, his natural inclination is to take his complaint to the person who introduced him to the one who did the foul deed rather than to seek legal redress. This explains why there is one lawyer to every 830 Americans but only one to every 14,000 Japanese. It also explains the basic objection of the Japanese to self-introductions *(jiko-shōkai)*.

Self-Introductions

There are, however, some situations in which it is not objectionable to introduce yourself to another—for example, to a neighbor whom you have often seen but never met. Here you should begin with, *"Shitsurei desu ga jiko-shōkai sasete itadakimasu"* (Forgive my rudeness, but I would like to introduce myself).

The classic self-introduction in Japan was that of the *yakuza* (gamblers). In days of yore, when the *yakuza* traveled about Japan, they were recognizable to each other by their attire and sometimes by tattoos. Then they performed their colorful rituals of self-introduction, which they described as *jingi wo kiru koto* to make the formal greeting customary among gamblers, especially when in the territory of another *oyabun*. One gambler would begin by kneeling on one knee and saying, *"O-hikae nasutte, o-hikae nasutte,"* meaning that he was lowering himself in the presence of a superior. The other would then answer, *"Sassoku o-hikae kudassutte arigatō gozaimasu"* (Thank you for kneeling so quickly). The first would then go into the actual self-introduction: *"Temē shōgoku hasshimasuru wa Kantō nite gozansu. Kantō to itte mo hirō gozansu. Tōkaidō wo zutto kudarimashite Odawara nite gozansu ..."* (Starting with my native province, let me tell you that it is in Kantō. Kantō, however, is very large. You go down the Tōkaidō to Odawara ...). He not only describes his home grounds in fine detail but also talks about the *oyabun* (boss) of his group of gamblers and the connections the *oyabun* has with other gamblers in Kantō. At last, he ends up by saying, *"O-mishiri oki-kudasaimashite igo go-bekkon ni negaimasu"* (Thank you for letting me make your acquaintance. Please let us continue to be friends). This routine is usually good for laughs in a cabaret if you use it—without, however, necessarily kneeling on the cabaret floor—when you introduce yourself to one of the hostesses.

When introducing himself, a Mr. Tanabe will say, *"Watakushi wa Tanabe desu"* (I am Tanabe) or *"Tanabe to mōshimasu"* (I am called Tanabe). Normally he will not use the word for name *(namae)*. Nor will he use it when asking another's name. Instead, he will say, *"Shitsurei desu ga nan to osshaimasu ka?"* (Excuse my rudeness, but what are you called?).

Although it is often avoided in this way, *namae* is usually the word that the beginning student learns for name, and it can mean either family or given name. When, however, you mean family name, you can prevent possible misunderstanding by using *myōji*. *Seimei,* the word used in applications, means full name. Other kinds of names to note are: *gimei* (false name; used for illicit purposes), *kamei* (assumed name; lit., temporary name), *hommyō* (true name), and *geimei* (stage name).

Family Names

In England, many family names derived from occupations. (Seward, for example, came from "sea warden," the coastal lookout who warned of the approach of Viking raiders). In Japan, however, family names *(myōji)* came from place names or descriptions of locations or objects. Before the commoner Gonsuke was allowed to possess a family name, he was identified by his first name and generally by the name or description of the place where he lived, i.e., Yamamoto no Gonsuke or Gonsuke of or from the base *(moto)* of the mountain *(yama)*. Later, when he gained the right to have a family name at the time of the Meiji Restoration, he dropped the possessive particle *no* and became Yamamoto Gonsuke. (Or he may have merely glanced around him and picked the first handy physical description that came to mind.)

Even today, when Japanese are paged aboard trains or among audiences, the surname and place of residence or employment are used: *Atami no Mochi-san* (Mochi-san of Atami), *Sapporo no Doi-san* (Doi-san of Sapporo), or *Mitsubishi Shōji no Matsudaira-san* (Matsudaira-san of Mitsubishi Trading Company). If a Japanese has more than one aunt, he will usually identify them by place of residence rather than name: *Ōsaka no obasan* (my Ōsaka aunt) or *Shibuya no obasan* (my aunt who lives in Shibuya).

There are 9,335 entries in the dictionary of Japanese family names compiled by I. V. Gillis and Pai Ping-ch'i. Suzuki is evidently the most numerous family name, there being about 7,000 listed in the Tōkyō telephone directory as well as over 4,000 Satōs. Other common family names are: Tanaka (inside the paddy), Yamamoto (base of the mountain), Katō (added wisteria), Hashimoto (foot of the bridge), Kobayashi (small forest), Matsuda (piney paddy), Takahashi (high bridge), Matsumoto (base of the pine), Yamashita (under the mountain), and Nakamura (middle of the village).

The importance of rice in the Japanese scheme of things is testified to by the many names containing *ta* (paddy). Some of these are: Ashida (reed paddy), Ikeda (pond paddy), Ishida (stone paddy), Taura (paddy beach), Ueda (upper paddy), Oda (small paddy), Okada (hill paddy), Iwata (rocky paddy), Osada (chief paddy), Kanda (god paddy or, perhaps, God's little acre), Tagawa (paddy river), Kuroda (black paddy), Sawada (marshy paddy), Shimoda (lower paddy), Tajima (paddy island), Takada (high paddy), Takeda (bamboo paddy), Tsuchida (earth paddy), and many, many more.

Because certain components of family names (such as *matsu, yama, mori, hayashi, kawa, oka, miya, mura, take, taka, shima, naka, hara, moto,* and *kuchi*) are used frequently and have one standard pronunciation, they render family names easier to read than given names, whose *kanji* and their readings tend to be unusual and nonstandard.

Occasionally we find a family name with some built-in humor, but a knowledge of *kanji* is needed to really appreciate these. The name Bamen, for instance, is written "horse face," and the name Mitarai is more commonly read *o-tearai* (toilet). The two *kanji* for *mezurashii* (rare) and *tamotsu* (maintain) form a family name which is correctly pronounced Jimbo. The more common *on-yomi* for *mezurashi* however, is *chin,* and many persons would probably make the disastrous mistake of reading the name as "Chimpo" (penis). Misreadings of this sort are reminiscent of an old Issei teacher in the language school I attended who persisted in mispronouncing classmate Pines's name as if the positions of the "i" and the "e" were reversed.

As suggested above, many names can also be place names, e.g., Nagano, Miyazaki, Matsuyama, Kagawa, Ishikawa, and Miyagi. Some place names are descriptions of the locale, e.g., Shirahama means white beach. Others originated in activities for which the region was known, e.g., Futsukaichi, Mikkaichi, and Yokkaichi are towns that once held market days every day with '2' or '3' or '4' in their nomination. (Futsukaichi, therefore, would mean a market held on the second, twelfth, and twenty-second day of each month.)

As many of our American place names are Indian in origin, so the names of many places in Japan can be traced to the language of the Ainu, the fair-skinned aboriginal inhabitants of Japan. This last category, however, can be misleading, because their present *kanji,* which are *ateji* (*kanji* that are assigned for their phonetic value rather than meaning), have overlain and concealed the original Ainu meaning. For instance, Enoshima, in the original *Ainu-go,* means Land's End, Karuizawa means Pumice Moor, Omori is Mound Place, Kamakura is Cross-over Hills, and Noboribetsu is Turbid River, all meanings different from those you would assume from reading the *kanji.*

Yagō is a unique kind of name that is given separate listing in many telephone directories, especially in the rural districts. It can be the name of a shop or it can be the name of a house. In the case of the latter, it may have little or no connection with the name of the family now occupying or owning the premises. Four generations ago a particular house may have provided a roof for a fishmonger's shop—we'll call it Uohachi—and for his family. Now the dwelling may be owned and occupied by one of the fishmonger's descendants—or by a complete stranger to the original family—who has no connection with the sale of fish, but still the house itself can continue to be known and identified by the old name of Uohachi. Or the house may have a name whose origin is lost in the obscure past, like the one that a friend of mine knows in Chiba. It (the house itself, not the occupying family) is called Mitsu-abu (Three Horseflies).

Foreigners' names can be written in Japanese phonetically, with *kana* or with *kanji,* using the *ateji* defined above. In the case of the latter, however, the *ateji* seldom make much sense. Even if they do, the meaning may not be felicitous. A friend of mine named Denton once asked a Japanese to choose appropriate *ateji* for his name. Mr. Denton did not, unfortunately, know *kanji* and for some months he distributed his new *meishi* around Tōkyō. The back side of his card carried the bold characters 田豚, which assuredly are read Denton but which mean field hog.

Here is one problem you will most likely have to cope with when you become proficient in this language. Suppose you are making a telephone call in Japanese and you identify yourself as Mr. Smith: *"Kochira wa Sumisu desu."* The quality of your Japanese speech causes the other party to assume that you too are Japanese or possibly a Nisei and he thinks that he has perhaps misunderstood your name, that it is really Sumida or something similar. So he says, *"Ē?"* (How's that?). You repeat your name, but he still does not catch it because he has on those mental blinkers and he is not considering the possibility that you are a foreigner.

This could go on and on, so what you should say is the Japanese equivalent of saying: "S as in Sue, M as in Man, I as in Italy, etc." My name, for example, becomes *Suwādo* in Japanese and the formula I use is: *"Suzume no su ni warabi no wa wo nobashite tokoya no to ni dakuten"* (*Su* as in *suzume, wa* as in *warabi*—lengthened—and *to* as in *tokoya*—with *nigori* marks). I recommend that foreigners living in Japan devise one for their name; it saves much anguish.

Given Names

The *kanji* for given names are often chosen from among those for qualities or conditions that the parents hope will fall to the lot of the child: Katsutoshi (to win cleverly), Noboru (to rise), Hideo (excellent male), Nagataka (everlasting filial duty), Chōkichi (long-lasting good luck).

Or the name may be based on the order of birth: Tarō, Ichirō, and Kazuo are names given to first sons; Eiji, Jirō, and Kenji are given to second sons; Saburō, Taizō, and Shūzō to third sons; and Gorō to fifth sons. The given name of one of my teachers was Gohachirō (five-eight male), and he was the thirteenth child in his family. Minako (three-seven child) is a girl's name that can be given to the tenth child. The famous Admiral Yamamoto's given name was Isoroku, which is written fifty-six, but I somehow doubt that he was the fifty-sixth child in his family.

Men's names usually end with one of the following: *o* (male), *zō* (storehouse), *emon* (guarding gate), *yoshi* (good), *suke* (assistance), *taka* (filial duty), *kichi* (good luck), *ji* (administration), *rō* (man), and *aki* (bright or autumn).

Some names, especially those involving kinds of animals, are reminiscent of American Indian appellations, like these: Kamenosuke (turtle's helper), Kumakichi (fortunate bear), Torao (tiger man), Itarō (wild boar's first son), Mima (pretty horse), Ogano (little deer field), Tobikuma (flying bear), Ōzuru (big stork), Hachiuma (eight horses), Bekki (long tree), Chikuma (bamboo horse), and Chikuma (thousand bears).

Japanese do not have middle names. At least not in Japan, with the exception of Japanese Catholics, who may take a saint's name as a second given (or taken?) name. Japanese born or living in foreign countries often do, however. This makes perusing telephone directories in places like Hawaii a memorable experience. Some Issei immigrants must have selected—before they knew much English—names for their offspring at random and from odd sources. Regard some of the classic examples I have found: Aiichirō Robespierre Yoneyama, Abercrombie Toyohiko Uchimura, Kanzō Baron Tada, Rikizō Cyrano Sakurai, and Blucher Shin Satō.

Dictionaries give "nickname" as the meaning of both *adana* and *yobina,* but these words need to be differentiated. *Yobina* (or, more formally, *aishō*) is a diminutive form of the correct given name, such as Fumi-chan for Fumiko. *Adana* is a nickname taken from a characteristic of the person. For instance, a person of dark complexion might be called Karasu (crow) and one of slow movements could be called Dongame (slow turtle).

Ko (child) is the most common ending for the given names of women, with *e* (inlet or tree branch) next, and *yo* (generation) a poor third. Such suffixes are evidently of fairly recent origin because one still finds that many women in the country have names like Hana, To, Teru, Shizu, Ju, Hide, etc. To address women with names like these, one prefixes *O* and suffixes *san* to get the normal form, e.g., O-Hana-san, O-To-san, and so forth. It is not unusual for a woman to change her name, often after consultation with an *ekisha* (fortuneteller). Such alterations can be legally made with comparative ease at the ward office.

The most numerous form of the female given name is in two syllables plus *ko* or *e*, i.e., Sachiko (happy child), Shizue (quiet inlet), Setsuko (child of fidelity), Fujiko (rich samurai's child *or* child of the wisteria). Girls' names, however, can have other forms, for example, Moshio, Haruyo, Ren, Masa, Yayoi, and Kaoru. Three-syllable female names never take *ko* as a final and fourth syllable.

A few names can be given to either sex, for example, Misao (fidelity), Sakae (prosperity), Kaoru (fragrance), Ayumi (pace, walk), Nao (honest, right).

One night in 1950 a Mr. Hori and I went to the Uruwashi Cabaret in the Ginza for the purpose of sporting. Six girls, unbidden, quickly joined us at our table. (Those were the days when we foreigners were considered big spenders.) The girls introduced themselves as Fumiko, Ruri, Sachiko, Midori, Yoshiko, and Sanae. It being a slow night on the Ginza, these stuck with us for quite a while, and Hori-san and I entertained ourselves by telling them monstrous lies.

I remembered all the six names correctly—except one. Instead of Sanae, I kept calling her Saneko. Since she was the sexiest, I said her name most often and most ardently. I soon noticed that whenever I said Saneko, I broke them all up. I thought I was pretty funny myself in those days, but I had never before enjoyed such success as I was having that night.

Toward the end of the evening, after I must have said Saneko's name fifty times, Hori-san took me aside and explained that the girl's name was actually Sanae—and that *saneko* meant clitoris.

CHAPTER 10

Numeratives and Numerals

Introduction

Although the Japanese numeratives (also called classifiers or counters) confound many students of the language, I must confess that I rather like them. Perhaps this is a fondness deriving from fascination with things macabre. Certainly the concept of these numeratives is formidable enough. Imagine—if you feel up to it—having to learn different ways of counting for persons, horses, plates, cars, birds, airplanes, pencils, ships, cats, nights, pistols, suits, and so on, *ad nauseam*.

Here, I suspect, is where we may separate the serious students of the language from the dabblers. But once you have mastered counting in Japanese, you will, I believe, experience a warm glow of satisfaction not unlike that you feel when you stagger up to the finish line of an obstacle course in infantry basic training.

Foreign students of English often shudder at our eerie orthography, our capricious pronunciation of proper names, and the many, diverse origins of our language (including Japanese and Chinese, e.g., kimono, tycoon, typhoon, and jingoism), but if they are speakers of a language that is burdened with such numeratives, they should be overcome with relief when they find that we make little use of them in English. Seven "head" of cattle and four "slices" of toast are two of the few exceptions.

Basic Numeral Systems

Before listing and discussing the numeratives, we should review briefly the basic numeral systems:

	NUMERALS OF CHINESE ORIGIN	NUMERALS OF JAPANESE ORIGIN
1	*ichi*	*hitotsu*
2	*ni*	*futatsu*

3	san	mittsu
4	shi (or yon)	yottsu
5	go	itsutsu
6	roku	muttsu
7	shichi (or nana)	nanatsu
8	hachi	yattsu
9	ku (or kyū)	kokonotsu
10	jū	tō

By "Chinese origin," I mean that when the Japanese, having none of their own, adopted the Chinese characters for writing their numerals, they also took over the Chinese way of pronouncing them, although they had their own "native" words for one, two, three, etc. The Japanese imitation of Chinese pronunciation, however, was imperfect, so we have today what can best be described as a Japanese adaptation of the Chinese pronunciation of the characters for numerals. You'll note that the native numerals extended only to ten, which makes one wonder what the early Japanese clan chiefs did when they wanted to summon their thirteen true loves, or order twenty bottles of o-sake for a shindig, or sing *The Twelve Days of O-Shōgatsu.*

With the introduction of a wide variety of Western techniques and customs, it is not surprising that, although they have their own, the Japanese have adopted some Western measurements. Commonly heard are measurements such as *ichi mētoru* (one meter), *ni senchi* (two centimeters), *san miri* (three millimeters), and *yon ton* (four tons). *Kiro* used alone may mean kilogram, kilometer, or kiloliter, depending on the context, and is also used in such combinations imported whole as *kiro-saikuru* (kilocycle), *kirowatto* (kilowatt), *kiroboruto* (kilovolt), and *kiroampeya* (kiloampere). Weather forecasters on radio and TV regularly broadcast (seemingly endlessly) atmospheric pressures measured in *miribāru* (millibars). Boxing fans will cheer (or jeer) for a *hyaku nijūroku pondo bokusā* (126-pound boxer) and golfers practice at neighborhood driving ranges to try to make *nihyaku yādo tonda tama* (200-yard drives). Stationers speak of *empitsu ichi dāsu* (one dozen pencils) and sporting-goods outlets sell golf and Ping Pong balls by the dozen and half dozen *(han dāsu)*. Note that it is the numerals of Chinese origin that are used to count imported units of measurement.

Although some texts mention three and even four sets of numerals, the additional one or two are modified forms of the native numerals, e.g., *hito* for *hi* or *hitotsu, futa* or *fu* for *futatsu,* and so on. An interesting example of one modified form is to be found in *Hifumi,* a man's name, which is written with the characters for one, two, three. The *hi* is from *hitotsu,* the *fu* from *futatsu,* and the *mi* from *mittsu.*

When counting, the Japanese numerals can serve alone or in combinations like those given in the chart on pages 88–89. Alone they are used as when a file of soldiers is ordered to count off: *Ichi! Ni! San!* and so forth. Examples of the latter would be *ichizen* (one bowl of rice), *itchō* (one pistol), and *ippai* (one cupful), in which the numerals are joined with numeratives.

The native numerals can also serve alone; one can count most objects with them: *hitotsu, futatsu, mittsu,* and so on. And, like the Chinese numerals above, these native numerals can combine with numeratives: *hitokire* (one slice), *futakire* (two slices), *mikire* (three slices). Unlike those of Chinese origin, they can be used, without combining, with the word for the object being counted. Note that there is no numerative in these examples: *futatsu no monogatari* (two tales), *Kiki-ukita jodan wo mittsu hodo kiite yatta ga* (I listened to three tired old jokes).

Using the possessive *no,* the native numerals can precede (although not necessarily immediately) the words they modify. Example: *Muttsu no kusatta ringo ga koko ni arimasu* (Here are six rotten apples). They can also come after the word they modify. Example: *Jukushite inai suika ga soko ni itsutsu hodo aru* (There are five watermelons not yet ripe).

Using Numeratives

The following is a list of numeratives and the things they count. It is not a complete list. While thumbing through *kanji* dictionaries, one will, with disconcerting frequency, come across other numeratives, but fortunately most of them will be obsolete, obsolescent, or archaic. The numeratives in this list, once mastered, should be sufficient.

NUMERATIVE   OBJECT

chaku   suits, dresses
chō   scissors, knives, pistols, saws, and similar objects with handles
dai   typewriters, pianos, beds, vehicles (except aircraft, which are counted *ikki, niki, sanki,* etc., and ships, which are noted below). *Dai,* in addition to *sei* (as in *nisei* and *sansei*), is also used to count generations, although the *kanji* is different.

Japanese Numeral-Numerative Combinations

NUMER-ATIVE	1	2	3	4	5	6	7	8	9	10	100	How Many?
						COMBINED FORMS						
chaku	itchaku	nichaku	sanchaku	yonchaku	gochaku	rokuchaku	nanachaku	hatchaku	kyūchaku	jitchaku	hyakuchaku	nanchaku
chō	itchō	nichō	sanchō	yonchō	gochō	rokuchō	shichichō nanachō	hatchō	kyūchō	jitchō	hyakuchō	nanchō
dai	ichidai	nidai	sandai	yodai yondai	godai	rokudai	shichidai nanadai	hachidai	kudai kyūdai	jūdai	hyakudai	nandai
fuku	ippuku	nifuku	sampuku sambuku	yompuku shifuku	gofuku	roppuku	shichifuku nanafuku	happuku	kyūfuku	jippuku	hyappuku	nampuku nambuku
hai	ippai	nihai	sambai	yonhai shihai	gohai	roppai	shichihai	hachihai happai	kuhai kyūhai	jippai	hyappai	nambai
hiki	ippiki	nihiki	sambiki	yonhiki shihiki	gohiki	roppiki	shichihiki nanahiki	hachihiki happiki	kuhiki kyūhiki	jippiki	hyappiki	nambiki
hon	ippon	nihon	sambon	yonhon shihon	gohon	roppon	shichihon nanahon	hachihon happon	kuhon kyūhon	jippon	hyappon	nambon
jō	ichijō	nijō	sanjō	yojō	gojō	rokujō	shichijō nanajō	hachijō	kujō kyūjō	jūjō	hyakujō	nanjō
kan	ikkan	nikan	sangan	yonkan	gokan	rokkan	shichikan nanakan	hachikan hakkan	kyūkan	jikkan	hyakkan	nangan
ken	ikken	niken	sangen	yonken shiken	goken	rokken	shichiken nanaken	hachiken hakken	kyūken	jikken	hyakken	nangen
ko	ikko	niko	sanko	yonko	goko	rokko	shichiko nanako	hakko	kyūko	jikko	hyakko	nanko
mai	ichimai	nimai	sammai	yomai yommai	gomai	rokumai	shichimai nanamai	hachimai	kumai kyūmai	jūmai	hyakumai	nammai

maki	hitomaki	futamaki	mimaki	yomaki	itsumaki	mumaki	nanamaki	yamaki	kyūmaki	tōmaki	hyakumaki	nammaki
mei	ichimei	nimei	sammei	yomei yommei shimei	gomei	rokumei	shichimei nanamei	hachimei	kumei kyūmei	jūmei	hyakumei	nammei
mon	ichimon	nimon	sammon	yommon	gomon	rokumon	shichimon nanamon	hachimon	kumon kyūmon	jūmon	hyakumon	nammon
nin	hitori	futari	sannin	yonin yottari	gonin	rokunin	shichinin	hachinin	kunin kyūnin	jūnin	hyakunin	nannin
satsu	issatsu	nisatsu	sansatsu	yonsatsu shisatsu	gosatsu	rokusatsu	shichisatsu nanasatsu	hassatsu	kyūsatsu	jissatsu	hyakusatsu	nansatsu
seki	isseki	niseki	sanseki	yonseki	goseki	rokuseki	shichiseki nanaseki	hasseki	kyūseki	jisseki	hyakuseki	nanseki
sho	ikkasho	nikasho	sankasho	yonkasho	gokasho	rokkasho	nanakasho	hachikasho	kyūkasho	jikkasho	hyakkasho	nankasho
shu	isshu	nishu	sanshu	yonshu	goshu	rokushu	shichishu	hachishu hasshu	kyūshu	jisshu	hyakushu	nanshu
sō	issō	nisō	sansō sanzō	yonsō shisō	gosō	rokusō	shichisō narasō	hassō	kyūsō	jissō	hyakusō	nansō nanzō
soku	issoku	nisoku	sanzoku	yonsoku shisoku	gosoku	rokusoku	shichisoku nanasoku	hassoku	kyūsoku	jissoku	hyakusoku	nanzoku
tō	ittō	nitō	santō	yontō	gotō	rokutō	shichitō nanatō	hachitō hattō	kyūtō	jittō	hyakutō	nantō
tsu	ittsū	nitsū	santsū	yontsū shitsū	gotsū	rokutsū	shichitsū nanatsū	hachitsū hattsū	kyūtsū	jittsū	hyakutsū	nantsū
wa	ichiwa	niwa	samba	yonwa yomba shiwa	gowa	roppa rokuwa	shichiwa	hachiwa	kuwa kyūwa	jippa	hyappa	namba
zen	ichizen	nizen	sanzen	yonzen shizen	gozen	rokuzen	shichizen nanazen	hachizen	kyūzen	jūzen	hyakuzen	nanzen

fuku	doses of medicine, puffs of tobacco smoke
hai	cups, glasses, bucketfuls, tubfuls, etc., of liquid
hiki	quadrupeds, insects, fish (*bi* is an older numerative for fish)
hon	things that are somewhat rounded and long in proportion to their thickness, such as trees, cigarettes, ropes, teeth, fans, legs, needles, pencils, cigars, bottles, fingers, poles
jō	tatami mats, batches of twenty sheets of dried, edible seaweed (written with a different *kanji*), quires of paper
kan	reels of a movie, individual volumes in a set of books
ken	houses, shops, buildings
ko	various objects for which there are no numeratives
mai	flat things, e.g., boards, paper, dishes, kimono, blankets
maki	rolls of silk and other cloth, scrolls
mei	persons. A more formal or literary way of counting persons than *nin* (see below).
mon	cannons
nin	persons
satsu	books, magazines
seki	large ships
sho	places
shu	poems
sō	small ships (although I have seen *sō* used for ships as large as submarines)
soku	footwear: pairs of shoes, *geta*, socks, *tabi, zori*
tō	large quadrupeds, whales
tsū	letters and documents
wa	birds. From this we get the classic mnemonic: *Niwa ni wa niwa no niwatori ga iru* (Two chickens are in the garden).
zen	rice bowls, pairs of chopsticks

The so-called Chinese numerals (*ichi, ni, san,* etc.) are the ones used with almost all of the above numeratives. In combining numerals and numeratives certain phonetic changes take place. *Ichi* becomes *it* before *ch, t,* and *ts; ip* before *f* and *h; ik* before another *k; is* before *s* or *sh. San* becomes *sam* before *f* and *h* (where *f* becomes either *p* or *b* and *h* becomes *b*), *m* and *b. Roku* becomes *rop* before *f* and *h* (where *f* becomes either *p* or *b* and *h* becomes *b*); *rok* before another *k. Hachi* becomes *hat* before *ch, t,* and *ts; hak* before another *k; has* before *s* and *sh. Jū* becomes *jit* before *ch, t,* and *ts; jip* before *f* and *h; jik* before another *k; jis* before *s* and *sh. Hyaku* becomes *hyap* before *f* and *h; hyak* before another *k*. **Sen** becomes *sem* before *f, h, m,* and *b*. After *sen* or *san,* numeratives that start with the letters *f, h, k, s,* and *sh* usually change: *f* becomes either *p* or *b* and *h* becomes *p, k* becomes *g, s* becomes *z,* and *sh* becomes *j*.

We find, however, exceptions to these rules because such alterations in sound would otherwise obscure the meaning of the numeratives. Because of the resulting complexity, some students find it easier to work with a chart such as the one given on pages 88–89. The chart is, admittedly, formidable. The student will not memorize it in one evening unless he is a linguistic genius with a cameralike memory. For the average student, however, it will no doubt be easier to consult this chart than to paw through a memory lane of ill-remembered rules. Alternately, the beginning student could make a copy of the chart and carry it with him until he feels secure in his knowledge of numeratives.

In the last vertical column on the chart, note that *iku* can be substituted for *nan* and still retain the same meaning: *ikuchaku* for *nanchaku, ikunin* for *nannin,* etc.

Note that the word *dai* (not the *dai* used to count vehicles) means "number" as in number one *(dai-ichi)* and number two *(dai-ni)*. But *dai-ichiban* also means "number one," the *ban* being "order." We could translate *dai-ichiban* as "number one in order" but this sounds redundant in English. Not content with this seeming redundancy, the Japanese can go on to add *me* to *dai-ichiban,* i.e., *dai-ichibamme,* which literally would be something like "number one in order in order."

No appreciable distinction exists between *ichibamme* and *dai-ichibamme,* except that the latter is slightly more emphatic, but there are differences in usage between *ichiban* and *dai-ichibamme*.

The above *dai* and *me* become part of ordinal numeratives in examples like this: *Dai-sansatsu-me no ero-zasshi wa sensei no desu* (The third pornographic magazine is the teacher's).

Sai is the numerative for counting people's ages, i.e., *nisai no kodomo* (a two-year-old child) and *rokujūnisai no bāsan* (a sixty-two-year-old woman). An exception to this rule is *hatachi* (twenty years old).

Students are designated with *nensei* (year-student) as in *shōgakko no ichi-nensei* (first grader) or *daigaku no san-nensei* (third-year university student). Months are counted *ikkagetsu, nikagetsu* (one month, two months), etc., and weeks are counted *isshūkan, nishūkan* (one week, two weeks), etc. The names of the months are derived from the Chinese numerals plus one of the suffixes for month *(gatsu),* e.g., *ichigatsu* (January), *nigatsu* (February), and so on, and are divided into three ten-day periods, *jōjun, chūjun,* and *gejun* (lit., upper, middle, and lower ten-day period). Weekend, end of the month, and year-end are *shūmatsu, getsu-matsu,* and *nemmatsu.*

Counting days is more complicated since the numeral pattern is irregular:

one day = *ichi-nichi*	nine days = *kokonoka*
two days = *futsuka*	ten days = *tōka*
three days = *mikka*	eleven days = *jūichi-nichi*
four days = *yokka*	twelve days = *jūni-nichi*
five days = *itsuka*	thirteen days = *jūsan-nichi*
six days = *muika*	fourteen days = *jūyokka*
seven days = *nanoka*	twenty days = *hatsuka*
eight days = *yōka*	twenty-four days = *nijūyokka*

Days which are omitted from this list are counted with the Chinese numerals plus *nichi*. *Kan* may be added to any of these words to emphasize the meaning "period of," although this is implicit without the *kan*. Thus, both *mikka* and *mikka-kan* mean a period of three days. To designate the days of the month use the numerals with which you count them, e.g., *mikka* (the third) or *jūyokka* (the fourteenth), except for the first day *(tsuitachi)* and the last *(misoka)*. *Ōmisoka* is the last day of the year.

Hours present little difficulty: take the words for telling time, e.g., *ichiji, niji, sanji* (one o'clock, two o'clock, three o'clock) and add *kan* to get *ichijikan, nijikan, sanjikan* (one hour, two hours, three hours). Minutes are counted with *fun: ippun, nifun,* and *sampun* are one minute, two minutes, and three minutes. Count seconds with *byō* as in *Sanjūbyō gurai kakarimasu* (It takes about thirty seconds).

CHAPTER 11

How to Sound Better
in Japanese Than You Are

The Fool Valve and the Imperial Rescript Ploy

Please understand that I would not be a party to the deception whose methods are described in this chapter if I did not firmly believe that there is ample justification for teaching foreigners how to make their Japanese sound better than it actually is.

The anecdote which follows will serve to illustrate my premise. Some years ago, a Nisei (American citizen born of Japanese immigrant parentage) lass and I made a trip to a hot-springs resort deep in Japan Alps country. We stayed in a *ryokan* (Japanese-style inn) and occupied separate rooms. (A disclaimer required by the publisher.) The parents of this girl (I'll call her Mary) died when she was a baby and she had been raised by a Caucasian family in Fresno, California. Mary had arrived in Japan only a few weeks before our trip to work as a secretary in one of the branches of SCAP. Her knowledge of the Japanese language was limited to a few words that she had learned since her arrival, such as *Nihon* (Japan), *Konnichi wa* (Hello), *takusan* (much), *arigatō* (thanks), *sukoshi* (little), and *sayōnara* (goodbye). While no one in the *ryokan* spoke any English, I had no reason not to believe that my Japanese would be more than adequate for the occasion.

Right from the start, the *ryokan* manager took us in hand because we were, I learned later, his first American guests since before the war. He hovered about us like a protective helicopter, barking staccato commands at the maids as soon as he understood our needs. And, right from the start, I said what little I had to say to him in what I thought was passable Japanese. He answered in Japanese but, as if not trusting my ability to comprehend, he invariably addressed himself to Mary.

Mary, despite her Japanese features, did not understand a word of what he said and always turned to me for an explanation. Or, in reverse, he would ask Mary a question in Japanese, she would turn to me, I would tell her in English what he had said, and then I would answer him in Japanese. Judging from his correct and immediate compliance with my requests, he had no trouble in understanding my Japanese, but he persisted in talking only to Mary, who, dumbfounded, could only stare blankly in return.

This comic cycle continued until it became distressing. At length, I told him: *"Hakkiri setsumei wo mōshiagemasu ga, kono musume-san wa Nihongo wo zenzen zonjimasen. Nihon ni kita bakkari desu. Nihongo no dekiru no wa kono watakushi dake da kara kochira ni o-hanashi kudasai"* (Let me explain clearly that this girl does not know any Japanese. She has just arrived in Japan. I am the only one who can speak Japanese, so please talk to me).

The *ryokan* manager chuckled, turned to Mary, and said, *"Kono gaijin wa Nihongo ga umai mon desu na!"* (This foreigner certainly speaks good Japanese, doesn't he!).

With that, I threw in the sponge or, as the Japanese would say, the spoon *(saji wo nageru)*. For the rest of the evening, I drank *sake* and entertained dark thoughts.

The situation had not improved the next morning, but in the late afternoon I had an idea. Knowing when the manager would come to take our order for dinner, I had one of the maids bring some ice to my room shortly before the time I thought he would appear. When she came, I pretended to be writing a letter in Japanese on the low table in the center of the room. While she was mixing a drink for me, I asked her, *"Chotto o-negai shimasu. Seika no ka wa dō yatte kakimasu ka?"* (Will you help me a minute, please? How do you write the *ka* in *seika?*).

The maid answered, *"Dono seika desu ka?"* (Which *seika* do you mean?).

"'Kore waga kokutai no seika' no seika" (The *seika* in "This is the glory of the fundamental character of our country"), I said.

That flustered the maid, who asked, *"Sore wa nan deshō ka?"* (What is that?).

"Ē? Kyōiku Chokugo wo shiranai?" (What? You don't know the Imperial Rescript on Education?), I asked in feigned surprise.

She started to blush and answered, *"Osoreirimasu ga ..."* (I'm afraid not ...).

I stared at her in pretended indignation and said, *"Konna koto wa hatsumimi da! Kyōiku Chokugo wo shiranai nante!"* (This is the first time I ever heard of such a thing! Imagine anyone not knowing the Imperial Rescript on Education!).

Motioning the maid to sit down beside me, I tore off a clean sheet of paper and began writing out the Imperial Rescript on Education, which was as familiar to pre-1945 school children in Japan as the Pledge of Allegiance to the Flag is to Americans: *"Chin omou ni waga kōso kōsō kuni wo hajimuru koto kōen ni ..."* (We believe that Our Imperial Ancestors have founded Our Empire on a basis broad and lasting ...).

At that moment, the manager bowed his way into the room and, with the white-hot curiosity that many Japanese have about anything a foreigner does, hastened to inquire of the maid what their foreign guest was doing. This gave me an excuse to stop writing—which was a good thing because I could not remember much more of the rescript.

With sparkling eyes, the maid excitedly explained to the manager that I was teaching her the Imperial Rescript on Education. He looked at her in utter disbelief, then scooted across the mats to regard what I had written. There was an audible, sharp intake of breath—and then he backed off, bowed deeply, and said *directly* to me,

"Dōmo shitsurei itashimashita. O-misore shimashita." (I have been very rude. I failed to recognize your ability).

After that, we had no more difficulty.

He simply had not been able to believe that I, an American, could really speak and understand Japanese. He probably thought—if he thought at all—that what I had said in Japanese had been a few words and sentences memorized parrot-fashion from some book like *How to Speak Perfect Japanese in Ten Easy Lessons.*

People like this *ryokan* manager have led me to believe that many (or most) Japanese have a kind of psycho-physiological, two-way valve in their ears which I have come to identify as the *baka-barubu* (fool valve). When an American or other Caucasian foreigner is sighted, this valve automatically opens for the audio-reception of English speech, while closing the channel for Japanese speech. The valve functions in accordance with visual—not auditory—stimuli. The sight of a foreign face switches the channel over from Japanese to English reception, but perversely, Japanese speech issuing from a foreign face will not cause it to switch back again. As long as the Japanese person is vis-à-vis a foreigner, the only way to cause his valve to change its reception channel from English back to Japanese is to say or do something so massively and so purely Japanese in nature that the shock of it—coming from a foreigner—causes the valve to spin on its stem and perhaps come back to rest with the Japanese channel open.

A word of caution is in order. This valve may tend to return, of its own accord, to the English channel time and time again, even when the Japanese is talking to a foreigner who, he knows, can speak Japanese. This often occurs when you meet a Japanese friend for the first time in a long while. You should prepare yourself for these emergencies by having ready a stock of ploys such as those described in this chapter.

The Imperial Rescript Ploy—or, as called by the irreverent, Seward's Sham—is obviously not for the beginner who has only a hundred words or so of Japanese. To follow through on the advantage gained, one must have a passable ability in the language.

Songmanship

There are, however, several ploys that can be used by beginners. One such device is Songmanship, which was originated and brought to perfection by a friend of mine whom I can identify only as Mr. K. Having a fine voice, he began learning Japanese songs soon after arriving in Japan. Within a year, he could count in his repertoire about two dozen songs that he knew the Japanese words to. Perhaps because the music itself takes care of the placement of accent and syllabic stress, Mr. K's Japanese—when sung—sounded quite good.

He and I worked together in those days. We were often invited to the same parties, where an evening seldom passed without him being called on to sing. His heartful rendition of old favorites like *Kōjō no Tsuki* (Moon over the Castle Ruins) would always earn gasps of sincere admiration and resounding applause.

Between songs he would busy himself keeping his *sake* cup filled— and refilling the cups of other guests. Whenever someone addressed a remark in Japanese to him, he would either smile enigmatically and say, *"Sā ..."* (Well ...) or lift his cup and shout, *"Kampai!"* In time he learned a little Japanese by osmosis alone, but he never studied the language—beyond his repertoire of songs. (And I doubt that he even knew the meaning of the lyrics.) Yet his device stood him in good stead for many years. To this day many Japanese who have heard him sing at parties mistakenly believe that he is fluent in Japanese.

You need not go to this extreme, of course, but you would be wise to memorize all the lyrics to five or six songs and sing them on appropriate occasions. This will go far in persuading your audience that your Japanese is better than it actually is. (The older the songs, the better. Your listeners will then assume that you've been long acquainted with Japan.)

Three Little Words

The Three Little Words device is one that approaches being one of those magic formulas that Madison Avenue crows about. It involves the memorization and use of the three words, *Yō, Dōmo,* and *Che.* Frequent use of these three—at the right time, of course—will persuade many people that you are on far more than slightly familiar terms with Japanese. Use them in the following way:

1. *Yō* is used between men who are approximate equals. It is a greeting similar to our "Hi!" An accompanying gesture is the right hand raised head-high. (In the same category with *Yō* is *Ossu* or *Ōssu,* a contraction of *O-hayō gozaimasu.*)

2. *Dōmo* means "very," "quite," "really." It appears in such locutions as these: *Dōmo arigatō gozaimasu* (Thank you very much), *Dōmo sumimasen deshita* (Please excuse me), *Dōmo shitsurei itashimashita* (That was really rude of me), and *Dōmo o-sewasama deshita* (I'm much obliged to you). It is used alone as an abbreviation of all of these—and herein lies its value. In situations where you are parting with a friend or thanking a person or apologizing to someone, all you need say to get by is the one word, *Dōmo.* (A slight bow makes it more effective.)

3. *Che* is used when you are suddenly irritated, disappointed, bested, or chagrined. The English word "Phooey" is as close as we can come to a good translation. It should be uttered with a short, semi-explosive sound. You should practice using *Che* in privacy so that it will sound natural when you have cause to say it before others.

Nichoson's Nictitation and Neely's Nimbus

Two more methods, which I should mention if only in passing, were devised by W. K. Nichoson and G. C. Neely and have come to be known as Nichoson's Nictitation and Neely's Nimbus. Both methods are strikingly simple but effective. The Nichoson system was based on the substitution of other words of scholarly tone for Japan, as in these examples: *Yamato* (Japan), *Shinkoku Nihon* (Japan, the Land of the Gods), *Sumeramikuni* (The Land Under Our Emperor's Rule), *Yamato Shimane* (The Island Country of Japan), *Ōyashima* (The Eight Great Islands [of Japan]), *Akitsushima* (Land of the Dragonflies), *Shikishima* (Japan), *Ōmikuni* (The Great August Country), *Shinshū* (The Divine Islands), and *Toyo Ashiwara no Chiaki no Nagaihoaki no Mizuho no Kuni* (The Land of the Luxuriant Reed Plains, of the Ripe Rice Ears, and of the Thousand Long Autumns).

One unforgettable night in Takatanobaba, Mr. Nichoson contrived to use all ten of these academic expressions in only five sentences, making an everlasting impression on his audience, of which I was lucky to count myself as one.

Neely's Nimbus is a method involving three locutions: 1. *Yoi korashō to!* 2. *Yattoko sa!* and 3. *Dokkoi sho!*

These three are used at moments of great physical exertion, as when lifting or moving something heavy, or immediately after such exertion. Uttered naturally and at the proper moment, Mr. Neely's three expressions are more effective for our purposes than ten or twenty times their number of complicated, technical vocabulary items.

Let us go on now to methods for use by students in the intermediate or early-advanced stages of study.

Edge's Edge

One such method was developed by G. Kenneth Edge while he was in residence at the Ueno Ryokan in Fukuoka in 1946 and was what he then called his "Say-the-Usual-in-an-Unusual-Way Method." He took twenty-seven commonplace expressions and, after some difficulty, discovered twenty-seven unusual ways (mostly literary) to communicate the same meaning. Sprinkled continually throughout his speech, they lent him the aura of a man so immersed in scholarly projects and all-night lucubrations that he could by no means rid his speech of them even while talking to laymen.

Subsequent scholars of the devious have wrought variations and (some say) improvements in what we later came to call Edge's Edge. The original twenty-seven, however, are still quite effective and should be preserved:

EDGE'S TERM	USED INSTEAD OF	MEANING
kuchinawa	*hebi*	snake
Iza-saraba	*Sayōnara*	Goodbye
saredomo	*keredomo*	however
ikuji	*nanji*	What time (is it)?
tare	*dare*	who

ikahodo	*ikura*	how much
o-habakari	*o-tearai, benjo*	toilet
samonakuba	*sō ja nakereba*	otherwise, if not so
kusushi	*isha*	physician
chigiru	*yakusoku*	promise
hōbai	*nakama*	friend
arinomi	*nashi*	pear
debana	*o-cha*	tea
wakōdo	*wakamono*	young person
akindo	*shōnin*	merchant
nakanzuku	*koto ni*	especially
sasa	*sake*	rice wine
Ikan tomo itashikata nai	*Shikata ga nai*	It cannot be helped
sukoburu	*taihen*	very
Kore wa katajikenai	*Arigatō*	I am grateful
ikutari	*ikunin*	how many persons
goran nasare	*goran nasai*	please look
kakubetsu	*tokubetsu*	special, especially
suru bekarazu	*shite wa ikenai*	should not
narō koto nara	*dekiru naraba*	if possible
shikaraba	*sō de areba*	if it is so
shikarazumba	*sō de nakereba*	if it is not so

An example of the later variations on Edge's Edge was the substitution of *kawaya* for *o-habakari*. Opponents of this substitution (and I am one of them) hold that frequent use of *kawaya* for toilet gives the user the air of a professional military man or possibly an ex-POW of the Japanese. Although this stance may be a desirable one under certain conditions, it is not, we opponents insist, at all in keeping with the scholarly cloak the originator strove to wrap himself in.

The Renne Reel

An innovator of the early nineteen-fifties, R.L. (for Lucky) Renne, introduced the Renne Reel, so named for the glib manner in which he reeled off *hayakuchi-kotoba* (tongue twisters), such as these:

1. *Nama-mugi, nama-gome, nama-tamago* (Unprocessed grain, unprocessed rice, and raw eggs).

2. *Kanda Kaji-chō no kado no kambutsuya de katsuo-bushi wo katte*

katakute kamenai kaeshite kaerō (I bought a dried bonito in a dry-provisions shop on a corner in Kaji-chō in Kanda but it was so hard that I couldn't chew it so I took it back and will now return home).

3. *Tonari no kyaku wa kaki kuu kyaku. Uchi no kyaku wa kaki kuwan kyaku. Kaki kuu kyaku to kaki kuwan kyaku* (The guest next door eats persimmons. Our guest does not eat persimmons. A guest who eats persimons and a guest who does not eat persimmons).

4. *Tokkyo-kyoka-kyoku kyoku-chō* (Head of the Department of Patent Approval).

5. *Bōsan ga byōbu ni jōzu na bōzu no bōshi no e wo kaita* (The priest skillfully painted a picture of a priest's hat on the standing screen).

Although Mr. Renne, who is, by the way, one of my most loyal saloon cronies, thought the Renne Reel to be effective when properly used, others found fault with it on two counts. First, unless the user practices his entire stock of tongue twisters several times daily (preferably in the privacy of his bath), he is apt to stumble over the words, thus spoiling the desired effect. Second, it is difficult to plan and arrange situations in which the seemingly casual reeling off of a tongue twister is appropriate. One could come to be regarded as eccentric if he were given to frequent repetition, however glib, of tongue twisters without apparent connection with the current topic of conversation.

Before we pass on to the final method, I would like to refer the reader to the chapter entitled "Proverbs," where he may avail himself of the material necessary for *kotowaza-otoshi* (proverb-dropping). Appropriately timed, proverb-dropping can draw heartwarming cries of *Umai!* and *Yoku shitteru nē!* from a bedazzled audience.

Dizer's Dialectic

One final method—one that has now fallen into disuse but not disrepute—was called Dizer's Dialectic, the term "dialectic" having in this case no connection with the discrimination of truth from error. Also referred to as Dizer's Dodge by the cognoscenti, it was devised by W. Haven Dizer.

The pith of DD was a frequent lapse into one of the dialects of Japanese. (For those who wish to try DD, please study the chapter titled "Dialects" in this book.) Mr. Dizer and his disciples believed that any Japanese who heard a foreigner speaking, for example, the Hakata dialect would presume that here was a foreigner so steeped in the ways of Japan that he had gone beyond—far beyond—the mere acquisition of standard Japanese and, entering esoteric realms, had mastered one of the difficult dialects.

Mr. Dizer's system, however, fell into its present state of disuse for three reasons: 1. Truly accurate imitation of any dialect is extremely difficult. 2. Some Japanese unfortunately twisted Mr. Dizer's premise around and assumed that he and his followers were learning the rural dialect *before* learning standard Japanese, the logic of which order they questioned. 3. Certain listeners did not recognize DD as a dialect at all, but thought that the user was merely mispronouncing what little Japanese he knew. (This was not true of Mr. Dizer himself but of some of his less learned disciples.)

Some students may, nevertheless, wish to experiment with DD or Renne's Reel. I can neither oppose nor support such experimentation. Although I can discern some validity in the objections to these two methods, I can also see the right thinking involved in the origination of both. (I was, in fact, closely associated with both Haven Dizer and Lucky Renne when they were inspired to invent their systems, and I may even have played a modest assisting role.)

Leaving DD and the Renne Reel to the discretion of the student, we still have the other methods offered herein to the serious pretender: the Imperial Rescript Ploy or Seward's Sham, Mr. K.'s Songmanship, the Three Little Words, Nichoson's Nictitation, Neely's Nimbus, and Edge's Edge. Given practice and correct usage, these should go far in convincing your listeners that your Japanese is much better than it really is.

CHAPTER 12

Imported Words

Importation and Malformation

In their pell-mell rush to introduce Western culture and technology into Japan during the twenty or thirty years following the Meiji Restoration in 1868, the Japanese also imported many words of American and European origin. Although this importation continues today, there have been periods of considerable resistance to such borrowing. The classic instance was during World War II, when the government, wanting to obliterate every trace of the enemy tongue, urged the substitution of pure Japanese words for those of English origin, such as *tōshu* (lit., throwing hand) for *pitchā* (pitcher) and *shōkōki* (lit., going up and going down machine) for *erebētā* (elevator).

A recent survey of ninety Japanese magazines found that four percent of the words used in these magazines were of foreign (other than Chinese) origin. Even though I suspect that this means four percent of the vocabulary amenable to foreign conversion, i.e., excluding the inflective and connective words, it is still a high percentage, and I am sure I have read many articles in which the percentage of *gairaigo* (imported words) was significantly larger. I do not, however, necessarily recommend that you memorize the *gairaigo* which follow; they are given here more in illustration of what dread malformations can befall innocent English words when they cross Japan's threshold: *appā-katto* (uppercut), *fain purē* (a fine play—in baseball), *naitoueia* (nightwear), *wan-suteppu* (one step), *fuandeshon* (a foundation garment), *raito ranchi* (light lunch), *rakki ringu* (lucky ring), *sēfutei fāsuto* (safety first), *furūtsu doroppu* (fruit drops), *kuraimakkusu* (climax), *raundo choko* (round chocolate), *apputsū-dēto* (up-to-date), and *appuru* or *rēzun pai* (apple or raisin pie).

Even though there are twice as many Japanese phonetic symbols *(kana)* as there are letters in our alphabet, it is nevertheless practically impossible to correctly reproduce the pronunciation or the spelling of English words with these symbols, as the above list would indicate. Since most Japanese first approach the study of English through these same symbols, it is little wonder that much Japanese pronunciation of English is abominable.

Be that as it may, the subject of *gairaigo* would not deserve a separate chapter in this book if it were not for one disturbing circumstance—that is, the average citizen of Japan who hears a Westerner (whom he usually presumes to be an American) fumbling about in Japanese often attempts—with disastrous results—to give that foreigner a helping hand by injecting as many *gairaigo* as he can muster into his speech. This kindness would be beneficial if the imported words were correctly used and correctly pronounced. Unfortunately, they seldom are. As a result, the Westerner is more in the dark than ever—and the Japanese becomes bewildered. After all, he did go out of his way to use *gairaigo,* didn't he? What's wrong with this foreigner? Doesn't he understand his own language?

Although eighty-seven percent of *gairaigo* are of English origin, these are by no means necessarily comprehensible to native English speakers in their misshapen Japanized form and less likely to be so to foreigners whose native tongue is not English. The remaining thirteen percent of non-English derivation come mostly from Dutch and Portuguese, since Holland and Portugal were most active in the early opening of Japan to the West, and from France and Germany, from whom Japan learned much about medicine, law, and military organization during the period from 1868 until the turn of the century. Some examples of non-English *gairaigo* are: *mesu* (scalpel, German), *abekku* (together or a couple; French), *buriki* (tin, Dutch), and *pan* (bread, Portuguese). Note that the Japanese intensify the Japanization of *pan* by confecting such forms as *shoku-pan* (lit., eating bread) (What other kind, one wonders, is there?), *kuro-pan* (black or dark bread), and *ampan* (a bun containing a purplish, repugnant bean jam).

Four things can happen to an imported word when entering Japan that can make it more confusing than the purely Japanese equivalent would have been:

1. The Japanese abbreviate it. Examples: department store = *depāto,* modern girl = *moga* (prewar slang), mass communications = *masu-komi,* permanent = *pāma,* engine stoppage = *ensuto,* apartment house = *apāto.*

The most extreme example that comes to mind is *bēa,* from *bēsu appu* (base up; to have one's base pay raised), which is usually used in writing and not in conversation.

2. The Japanese mispronounce the imported word. This, of course,

is to be expected of a people whose language training requires them to say "silver" as if it were *shirubā*, "gesture" as if it were *zesuchua* or *jiesucha*, and "love scene" as if it were *rabu shiin*. The problem here is that there is a wide—very wide—disparity between "I love you" and *Ai rabu yū* (I rub you?).

3. The Japanese change the meaning of the word during the process of importation. For example, they took the word "demagogue," shortened it to *dema*, and then arbitrarily assigned to it the meaning of false rumor, (which is, to be sure, a weapon in the demagogue's arsenal).

Again, on the Ginza, I recently saw a large sign that read (translated into English) "Please visit our rooftop rathskeller."

4. They take an English verb, shorten it, and then decline it as if it were a Japanese verb. Taking the first four letters (*nego*) of the English verb negotiate, the Japanese verbalize it by adding *ru* (i.e., *negoru*) and then use such locutions as, *Kare to negotte miyō ka?* (Shall I negotiate with him?).

In all fairness, however, I should make mention of one legitimate function these imported words can occasionally perform—namely, they can be used to distinguish between something that is basically a Japanese object or institution and something that is foreign. For example, *hirumeshi* (noon rice) is a lunch of Japanese food and *ranchi* (lunch) is a Western-style noon meal, *ryokan* is a Japanese-style inn and *hoteru* is a foreign-style hotel, *chirigami* is Japanese toilet paper, which comes in flat, single sheets, and *toiretto-pēpā* is foreign-style toilet paper that comes in rolls.

Even after you have gained considerable proficiency in Japanese, the problem of understanding the many *gairaigo* that will come your way does not necessarily diminish. If anything, it increases. You will hear an imported word and, not recognizing it immediately as such, you will often assume that it is a word of native Japanese origin. The resulting confusion can create situations that are truly *yūmorasu* (humorous).

Once when I was making a reservation for a room in a *ryokan* in Kagoshima, the Japan Travel Bureau agent asked me if I wanted a *basutsuki no heya* (a room with *basu*). Maybe I should have known what he meant, but it had been a hard day and I took *basu* to mean bus. Stranger things than a hotel room with a bus attached have happened in Japan, and, anyway, I thought it probably meant that guests in that *ryokan* had the privilege of a daily tour by sightseeing bus. As you have probably guessed, it turned out to be just a room with bath *(basu),* but

I still don't see why the JTB agent couldn't have used *furo* instead of *basu* for bath.

Another time, I was host to a group of Japanese and American academics, most of whom were somewhat bilingual. The talk that evening kept shifting from Japanese to English and back again, and, in the midst of one heated discussion, a Japanese professor called out several times, *"Hiya, hiya!"* Since *hiya* (or *o-hiya*) means a glass of cold water in Japanese, I sent my maid to the kitchen to fetch a pitcher of ice water and glasses, but when she offered him a glassful, he looked at her in surprise and said he did not want any. Later, I learned that he had been enthusiastically supporting the views of a colleague by repeatedly calling out, "Hear, hear!"

And I would prefer not to relate in detail the scene in the Seibo Hospital, in which a nurse kept talking to me about *goshippu* and I thought she meant "honorable compress" *(go-shippu)* instead of ordinary gossip.

The worst aspect of all these *gairaigo* is that, with the exception of certain basic expressions, many Japanese do not understand them, either. Here I cannot substantiate my point with exact statistics, but I remember a magazine article of several years ago that made excessive use of imported words. I showed the article to eight persons chosen at random in the Japanese company in which I worked and found that, on the average, these eight understood less than half of the words in question.

But Still the Tide Flows In

Is there a counterploy? Since, in many instances, your Japanese friend is using these imported words for your benefit, albeit from a misguided sense of kindness, it would hardly be proper for you to use any harsh devices in calling his attention to the error of his ways. For years I tried the gentle method of merely repeating the same word back to him in Japanese, hoping that he would understand and appreciate my desire that we speak in pure Japanese, but this method was not very efficacious. What often resulted was an exchange like this:

JAPANESE FRIEND: *Nē, Suwādo-san, anata kara no kanai-ate no rabu-retā wo yonda yo!* = Say there, Mr. Seward, I read your love letter to my wife.

SEWARD (exposed and shaken): *Sō desu ka? Boku no koi-bumi wo yomi-mashita ka?* = Oh? So you read my love letter, eh?

JAPANESE (no longer a friend): *Ē. Rabu-reta wo yonda* = Yes, I read your love letter.

Curtain falls as Seward makes hasty exit.

To one Japanese friend (not the ex-friend mentioned above), I once mentioned this problem and he was most sympathetic. He fully agreed that I had a legitimate complaint. He proposed that in the future he and I should always converse with each other in pure Japanese.

Later, as our Saturday night on the Ginza was ending, he said to me: *"Nē, Suwādo-san, ashita wa sandei da kara uchi no waifu to issho ni chāchi ni itte sono ato doraibu ni dekakete sono kaeri watakushi no hōmu ni tachiyotte ranchi tabemasen ka?* (Mr. Seward, since tomorrow is Sunday, let's go to church with my wife and after that, we can go for a drive. On the way back, we can stop off at my house for lunch. All right?) Note that he used the imported words for Sunday, wife, church, drive, home, and lunch, for which there are perfectly good Japanese equivalents.

CHAPTER 13

Colors in Japan

Colorful but Confusing

The Japanese words for colors can be confusing. With certain ones, it seems as if the Japanese view the world through glasses so tinted that they see the same outlines we see, but in different shades. For example, the green light in a traffic signal looks very green to me, but the Japanese (until 1968) called it *aoi* (blue), even though they had a fine, upstanding word for green *(midori-iro)*.

Also, in the abstract sense, the qualities given to colors by the Japanese differ from ours, which is not strange for two languages which grew to maturity in complete independence of each other. In illustration, yellow is a disreputable color to us: witness yellow journalism, a yellow streak, and the yellow flag of quarantine. When we want to describe a yellowish object that we like, we tend to shun the word yellow and call the object golden. But to the Japanese, yellow is a perfectly respectable color. Nor does this have any connection with the color of their skins, which is not truly yellow to begin with, and which they do not think of as being yellow. The word *ōshoku jinshu* (lit., yellow race) was coined after early Western visitors began referring to the Japanese as members of the "yellow race."

The Color of Love

Let's begin by regarding the word for color itself: *iro.* Say it twice, *iro-iro,* and it means "various." *Iro* is also often used to mean love or passion. Its *kanji* has the variant readings of *shoku* and *shiki.* Note its usage in these examples:

iro-onna = mistress or fancy woman
iro-otoko = male lover or lady-killer
iro-goto = love affair

107

Iro wa shian no hoka = Love is beyond reason
Eiyū iro wo konomu = Heroes are romantic
sake to iro ni tandeki suru = to be addicted to sensual pleasures
kōshoku bungaku = pornographic literature (*kōshoku* is written with
    the characters *konomu,* meaning "to like," and *iro*)
shiki-jōkyō = nymphomania

A Spectrum of Chromatic Meanings

The following is a list of the more common colors with examples of
how they are used. An asterisk after the example word tells that the
word or phrase is used more in the written than the spoken language.
These colors are listed here to give the reader an idea of the spectrum
of shades of meaning in each example. Note that the adjectival form of
the color is given first with the noun or combining form next, followed
by the variant readings of the *kanji,* and the English equivalent. The
literal meaning of an example appears in parentheses.

I. BLUE

aoi, ao, sei = blue, pale, unripe; this color also connotes purity.
aoi me no gaijin = Caucasian foreigner (blue-eyed outsider)
seinen = youth (blue years)
aomonoya = vegetable shop (blue-things shop)
aonisai = callow youth (blue two-year old)
aogoke = green moss (blue moss)
ao-iki = anxious sigh (blue breath)
*aohyō** = opposing vote (blue ballot)
*seiryō** = brothel (blue tower)

II. GREEN

midori-iro no, midori-iro or *midori, ryoku, roku* = green. These refer to
the word which we foreigners usually use when we mean green, although
in similar situations the Japanese would use *aoi.* Considering the Japanese penchant for describing the stages of youth with colors (see *aonisai,*
above; *akago,* below), one could reasonably assume that *midori-go* (in-

fant) is written with the *kanji* for green child, but the *midori* in *midori-go* is written with a different *kanji*, that has, of course, a different meaning.

*midori gyokuzui** = chrysoprase quartz (green jewel marrow)

*ryokuen** = evening haze (green smoke)

*rokushō** = green rust (green blue)

III. RED

akai, aka, seki = red. Red is the *o-medetai* (congratulatory) color in Japan and is used in decorations for festive occasions. It is also the color of youth; an older person wearing much red clothing would be considered odd.

akago, akachan, akambo = baby (red child)

makka na uso = bare-faced lie (pure-red lie)

sekimen = blush (red face)

akasen-kuiki = red-light district (red-line district)

akamon = entrance to Tōkyō University (red gate)

aka-daikon = radish [as we know it in the U.S.], lip communist, i.e., red ouside and white inside (red big root)

sekirara = stark naked (red naked naked)

aka no tanin = a perfect stranger (red stranger)

*akai kokoro** = sincere heart (red heart)

*akahon** = dime novel (red book)

*sekishu** = bare or empty hands (red hands)

*sekihin** = extreme poverty (red poverty)

IV. BROWN

cha-iro no, cha-iro = brown. Brown is perhaps the most difficult color to come to terms with. *Cha-iro* (lit., tea color) means brown, but consider the many shades of tea, some of which appear to me to be green (or should I say blue?). *Kitsune-iro* (fox color) means brown, but there are silver foxes and red foxes as well as white and blue foxes. *Tsuchi-iro* (earth color) is brown, but think of all the shades of color in the earth. *Kasshoku* (as in *kasshoku jinrui,* the brown or Malayan race) is brown, but the same characters can be read *kachi iro,* in which case the meaning changes to "dark blue."

kuro-zatō = dark-brown sugar (black sugar)

akai kutsu = brown shoes (red shoes). This refers to shoes for men, as nowadays *akai kutsu* for women are actually red.

akai inu = brown dog (red dog)

aka-zatō = light-brown sugar (red sugar)

tobi-iro = dusky brown (kite [the bird] color)

yaite kitsune-iro ni naru = turn green with jealousy (become toasted brown with jealousy)

kongari-to kitsune-iro ni yakeru = to become beautifully sun-tanned (to burn in the sun and become fox-colored)

V. BLACK

kuroi, kuro, koku = black. One phrase which I like to use is *me no kuroi uchi ni*, as in *Ore no me no kuroi uchi ni kono bessō ni ashibumi sasenai zo!* which means "I'll not let you set foot in this villa as long as I'm alive." The literal rendering of *me no kuroi uchi ni* is "as long as my eyes are black," and though my eyes are blue, I seldom evoke so much as an eyelash flicker when I say this.

hara ga kuroi = crafty, wicked (black-stomached)

kokujin = Negro (black person)

kurōto = a professional (an abstruse or black person)

kuroyama = large crowd (black mountain)

kuro-shiro = black and white, right and wrong (black-white)

kuro-bune = Commodore Perry's ships (black ships)

kuro-ichigo = blackberry (black strawberry)

*kokui-saishō** = a Buddhist priest who has become a cabinet minister (a black-clothed cabinet minister)

VI. WHITE

shiroi, shiro, shira, haku = white

shirōto = amateur (white person)

hakumai = polished rice (white rice)

shiraga = gray hair (white hair)

hakujin = Caucasian (white person)

hakujō = confession (white letter)

shirafu = sober (white face)

Hakuakan = the White House (chalkstone building)

Shirakawa yofune no uchi ni = while sound asleep (while passing Shirakawa aboard a night ship [a phrase from the *Kefukigusa,* a collection
of *haikai*])
hakusen = hand-to-hand combat (white fighting)
shiro-kubi = prostitute (white [powdered] neck)
shirajirashii uso = bare-faced lie (white-white lie)

VII. GOLD

kin-iro no, kin-iro, kane, kon = gold. The character for gold also has
the meanings of money and metal.
kinketsu-byō = short of funds (gold-shortage sickness)
kinshi gyokuyō* = the imperial family (leaves of jewels on branches of
gold)
kanekui = spendthrift (gold eater)
kintama = testicles (gold balls)

VIII. SILVER

gin-iro no, gin-iro, shirogane, gin = silver. Not only is the Ginza Tōkyō's
most famous street and district but there are also 560 more Ginza
streets—mostly shopping centers—in Japan to attest to the popularity
of the name. The *kanji* for Ginza are those for silver and for seat, the
"seat" in this case being used as in "seat of government." Somewhere
in the present Ginza district, during the Keichō era (1596–1615), the
Tokugawa shogunate established a mint, and the present characters for
Ginza were stamped on the silver coins minted there.
ginkō = bank (silver-dealer)
shirogane = silver (white metal)
Gimbura = a stroll on the Ginza (silver stroll)
gin-sekai = snow scene (silver world)
gin-nagashi* = fop, dandy (one who lets silver flow)

IX. PURPLE

murasaki-iro no, murasaki-iro or *murasaki, shi* = purple
murasaki = soy sauce (purple)

*shien** = tobacco smoke (purple smoke)
*shiden** = flashes of lightning (purple electricity)

X. YELLOW

kiiroi, kiiro, ki, kō, ō = yellow
kimi = egg yolk (yellow body)
kiiroi koe = shrill voice (yellow voice)
kuchibashi ga kiiroi = inexperienced (to have a yellow beak, i.e., like a chick)
*kōkō** = greenhorn (yellow mouth)
*kōka** = the yellow peril (yellow calamity)
kibyōshi = pornographic novel (yellow cover)

CHAPTER 14

Male and Female Speech

Men Who Follow Feminine Forms, Beware!

Many foreign men learn much of what Japanese they know from Japanese wives or girl friends, who are sometimes facetiously called *ne-jibiki* (sleeping dictionaries). Although such fonts of linguistic knowledge can be both pleasant and inspiring as well as instructive, they can also seduce unwary men into hard-to-correct patterns of feminine speech. There are certain clear-cut distinctions between the way a man talks and the way a woman talks in Japan, and the foreign student who learns his Japanese from a woman will tend to imitate her speech patterns.

Herein we have two dangers or disadvantages. The first and more obvious is that any man sounds ridiculous when he uses such feminine expressions as, *Iya da wa!* (I don't like it, No, I refuse, etc.) or *Sō na no?* (Is that so?). The second is that the average Japanese will often assume, quite possibly mistakenly, that the speaker has learned his Japanese from a Tachikawa or Yokosuka (or Chitose or Sasebo) bar girl with whom even now he may be living in sin.

The Japanese weeklies, in their unflagging search for the lurid and sensational, have always pounced upon the offenses, both major and minor, of U.S. servicemen and ex-servicemen and have published these stories, replete with half-truths and pandering to popular prejudices, in fulsome detail. From this mass has emerged one clear image that has become firmly fixed in the popular imagination—namely, the American GI who becomes attached (he is seldom depicted as being capable of sincere love) to a Japanese girl during a tour of duty in Japan. He returns to the U.S. for military discharge (often abandoning his erstwhile mistress and perhaps an illegitimate child or two), but the good life in Japan, based on a permissive sexual atmosphere, lures him back like Kipling's ten-year soldier who hears the voices singing, "Come ye back to Mandalay."

Back in Japan, he may not return to the lonely (?) arms of his previous girlfriend, but never mind, there are other bars and other bar girls.

113

To remain in Japan, he has to do something beside drink *o-sake* and pitch woo to obtain a visa, so he either teaches English (the blind leading the blind?) or he engages to sell encyclopedias. But these enterprises, it seems, seldom prosper and, yielding to temptation, he engages in one of the traditional occupations of *furyō-gaijin* (delinquent foreigners); namely, smuggling, black-marketing, or spying. The forces of right, naturally, catch up with him sooner or later—and this is when he gets a lot of free publicity in some of the forty or more Japanese weekly magazines *(shūkan-shi)*.

This ex-GI, having learned what Japanese he knows from his mistress(es), uses a number of feminine expressions in his speech and this is duly reported to Japanese readers, who are always eager to believe the worst of foreigners. What finally emerges is this equation:

Use of feminine expressions = extensive, illicit relations with the bar girls of Tachikawa or Yokosuka = ex-GI who is now a gold smuggler, spy, or thoroughly corrupt rascal.

If you suspect that you may use such feminine expressions—from whatever source—and if you care at all what others think, then it behooves you to take unhesitating measures to defeminize your speech.

Feminine Japanese

Feminine Japanese is characterized by inflectional style, comparatively more extensive use of polite forms, and by certain interjections and pronouns. Japanese women generally inflect their voices more than the men. We Americans tend to do the same in speaking any foreign language, so all the more reason we should try to speak Japanese in an even pitch. Also, Japanese women use more polite forms in their speech than men, although the men can be extremely polite when the occasion requires. But it is principally by certain pronouns and interjections that male and female speakers are most easily distinguished (aside, of course, from vocal timbre). Here are some examples of pronouns *(daimeishi)* and interjections *(kantōshi)*.

I. FEMININE PRONOUNS

watashi = I (more feminine in feeling than masculine, although some men use it) *atakushi, atashi* = I (feminine contractions of *watakushi*, which is used by both men and women)

atai = I (sometimes used by young girls)

II. FEMININE INTERJECTIONS

wa. Used at the end of a sentence, this interjectional post-particle is the most distinctive mark of female speech. (Note, however, that men in Kansai use it dialectally.) Example: *Ano otoko-tteba hidoi wa!* = Speaking of that man, I think he's awful!

Mā. Meanings are "My," "Oh dear." Example: *Mā, kono kanjō wa baka ni takai, nē* = My, this check is awfully high, isn't it? (Shortened to *ma*, it is sometimes used by older men as well.)

wa yo. Like *wa*, above, this is used at the end of a sentence and the *yo* makes it more forcible. Example: *Ii wa yo! Hottokinasai!* = It's all right! Let it alone!

Ara. This interjection stands alone and means "Well," "You don't say," "My," "Indeed," "Listen," and so forth. Example: *Ara! Uchi no niwashi ga wani ni kuwarete iru yo!* = Look! Our gardener is being eaten by a crocodile!

Ara mā. A combination of the two given above. Example: *Ara mā! Ano henshitsusha wa renkō sareru toko da!* = My goodness! That degenerate is being taken to jail!

no. More often than men, women use *no* in place of *ka* as the interrogative particle or spoken question mark. Example: *Asu Kimi-chan mo iku no?* = Kimi-chan, are you going tomorrow, too?

nē. Used for sentence endings like "isn't it," "aren't we," "haven't we," etc. One text tells us that *nē* characterizes the speech of women and children, thus its entry here. Nevertheless, it is used frequently by men and I do not feel that its use seriously impairs the masculinity of one's speech, although *nā* is admittedly rougher. Example: *Tadagoto ja arimasen, nē?* = This is no trivial matter, is it?

Sō na no? Is that so? Example: *Sō na nō? Ii kimi da wa!* = Is that so? It serves him (her) right!

Ē. Like *Hai*, this word means "Yes," "I'm listening," "I agree," "Uh-huh," "Go on," "I hear you," etc. *Un* and *Ē* are both substitutes for *Hai*, the former somewhat masculine in tone and the latter somewhat feminine. These are used so extensively by both sexes, however, that I note these distinctions only with hesitation. Example: *Ē, sō desu.*

Shujin wa jūnen-mae kara shitsugyō shite orimasu = Yes, that's true. My husband has been out of work for the past ten years.

koto. Coming at the end of a sentence, this word is emphatic. Example: *Mā, ii tenki desu koto!* = What fine weather!

mono. Like *koto,* above, *mono* is suffixed to a sentence or phrase; it means "because." Example: (A) *Naze kare wo sonna ni nikumu ndesu ka?* (B) *Moji-dōri no kyūketsuki desu mono* = (A) Why do you hate him so much? (B) Because he's a veritable bloodsucker.

Masculine Japanese

The speech of Japanese men is generally rougher, coarser, and blunter than that of the women. In addition, some Japanese men emphasize the masculinity of their speech by adopting a deep-voiced, guttural mode of speaking which is often accompanied by stern faces and stiff postures. In his gestures and speech, the film star Toshirō Mifune sets a good example of *otoko-rashii* (masculine) behavior.

I. MASCULINE PRONOUNS

washi = I (used mostly by older men in the rural districts)
ware-ware = we (formal) (women prefer *watashi-tachi* or *watashi-domo*)
boku = I (used mostly by boys and young men)
ore = I (rough)
kimi = you (a familiar pronoun used by men to men)
temae = you (rough; used by men to men)
kisama = you (rough; used by men to men)

II. MASCULINE INTERJECTIONS

zo. Used at the end of a sentence or complete thought. This interjectional particle is both rough and emphatic. It is distinctly masculine. Example: *Kora! Te wo komanuite bōkan shiteru toki ja nai zo!* = Hey! This is no time to fold your arms and look on idly!

ze. Similar to *zo,* above. Example: *Bāten-san! Kore wa Hakutsuru ja nai nja nai ka? Dōmo imo-jōchū no yō da ze* = Bartender, this is not

Hakutsuru [a brand of *sake*]. It tastes more like *imo-jōchū* [home-brew made from potatoes].

nā. A rough equivalent of the feminine *nē*. (Some women, however, use *na* in expressions which end with *kudasai na*.) Example: *Dosha-buri ni futte iru nā?* = It's raining cats and dogs, isn't it? (Lit., It's raining earth and sand, isn't it?)

Yā. Often used as "Hello there." Also means "Well, I'll be ..." Example: *Yā, Morita-kun! Shibaraku da na. Dō da, mizumushi wa mada naoran kai?* = Hullo, Morita! It's been a long time, hasn't it? Say, hasn't your athlete's foot cleared up yet?

ja nai ka? More politely, *ja arimasen ka?* Used at the end of a sentence, this phrase is argumentative in tone as in "Can't you understand that?" or "Don't you see that?" etc. Example: *Ii nja nai ka?* = Can't you see that it's all right?

Un. See *Ē* in FEMININE INTERJECTIONS, above. Example: *Un. Kizuke no tame ni ippai yarō!* = Let's have a glass of "encouragement."

Ja. Contraction of *de wa*. Meanings are "Well," "Well then," "In that case." Example: *Ja, iya-garase wo iu nara mikudari-han wo yatchaō!* = Well then, if she's going to make nasty comments, I'll give her a letter of divorce. *Mikudari-han* is an old word meaning letter or statement of divorce. The literal meaning is three-and-a-half lines, which was the prescribed length of the divorce letter. The writing of the short letter was all that the husband had to do to be legally divorced. (Ah, the good old days.)

In addition to the defeminization measures already given, the student should take note of *chōdai* and *mashi*. *Chōdai* means "please give" or "please do" and is the equivalent of *kudasai*. Although it is also used by men, it is somewhat more feminine in tone than *kudasai*. The verb suffix *mashi* (or *mase*) is affixed to *kudasai* (not to *chōdai*) and intensifies its politeness. Ordinarily men will use *kudasai* alone, but when formal occasions require they will use *kudasai-mase*, whereas women will use *kudasai-mashi*, e.g., *O-kane wo zembu kudasai-mashi* (Please give me all your money).

III. MASCULINIZING JAPANESE SPEECH

Having examined the general distinctions between masculine and feminine forms of speech, we can now consider some specific methods for the male student to masculinize his speech. Since these suggestions are addressed chiefly to men, women may be tempted to skip over this section, but in order to understand Japanese men and to avoid using embarrassing masculine forms, it is recommended that they familiarize themselves with the material presented here.

1. For I, use *watakushi* and for we, use *ware-ware*. Be chary in your use of *anata* (you); use the person's title or name. Eschew pronouns and indicate of whom you speak through polite and nonpolite verb forms and nouns. If you are young or on particularly close terms with another man of your age, you can use *boku* for I and *kimi* for you without detriment. You should, however, absorb the chapter on polite and nonpolite forms first.

2. Prefer *nā* to *nē*.

3. Use *Un* in place of *Hai* for Yes, unless speaking to *o-rekireki* (very important people).

4. Use *Ja* for "Well," "Well then," etc.

5. The use of *zo* or *ze* at the end of sentences will lend a very rough, masculine tone to your speech, but you may prudently decide that it is better not to use these interjectional particles to many of your acquaintances. If, for example, your Japanese boss tells you to go to the airport at Haneda to meet someone and you tell him *Itte kuru zo!* (I'm on my way!), you might as well just keep on going because it is doubtful that you will have a job to come back to. You can, however, use these interjections in an indirect fashion and accomplish your purpose. Example: *Kare ga sakujitsu uchi ni kita toki, omae nanka aite ni shinai zo to itte opparatte yatta ndesu yo* = When he came to my house yesterday, I told him that I would have nothing more to do with him and sent him on his way. Herein you have quoted your own use of *zo* but have maintained a decent level of politeness to the person to whom you are speaking by finishing the sentence with *ndesu yo*.

6. Use *ja nai ka* in lieu of *ja arimasen ka,* which is polite, and *ja nai no,* which is feminine, where appropriate. Remember that it is informal in tone.

7. Use *Yoshi* (All right, O.K., Fine) when an informal and fairly rough tone is permissible.

8. Make use of *Sayō ka?* (Is that so?) now and then instead of *Sō desu ka?* Whereas *Sō ka?* is very rough, *Sayō ka?,* while still masculine, is softened somewhat by the use of *sayō,* which has a strong association with formal, polite speech, albeit a bit old-fashioned.

9. Use *kotta* occasionally in place of *koto da,* e.g., *Iya na kotta* for *Iya na koto da* (It's an unpleasant thing) or *Nante kotta?* for *Nan to iu koto da?* (What's this all about?).

10. Be sure to use *ka* at the end of all interrogative sentences or phrases. *Ka* has a bold, masculine sound to it. Women may use *ka,* but frequently they substitute *no* for it or omit an interrogative particle altogether.

11. When hungry, say *Hara ga hetta* rather than *Onaka ga sukimashita.* For "to eat," use *kuu* in place of *taberu.* Example: *Hara ga hetta kara, kui ni ikō ja nai ka* = I'm hungry. Let's go somewhere and eat.

CHAPTER 15

Polite and Nonpolite Speech

Speech Gradations and Social Relationships

A subject deserving your careful attention is that of the varying degrees of politeness and impoliteness in Japanese, of which there are four discernible gradations: impolite (or abrupt), familiar, polite, and extremely polite.

The extremely polite speech, including but by no means limited to the words once used only to or about the imperial family, has suffered setbacks since 1945, during the so-called democratization of Japan. Since extensive use of it was limited to a small segment of the people to begin with, it is best omitted from this discussion. Of the three remaining gradations, I will combine the impolite and the familiar forms into one classification (to be called the nonpolite), both for the sake of simplification and because their lines of demarcation become blurred at a number of places.

The distinguishing characteristics of the two remaining forms, the polite and the nonpolite, are to be found in personal pronouns, verbs and assorted verbal constructions, honorific prefixes, and certain words for relatives, home, employer, and so forth.

To those readers for whom English is their native and perhaps only tongue, these polite and nonpolite forms may present, as they did to me, an outlandish and somewhat frustrating concept in speech. To us, before we came to grips with Japanese, there was only one word for the person to whom we were speaking and that one word was "you." In Japanese, however, instead of one word, we found that we would be working with *anata, kimi, omae, kiden, kisama,* and *otaku.* Instead of one short, easy word like "I," we found them coming at us with *boku, ore, sessha, uchi, kotchi* or *kochira,* and *watakushi,* the last having variants like *watashi* and *washi.* There was even one word that, according to *Kenkyūsha's New Japanese-English Dictionary,* means *both* "you" and "I," i.e., *temae.*

The choice of which word to use is determined by the speaker's relationship to or position vis-à-vis his auditor or the person about whom he is talking. In Japan, very few people are considered exactly equal. To be so would require the unlikely coincidence of having been born at the same time, having the same education, being from families of nearly identical means and reputation, having the same position in companies or government offices of similar importance, and so forth. Such coincidences being seldom obtained, it follows that all Japanese have to talk up or down to other Japanese. Accordingly, a man might address a serving wench—or his wife—as *omae,* which leaves no doubt where she stands in relation to him. A wife might address her husband as *anata,* but seldom by his name, which would show exceeding familiarity. (Some young persons today, however, are trying to show how up-to-date they are by violating this old custom.) A maid should not address her employer by any personal pronoun or even by name. Properly, she should call the wife of the house *Okusama* (Honorable Interior) and the man *Dannasama* (Honorable Master), although some snippy young things these days have shortened that to *Danna-san* (Mr. Master?). If a man brushes rudely against you on the Moto-machi, you may feel justified in expressing your antagonism toward him by calling him *kisama,* but if you do, stand ready for a bare-knuckle fist fight.

One justification for the prevalent use of business cards *(meishi)* and letters of introduction *(shōkai-jō)* is that they enable one person to know how to speak to another socially. When meeting a person, one needs to know, in addition to such visible differences as age and mode of dress, such other details as position and company affiliation (provided by the business card) and the extent, if any, of one's pre-meeting indebtedness, incurred through, for instance, favors extended to friends and relatives. This information is generally provided by the introducer or the letter, of introduction.

One can, of course, carry on a dialogue with a man one is meeting for the first time without being aware of all the background data. Not knowing them, however, does impart to the average Japanese a feeling of awkwardness and unease, of conceivable impending and irretrievable faux-pas. He cannot afford to be too curt for fear that the father of the young man touching his forelock in front of his desk may have befriended a member of his own family in the past. On the other hand, he balks at the easy escape of blanket politeness to one and all, since he would feel like a fool if he spoke politely to this same man who turned out to be his scullery maid's country cousin come to Tōkyō to humbly beg assistance in finding employment.

So, our Japanese friend reasons, the only sane course is to avoid un-expected meetings with strangers and to somehow learn the essential facts about persons to whom he expects to be introduced. I have attended social gatherings where all guests were told in advance who else would be there and were given biographical summaries of anyone not already known to them. With the notable exception of the mammoth cocktail parties popular these days, however, it is not considered good form to invite too many people who are strangers to each other to the same social occasion, the desire being to avoid the obvious complications.

Restricted Pronoun Usage

If the forementioned plethora of I's and you's in Japanese is per-plexing, there is one amelioration for which we should be thankful—the Japanese do not use them, comparatively speaking, as often as we would use such pronouns in English. If the English sentence, "I like girls," is denuded of its subject "I," it sounds like a command to become fond of young females. In Japanese, however, if one said, *Musume ga suki da* (Girls as for, like), there is no doubt that it is the speaker who likes girls, even though he has not used any of the words for "I" at all.

When starting out in Japanese, the foreign student should be par-ticularly cautious about his use of personal pronouns. Overusage of *watakushi* and *anata* is one of the most common faults of the beginner. Once you get your feet on the ground in Japanese, it would be excellent training to practice composing and using sentences without the pro-nouns for "I" and "you."

There are, of course, exceptions. One Japanese man of my acquaint-ance used the pronoun *anata* every fifth or sixth word, it seemed, just as some Americans overuse "you know" and "I mean" and "d'ya un-derstand?" The norm, nevertheless, is very restricted usage. No one apparently noticed, for example, that there were no personal pronouns at all used in a novelette written by a distinguished Japanese writer until he himself pointed out his deliberate omission in a magazine article. What makes this possible are certain verbs and verbal constructions, honorific prefixes, and what not, by which the speaker can clearly in-dicate about or to whom he is speaking without necessarily making fre-quent use of names or personal pronouns.

There are verbs in which the subject is implicit, such as *mairu,* mean-ing "to go." When using it, no personal pronoun as subject is necessary.

Mairu alone means "I (or someone inferior to the person addressed) go." Reversing our social direction, we see that the same is true of verbs such as *irassharu* and *o-ide ni naru*, both of which mean "to go" or "to be present." *Irassharu* or *o-ide ni naru* alone means "you (or the superior party about whom we are speaking) go." In like ways, *mōshiageru* alone means "(I) speak," and *ossharu* alone means "(you) speak."

There are verb constructions which will accomplish the same end. *Iku*, for example, means "to go," and *ikareru*, from the same verb root, means both "to be able to go" and "(you) go." *Hanasu*, for example, means "to talk." *Hanasareru* has both passive (to be spoken) and potential (to be able to speak) meanings as well as a polite meaning—"(You) speak." Or we can take the root of the verb, which for *hanasu* is *hanashi*, and, by adding *ni naru* (*naru* meaning "to become"), confect another polite form, *hanashi ni naru* (or, more commonly, *o-hanashi ni naru*), which, without the use of a personal pronoun or other expressed subject, means, "you (or someone the speaker respects) talk."

All this may appear hopelessly intricate to the beginning student. If so, he should let it go for the time being. My purpose here is not to lay down precise rules for the grammatical construction of polite Japanese but rather to offer a general concept of how such speech is achieved.

Honorific Prefixes

The *kanji* 御 has a number of readings, five of which are what we call the honorific prefixes. These five are *go, gyo, o, on*, and *mi*. You are doubtless familiar with the word *Mikado*, of Gilbert and Sullivan fame, which means either the emperor or the palace gate. *Mikado* is written with the same *kanji* (御) together with that for gate (門). The reading *on* is most frequently seen on envelopes in the word *onchū*, meaning "and Company" or "Messrs." *Gyo* is found in such words as *gyo-i* (御衣) meaning the imperial clothes and *gyo-i* (御意) meaning your will or intent.

For our present purposes, we can ignore the three readings, *gyo, on*, and *mi*, and concentrate on *go* and *o*. Prefixing either *o* or *go* to a noun indicates generally that the thing itself is either the property of or is something concerned with the person to whom you are speaking or a superior person about whom you are speaking. (Please bear in mind throughout this discussion that when I write "superior" or "inferior," I am not referring to absolute values but rather am using these terms within the framework of Japanese society, in which nearly everyone is either above or below you, but seldom at the very same level.)

Translators of Japanese to English sometimes use the device of translating *o* and *go* as "honorable" whenever and wherever these prefixes appear. I have had to follow suit at several places in this book to emphasize the existence of an initial *o* or *go* or to distinguish one of them from an *o* or *go* written with other *kanji*. But in English it sounds silly to say or to write such sentences as: It is honorably early *(O-hayō gozaimasu)*. Are you honorably healthy? *(O-genki desu ka?)*. Having honorably returned from a long, honorable trip, you must be honorably tired *(Nagai go-ryokō kara o-kaeri ni natte sazo o-tsukare-sama de gozaimashō)*.

This was the ploy used to introduce the rather strained humor in a book called *The Honorable Picnic*. In the foreign author's eagerness to call anything and everything "honorable," according to what he imagined to be the true Japanese fashion and intent, he even worked it into the book's title although the Japanese do not regard a picnic as something that is potentially either honorable or unhonorable and do not, therefore, say *go-ensoku* or *o-ensoku*. (*Ensoku,* the word commonly used to mean picnic, is written "distant legs," which conceivably could mean merely a long outing without a picnic basket, although the Japanese will rarely make even short trips without assuring themselves of a supply of food with which to fortify themselves and to litter train aisles and parks.)

The Japanese attach *o* and *go* to certain words seemingly instinctively just as we know when to use "an," "the," or "a" without stopping to ponder the choice. Also, *o* and *go* are both very short sounds, so it is not quite fair to align them for comparison with a much longer English word like honorable.

Four comments or caveats should be noted about the use of the honorific *o* and *go:*

1. The *o* and *go* honorifics are not normally prefixed to any of the many words in Japanese of foreign derivation, such as *apāto* (apartment), *erebētā* (elevator), *arubaito* (side job), *moga* (modern girl), *pan* (bread), *mesu* (knife), *abekku* (a couple), *depāto* (department store), *dezāto* (dessert), or what have you. There is, however, an arcane line, and occasionally one of these *gairaigo* (imported words) crosses over it to become worthy of the accolade of the honorific prefix. *Biiru* (beer) or *o-biiru* is such a word, as is *kōhī* or *o-kōhī* (coffee).

2. When composing your own sentences, you will want to know when to say *o* and when to say *go*. The only rule, observed often in its breach, tells us to use *go* with what are called the *on* (from a different *kanji* than

the *on* noted above) or Chinese readings of the *kanji* and *o* with the *kun* or native Japanese readings. This certainly holds true for such words as *Go-sokurō-sama* (Sorry to have made you come so far) and *go-enryo* (reserve, restraint) but not for *go-mottomo* (reasonable) and *o-genki* (healthy). But this rule will not be of any help to you at all unless you have advanced a considerable distance in the study of the written language—to the point where you can distinguish between *kun* and *on* readings. In either case, I believe that the best method is the memorization of pattern sentences.

3. When you have learned *kanji* and come across the ideograph for *o* and *go* (御), you will want to know which reading to give it. The advice given in comment 2 must apply here as well.

4. As pointed out above, *o* and *go* should not be used with or about one's own possessions. This is a valid basic rule, but bear in mind that it too bears its burden of violations. We say, for example, *O-cha ga nomitai nā* (I want to drink some [honorable] tea). (I once knew a tea merchant in Fukuoka who assiduously avoided the use of the honorific prefix with *cha* [tea]. For him, it was always *cha* this and *cha* that, and his acquaintances regarded him with some suspicion for this deviation from right thinking.) A mother calls to her family, *Go-han ga dekimashita yo!* (Dinner [honorable rice] is ready!). The father tells his family, *Ima kara o-furo ni hairu* (I'm going to take a [honorable] bath now). In these three instances, although the bath, tea, and dinner are part and parcel of one's own domain, the *o* or *go* is almost obligatory. Although the interests of euphony may be partial justification for some such violations, the best explanation is that tea, rice, and the bath are foundation stones of all that is right and good in Japan and that therefore they should be regarded with a proper degree of reverence, even though they may be on one's own side of the fence.

O and *go* can even be prefixed to some words that we Westerners find hard to regard as polite in any context whatsoever; for example, *o-shikko suru* (to pass [honorable] water), *o-benjo* ([honorable] toilet), *o-heso* ([honorable] navel), and some other anatomical descriptions which I will not treat for fear of losing more sensitive (honorable) readers.

Yours and Mine

This leaves us, in our explanation of words which can be used to express distinctions in polite and nonpolite speech, with those for relatives, home, etc., which are treated (although by no means exhaustively) in the following list:

o-taku = your home, you

uchi = my home, I

go-shujin = your husband, master

otto, taku, shujin = my husband

okāsan, okāsama, obodōsama your mother

haha, o-fukuro = my mother (lit., the latter means "honorable bag")

okusan, okusama = your wife

kanai, tsuma, sai, gusai = my wife (lit., *gusai* means "stupid wife")

o-kami-san = your wife (never used in polite society; a locution of the lower classes)

kami-san = my wife (not commonly used)

musuko-san, onzōshi = your son (the latter is very polite, originally it meant the scion of a noble house)

musuko, segare = my son (the latter term is a rough word)

otōsan, otōsama, go-sompu-sama = your father

chichi, oyaji = my father

o-ko-san, o-ko-sama = your child

tonji = my child (lit., pig child)

o-niisan, o-niisama = your elder brother (but often used when addressing one's own elder brother)

ani, aniki = my elder brother

o-nēsan, o-nēsama = your elder sister (also used when addressing one's own elder sister)

ane = my elder sister

ojisan, obasan = your uncle, your aunt (also used in addressing one's own uncle and aunt)

oji, oba = my uncle, my aunt

o-jiisan, obāsan = your grandfather, your grandmother (also used in addressing one's own grandfather and grandmother)

sofu, sobo = my grandfather, my grandmother

otōto-san = your younger brother

otōto = my younger brother

o-imōto-san, imōto-san = your younger sister

imōto = my younger sister

It hardly seems that it should be necessary to caution the student that *okusan* is never used to refer to one's own wife. Nevertheless, we hear it so misused with disconcerting frequency, evidently by persons who are devoted to ignorance for its own sake. (I have even heard it used a few times among the Japanese themselves, perhaps in an attempt to demonstrate the extent of their acquaintanceship with Westerners.) It should also be noted that the initial *o* in *okusan* is not the *o* of *keigo* (polite speech) but rather an intrinsic part of the word for interior, *oku: okusan* thus literally means Mrs. Interior.

Polite or Nonpolite?

As you come to use Japanese with increasing ease and frequency, you may find that the question of when to be polite and when not to be will perplex you. One cause of the difficulty is that most Westerners learn Japanese in an unnatural order, i.e., we learn the polite speech first, whereas Japanese children cut their teeth on the nonpolite forms. What this means, in a rather extreme example, is that if you or I were about to fall off Tōkyō Tower, we would probably shout, *Tasukete kudasai!* (Please save me!) whereas a Japanese would more efficiently yell only, *Tasukete!* (Help!).

Because Japanese children learn the nonpolite forms first, it is perhaps natural for most Japanese to use these same forms when speaking to a foreigner whose Japanese is obviously rudimentary. By speaking to us as if we were children, they think to assist us in comprehension. But this often results in half-tragic, half-ludicrous scenes in which the foreigner is struggling to get his meaning across in the only Japanese he knows —a few polite words and phrases—while the Japanese is talking in the nonpolite speech, thinking by doing so to facilitate comprehension but actually rendering it all the more difficult. This can ruffle one's feathers a bit, especially if you are vis-à-vis a callow, bepimpled delivery boy, for example.

Although no language school could afford the time to take you in hand and retrace the exact steps that a Japanese child follows in learning this language, a full-time course of language instruction should, ideally, place more emphasis on the nonpolite forms than has generally been done in the past. Not only should you learn many of these forms early in the course but, equally important, you should be taught precisely when and how to use them.

This puts me in mind of a young American businessman who had been in Japan for several months and who had learned such seemingly unavoidable words as *takusan* (much), *hanchō* (boss, leader of a squad or section), and *sukebei* (wolf, womanizer, lecher). His company was involved in a joint venture with a leading Japanese manufacturer and this young man, although still of comparatively low rank, had several times met at social functions Mr. Doi, the president of the Japanese partner company. Mr. Doi, I should add, was a staid, rather imperious Japanese of the prewar school. At the particular cocktail party I have in mind, our young American friend had just drained his second martini when he sighted Mr. Doi. Thinking to cement beyond the point of any possible future rupture the bonds of Japanese-American friendship in general and those ligatures that wedded his company to Mr. Doi's in particular, he determined to break down the barriers of reserve that stood between him and this forbidding gentleman by cheerfully saying to him something like, "Good to see you, Doi, you ole son of a gun!"

Having plotted this strategy and selected from his scant stock those Japanese words that might convey an approximately similar meaning, he gulped down his third martini, approached the stern presence, clapped him heartily on the back (a gesture in itself offensive to most Japanese in general and to our Mr. Doi in particular), and, winking largely, said in a clear, ringing voice: *"Kora, Doi, takusan sukebei hanchō-san, ne!"*

Mr. Doi's face turned an ashen gray and he stalked out of the party. Within two days, he had made representations to the president of the U.S. partner company to have our well-meaning young American sent home—or any place except Japan—and he was successful in this. A free translation of what had enraged Mr. Doi would be, "Hey, Doi, you very lecherous boss-man, you!"

Sukebei is a word more revolting to the Japanese than the translation "wolf" or even "lecher" would appear to justify. Your best course is to shun the word, and if you are ever called *sukebei* in a bar or night club, it will be a good indication of the kind of place you are in, the character of the girl who called you *sukebei,* and the nature of your own words and actions leading up to her remark.

The moral of my sad but true anecdote is: don't experiment recklessly with the nonpolite forms until you are certain that you know what you are doing. If you want to practice them, do so with a close friend, fellow student, teacher, or someone who understands your situation and will not take offense when otherwise unforgivable insults are voiced.

Nor should you allow yourself to be tempted to use certain nonpolite words and phrases simply because you have heard a Japanese use them under similar conditions. There is too much involved here—the whole Japanese social system of precise balances and counterbalances. Like an iceberg, the visible portion above the surface is only a small part of the whole. Eventually you will, I trust, be able to use these forms properly—but not from the beginning and not without considerable guidance.

One factor that muddies up the water in this vicinity is that the Japanese expect the foreign student of their language, especially after he has passed the kindergarten stage, to use only the polite forms. Perhaps "expect" is too weak a word. They almost demand it of us. And by denying us the opportunity to learn and practice the use of nonpolite forms, well-meaning people effectively render us incapable of coping with such expressions when they come our way in the future, as they inevitably will.

Many, many times during the thirty-nine years since I began the study of Japanese, I have, on hearing a nonpolite or abrupt word that I did not understand, asked my Japanese companion of the moment to explain it to me, but, at best, the desired explanation was given only grudgingly, and then with the warning, *Suwādo-san, sonna warui kotoba wo shirunai hō ga ii ndesu yo"* (Mr. Seward, you shouldn't know such a bad word).

Most Japanese, it seemed to me in the depths of my frustration, regard polite and nonpolite as synonyms for good and bad. Patiently, I would protest to them that it was necessary for me, in my efforts to understand all facets of Japanese life, to comprehend the speech—both good *and* bad—of *all* the people; that I could not live in Japan meeting only "nice" people, sipping tea in *o-chaya* with cultivated friends, and making polite murmurs about the quality and age of the *o-chawan* (tea bowls).

Seldom did my protests bear fruit. My Japanese companions, usually amenable and ready to oblige me in my barbaric vagaries, suddenly turned hard and unyielding. No, they would not contribute to the language delinquency of a foreigner. No foreign friend of theirs was to be allowed to go around using such words—or even knowing them. I promised that I would practice them in a small voice, alone, in the darkness of my three-mat room. But to no avail.

Maybe it was this that led me to abandon the more ethereal environs of Tōkyō and to seek life in the raw in Shinjuku and Asakusa. Eventually I learned what I wanted to know, but even today the desire of many

Japanese to have foreign students of their language be acquainted with only the polite speech is something of an enigma to me.

The "Courteous" Japanese

Comment on the "innate" politeness of the Japanese people deserves some space, I believe, in this chapter. It is a topic about which we seldom encounter moderate views. On one hand we find the simpering tourist who is leaving Japan after a one- or two-week tour and who writes an open letter to the Japanese people (printed in one of the English-language dailies) thanking them from the bottom of his heart for showing him a wonderful, wonderful time! For the first time in his life, he writes, he has learned what true politeness and kindness really are.

On the other hand, we find the bitter ex-serviceman who has returned to Japan as a civilian to be near his light-of-love and who has to ride the subways with the rest of us peons and drink low-cost Tory's highballs in sleazy neighborhood bars. If he understands enough Japanese to know what is really going on about him, he is likely to swear that the Japanese are the rudest people in the world.

The distinction is easy to explain. We Americans want to extend our courtesy and politeness to everyone. The young man who helps an old woman across the busy street, even though he has never seen her in his life, is a shining example we hold up to our children. But the average Japanese wants to conserve his fund of courtesy (as if he doubts that he has enough to go around) for those who deserve it, according to his scheme of things. To those on his "deserving list," he will be extremely polite. To those not on this list, he will give as much attention as he would give to a clod of earth.

Nor is the average Japanese at all eager to enlarge, at least not indiscriminately, the list of people to whom he should be courteous. This is where the Japanese concepts of *on* and *on-gaeshi* enter the picture. *On* is a favor or kindness and *on-gaeshi* is the returning of a favor. And your circle of acquaintances—that is, those to whom you should be courteous —is like a club in which one can ask and expects to be asked for favors. Japanese society is one in which its members seem to depend much more on "special favors" than we do, and the Japanese take the business of favor-giving and favor-accepting with great seriousness. If you receive a favor from a person, you have to return a favor—or be called *on-shirazu* (ungrateful), a very heavy charge, indeed. Now where this whole picture begins to fall out of focus, it seems to me, is the lack of a reasonable scale that would indicate approximately how much you should do for a person who has done such and such a thing for you in the past. If Mr. Tanaka lends Mr. Hashimoto a carton of cigarettes one day, he will not expect Mr. Hashimoto to lend him his wife the next day. The Japanese do not go quite to those extremes. But there is a definite imbalance in the comparison of what one can reasonably expect to receive for what one has given. In fact, it is even considered somehow improper and unbecoming to consciously assess the value of the favor received in comparison with the value of the favor being asked.

So this is why the Japanese do not like to receive favors, especially favors that they did not ask for to begin with. They fear what they might be asked to do in return.

One night some years ago in Ōsaka, I had dinner with a fellow American, who was new to Japan and could not speak any Japanese. It was a warm, pleasant evening and after an early dinner at the Alaska, we struck out on a long walk east toward Nakanoshima Park and Ōsaka Castle.

At that hour, many shops were still open and we soon came to one in front of which a Japanese mother and her little boy stood looking at a tricycle. The boy was begging his mother to buy the tricycle for him and she was telling him that he could not have it. She tried to pull him away but he clung to the tricycle and started to cry. My friend, who was in an expansive after-dinner mood, asked me to find out how much the tricycle cost. The price tag said ￥2,200 (about $6.00) so my friend handed me that amount to give to the shopkeeper while he picked up the tricycle and tried to give it to the little boy.

But when the little boy reached happily for the tricycle, his mother snatched him up in her arms and, casting fearful glances over her shoulder, started up the street at a fast walk. My friend thought that she had somehow misunderstood his intentions, so, carrying the tricycle, he started after her and the boy. And, although I already knew what the trouble was, I ran after them and finally succeeded in stopping the woman. At my friend's insistence, I carefully explained to her that we could see that the little boy wanted the tricycle very much and that my friend simply wanted to give it to him to make him happy.

The mother, however, could not accept such an explanation. In her world, people did not act so generously on the spur of the moment. There had to be another reason. She kept asking, *"Dōshite? Dōshite?"* (Why? Why?). What, she was thinking, would this strange American expect of her in return? Nothing I could say would lay her fears to rest so finally she and the little boy walked off into the night leaving two Americans standing there on the sidewalk holding a little green tricycle.

In the U.S, we tend to equate politeness with affability—and affability with smiles, which brings us to the old enigma, the Japanese smile.

The Japanese, like us, smile when they are pleased, when they are happy, and when they see something that amuses them. But they also smile when they are embarrassed and when they are sad and wish to shield others from their sadness. And when they are perplexed and when they are angry.

It is difficult for an American to smile when he is really angry or sad. (Try it sometime.) It seems to be natural, however, for the Japanese. I have seen Japanese smile when telling me of the death of a close friend or relative. And I have seen a delivery boy almost double over with laughter after dropping ten bowls of *udon* (noodles)—and losing a week's pay. But in situations like these, they are concealing their inner consternation and sadness, the exposure of which would be impolite.

CHAPTER 16

Parts of the Body

Anatomy, Powers, and Qualities

Where an American would say, "Who, me?" and point his forefinger toward his heart, a Japanese would say, *Boku desu ka?* and point to his nose. This latter gesture has its genesis in the idea that the spirit entered and left the body through the nostrils. If asked where in the body the spirit lodges, a Japanese of the past would probably have replied that it is the abdomen.

In like wise, the powers and qualities attributed to parts of the body by the Japanese differ in varying degrees from those we conceive in the Western world. In the list which follows here, I have selected thirty-three parts of the body for which there are colorful examples of these differences in the idiomatic speech. Literal translations appear in parentheses following English equivalents.

1. *atama* = head
Kare wa atama ga tarinai. = He is not too smart (He hasn't enough head).
atama ga sagaru = to be respectful (the head hangs down)
Kanojo wa nani ni de mo atama wo tsukkomu. = She involves herself in everything (She pokes her head into anything).
2. *kao* = face, countenance
kao wo tateru = to save face (to set up face)
kaoyaku = a man of influence (face service)
kao ga kiku = to be influential (the face has effect)
kao wo uru = to extend one's influence (to sell one's face)
3. *ha* = tooth
hagayui or *hagaii* = tantalizing (the teeth itch)
hagire ga ii = crisp speech (the teeth cut well)
4. *mimi* = ear
mimi-tabu ga ōkii = passionate, lucky in money matters (to have large ear lobes)

133

pan no mimi = crust or heel of a loaf of bread (bread ear)

Nisen-en yori chotto dake mimi ga dete iru. = I have a little over two thousand yen (An ear extends a little beyond two thousand yen).

mimi-gakumon = knowledge casually picked up (ear learning)

5. *kuchi* = mouth. (A dictionary definition that I like is the one for *kuchi-nagusami wo suru* meaning "to relieve tension by reading poetry or munching food." It is disappointing that it is not in common use.)

kuchi ga kusai = to have bad breath (the mouth is smelly)

kuchi-kazu ga ōi = to talk a lot or to have many mouths to feed (mouth-number numerous)

yoi no kuchi = early evening (evening's mouth)

Onna wa kuchi ga heranai. = Women have the last word (The mouths of women do not run down).

kuchi-sagashi = job hunting (mouth-searching)

kono kuchi no shina = this kind of merchandise (goods of this mouth)

hito no kuchi-guruma ni noru = to be talked into something (to take a ride in someone's mouth wagon)

kuchizumō = war of words (mouth *sumō*)

6. *hana* = nose

hana ga takai = to be proud (the nose is high)

hana no shita ga nagai = to be always chasing after women (The space between the nose and mouth is long.)

hana wo hojikuru = to pick the nose (to dig at the nose)

hito no hana wo akasu = to foil someone (to reveal a person's nose)

hana wo oru = to humble a person (to break [someone's] nose)

hana-iki ga arai = imperiously proud (the nose-breathing is rough)

hanagusuri = bribe (nose medicine)

7. *kuchibiru* = lips

kuchibiru ga kawakanai uchi ni = before the words were out of my mouth (before my lips were dry)

8. *me* (also *manako*) = eye

mekata = weight (eye-direction)

hosoi me = suspicious eyes (narrow eyes)

me wo hosoku shite ureshigaru = to be delighted (to squint with delight)

Rondon-Pari me = walleyes (London-Paris eyes)

me ni doku da = something very tempting (poison to the eye)

me ga koeru = to have good judgment (to have fat eyes)

sara-manako = round eyes; wide-open eyes (saucer eyes)

onna ni me ga nai = to be very fond of girls (to have no eyes for women) *me-kubase wo suru* = to cast a significant look (to distribute with the eye)

9. *shita* = tongue

shita ga mawaranai = to be tongue-tied (the tongue does not go round)

shita wo narasu = to clack the tongue (to make the tongue sing)

sanzun no shita wo furuu = to speak eloquently (to wield a three-inch tongue)

10. *kubi* (also *shu*) = neck. In school, I first learned "neck" as the meaning of *kubi* and I suppose I will always regard it as the basic meaning, as in *kubi-kazari* (necklace) and *kubi-suji* (neck tendons). But the reader will see from the examples below that there are some instances in which "head" would be a more apt translation.

kubi ni naru = to be discharged from a job (to become a neck) [to get it in the neck?]

kubi wo nagaku shite matsu = to wait eagerly (to wait with the neck stretched out)

shakkin de kubi ga mawaranai = to be tied down with debts (the neck will not turn because of debts)

shufu = capital city (head government office)

shushō = prime minister (head minister of a state)

kubi-kiri = decapitation (neck cutting)

kubi-gari = headhunting (neck hunting)

kubi jikken = to examine a cut-off head for identification purposes (actual examination of a neck)

11. *nodo* = throat

nodo kara te ga deru hodo hoshii = to want something so much that one's mouth waters (to want something so much that a hand comes out of the throat for it)

nodo-botoke = Adam's apple (the Buddha in the throat)

nodobue = windpipe (throat flute)

12. *kata* = shoulder

kata de iki suru = to pant heavily (to breathe with the shoulders)

kata de kaze wo kiru = to walk with a swagger (to walk cutting the wind with the shoulders)

13. *kokoro* (also *shin*) = heart, mind, motive, core. The Japanese have a large number of expressions built around the word *kokoro*. For the most part, upon direct translation, those expressions are readily comprehensible to us. Only a few, such as those that follow here, present somewhat alien concepts.

kokoro-nokori = regret (something remaining in the heart)

kokoro-bosoi = helpless, forlorn (thin heart)

shinsuisha = fan, enthusiast (heart-drunk person)

kokoro-garui = rash (heart-light)

kokoro-samui = deeply impressed (heart-cold)

14. *shinzō* = heart. *Shinzō* and *kokoro* can both be translated as heart, but when a doctor tells you that you have a bad heart, he says, *shinzō ga warui*. Although many idioms use the word *kokoro,* the only one I know which uses *shinzō* is, *Aitsu wa shinzō da* (He has his nerve. He is impudent). Thus, where we would say "cheeky," the Japanese would say "heart-y." In this sense, *shinzō* can be reinforced by prefacing it with the word *tōchika* (from the Russian word *tochka,* pillbox). The resulting combination, *tōchika shinzō,* means "very brassy' and is most often used by schoolgirls.

15. *mune* (sometimes *muna*) = chest, breast, heart, mind, feelings

muna-sawagi ga suru = to have vague apprehensions (the breast clamors)

mune wo uchi-akeru = to unburden oneself (to open up the breast)

Aitsu wo miru dake de mune-kuso ga waruku naru. = The mere sight of him makes me sick at my stomach (Just looking at him makes my chest-excrement turn bad).

mune wo odorasu = the heart leaps joyfully (to cause the breast to dance)

mune wo kogasu = to pine for (to scorch the breast)

16. *heso* = navel

hesokuri-gane = pin money; money saved from allowances for personal purposes (navel-reeled money)

o-heso ga yadogae suru = to laugh oneself into convulsions (the navel changes its lodging place)

heso-magari no hito = a contrary person (twisted-navel person)

17. *kimo* = liver. *Kanzō* is the doctor's word for the human liver, whereas *kimo* is used for the livers of such creatures as chickens and eels. However, when using liver idiomatically to describe a person's characteristics, *kimo* is the right word.

kimo ga chiisai = to be cowardly (small-livered)

kimo ni meijiru = to impress on the mind (to engrave on the liver)

kimo wo hiyasu = to curdle the blood (to chill the liver)

kimo-iri = promoter; go-between (parched liver)

kimo-sui = eel-liver soup

18. *hara* = belly, stomach. The Japanese call the stomach *i* and the stomach cavity *i-bukuro* (lit., stomach bag). The abdomen or belly is commonly called *hara* or *o-naka* (both are readings of the same *kanji*) or, as doctors would say, *fukubu.* Everyday parlance, however, bypasses such precise distinctions and the Japanese say *Hara ga herimashita* and

O-naka ga sukimashita (My stomach [abdomen] is empty) when hungry and *Hara ga ōkii desu* and *O-naka ga ōkii desu* (the stomach [abdomen] is big) when a woman is pregnant. No abstract qualities in particular are attributed to the *i,* but the *hara* is regarded as a receptacle of courage, anger, magnanimity, spirit, and intentions.

hara ga kuroi = wicked (to have a black abdomen)

hara ga tatsu = to be angry (the abdomen stands up)

hara wo yomu = to understand one's intentions (to read the abdomen)

jūyaku-bara = large stomach (a company director's stomach)

biiru-bara = beer belly (beer abdomen)

hara wo kimeru = to make up one's mind (to decide the abdomen)

hara ni ichibutsu ga aru = to have a devious motive in mind (to have one thing in the abdomen)

Kanojo no hara to kuchi to wa chigau. = She doesn't say what she means (Her abdomen and mouth are different).

hara wo watte hanasu = to speak frankly (to break open the abdomen and talk)

Hara no mushi ga osamaranai. = Something within me isn't satisfied (The abdominal bug will not be still).

hara-kiri = suicide by disembowelment. *Seppuku* (lit., cutting belly) is the correct term for ritual disembowelment. *Hara-kiri* (lit., belly cutting) is never pronounced Harry Cary.

taiko bara = potbelly (drum abdomen)

fukuwajutsu = ventriloquy (abdomen-talk art)

tanden ni chikara wo ireru = to devote oneself completely to a project (to put one's strength in the abdomen) [*Tanden* means abdomen, although it is written with different characters.]

19. *harawata* = intestines

harawata ga kusatta kaizoku = a depraved pirate (a pirate with rotten intestines)

20. *fu* = bowels, viscera

Fu ni ochinai. = I don't understand (It doesn't fall into my bowels).

21. *koshi.* One dictionary lists all the following meanings for this word: loins, hips, waist, small of the back, and pelvic region. *Koshi,* then, might best be described as the lower part of the trunk of the body. The Japanese regard this region as a prime source of strength.

koshi ga nukeru = to be surprised or scared, and unable to stand up (the *koshi* slips out)

koshinuke = coward (without *koshi*)

koshi ga hikui = humble (having low *koshi*)

koshi-bone = hip bone (*koshi* bone)

koshiben = low-ranking official or employee (*koshi*-lunch) [These men carried their *bentō* (lunch boxes) tied about their *koshi*.]

22. *shiri, ketsu* = buttocks, ass. *Ketsu,* a vulgar word, is found in few idioms; one of them is, *Boku wa karakketsu da,* which means "I'm broke" or, literally, "My ass is empty."

shiri ga nagai = to overstay one's welcome (to have long buttocks)

Shiri de mo kurae! = I dare you to try it, you dog! (Eat my backside!).

shiri wo makuru = to roll up one's skirt (to roll up one's buttocks)

shirimochi wo tsuku = to take a pratfall (to fall on one's backside with a thump [as when pounding steamed rice into cakes])

shiri no karui musume = a girl of loose virtue (a light-hipped girl)

shiri ga omoi = lazy; slow to move (to have heavy buttocks)

kanjō no shiri-nugui wo saserareru = to be left to pay the check (to be made to wipe the buttocks of the check)

shiri ga yoku kuru = to receive many complaints (buttocks come often)

hito wo shirime ni kakeru = to look at someone contemptuously (to hang a person before the eyes of the buttocks)

nyōbō no shiri ni shikareru = to be henpecked (to be spread under one's wife's buttocks)

shirigomi wo suru = to shrink back; flinch (the buttocks recoil)

shirikire-tombo ni naru = to be left half done (to make into a cut-buttocks dragonfly)

shiri ni hi ga tsuku = to be pressed by urgent business (the buttocks are set afire)

23. *mata* = thigh, crotch

matatabi = the nomadic life of gamblers (thigh trips)

sekai wo mata ni kakeru = to travel all over the world (to hang the world between one's thighs)

24. *kyokubu, imbu* = private parts [used for both sexes]. *Immō* is pubic hair. The breasts are called *oppai* or *chichi,* the nipples *chibusa.* *Chitsu* and *inkaku* are the medical textbook terms for vagina and clitoris, while *o-manko* and *saneko* are vulgarisms for the same. The scrotum is *innō,* and the testes are *kōgan.* The penis is called variously *inkei, nankon, dankon* (male root), *otoko no shōchō* (male symbol), *ichibutsu* (the one thing), *mara,* and *chimpo,* in descending order of refinement.

Note should also be taken of a contemporary development in cosmetic surgical techniques in Japan. At least thirty doctors in Tōkyō alone now perform what they call the *jinkō shojo shujutsu*—the man-made (or artificial) virgin operation. In this twenty-minute operation, the membranous tissues of the remnants of the *shojo-maku* (maidenhead) are sewn together or partially reconstructed with light, malleable plastic.

25. *ude* (also *wan*) = arm

ude ga aru = to be proficient in (to have an arm for)

ude-dameshi = test of strength (trying the arm)

teikyū no ude wo ageru = to improve one's ability in tennis (to raise one's tennis arm)

wanryoku ni uttaeru = to resort to force (to appeal to the strength of the arm)

26. *hiji* = elbow

hijideppō wo kuu = to be rebuffed (to eat an elbow rifle)

27. *te* = hand

te ga kireru = to break off relations (the hands are cut)

te ga nagai = to be given to stealing (to have a long hand)

te ga hayai = to be quick to strike people (to have a fast hand)

te wo kaeru = to change methods (to change hands)

tekuse ga warui = to have light fingers (bad hand habits)

shijūhatte = every trick in the book (forty-eight hands)

teguchi = way of doing something (hand-mouth)

te wo narasu = to call by clapping the hands (to make the hands sound)

tegirekin = alimony, heart balm (hand-cutting money)

tebana wo kamu = to blow the nose with the fingers (to blow the hand-nose)

teashimatoi = encumbrances, dependents (objects wrapped around the hands and feet)

28. *tsume* (sometimes *tsuma*) = nail, fingernail, toenail

tsuma-hajiki sareru = to be shunned (to be given a flick of the fingernail)

ashi no tsume ga niku ni kuikomu = to have an ingrown toenail (to have one's toenail eat into the flesh)

Kare no tsume no aka de mo senjite nomeba ii desu. = You should take him as your model (You should even boil the dirt from under his fingernails and drink it like tea).

29. *hiza* = knee

hizakurige de iku = to go by shanks' mare (to go by knee-chestnut hair)

30. *ashi* (also *soku*) = leg, foot

fusoku = deficit, insufficiency (no legs)

ashiyubi = toe (foot-finger)

ashikubi = ankle (leg-neck)

ashidai = travel expenses (leg charges)

ashi wo arau = to give up an evil way of life (to wash the feet)

Kyōto made ashi wo nobasu = to go on to Kyōto (to extend the leg to Kyōto)

o-ashi ga nai = to be broke (to have no [honorable] legs)

ashi ga deru = to show a deficit (legs come out)

31. *sune* = shin

oya no sune wo kajiru = to be dependent on one's parents (to gnaw the shins of one's parents)

sune ni kizu wo motsu = to have a guilty conscience; to be a fugitive from justice (to have a wound on the shin)

32. *hifu, kawa* = skin, integument, fur. *Hifu* is used for the skin of human beings and *kawa* for that of other animals. There are a few exceptions, however, as the following examples show.

tsura no kawa ga atsui = brazen (The skin of the face is thick.)

ningen no kawa wo kabutta chikushō = a beast in human form (a beast covered with the skin of a human being)

Bi mo kawa hitoe. = Beauty is only skin deep (Beauty has only one layer of skin).

33. *tamashii, kompaku* = soul. Both mean soul, but *tamashii* is the more common word.

tamashii ga suwatte iru = to be self-possessed (The soul is set firmly in place).

tamashii wo irekaeru = to reform (to get a new soul)

Mitsugo no tamashii hyaku made mo. = The child is father to the man (The soul of a child of three remains the same even if he lives to be one hundred).

Hotoke tsukutte tamashii irezu = to fail to put the finishing touch on a job (to make a statue of Buddha but to fail to add a soul)

Issun no mushi ni mo gobu no tamashii = Even a worm will turn (Even in an insect one *sun* long, there is a half-*sun* soul).

Kompaku kono yo ni samayou. = The soul is earthbound (The soul wanders about in this world).

Firsthand Observations

One of the best places for firsthand observation of the parts of the body is the public bath. Sadly enough, however, the number of places where one can enjoy *konyoku-buro* (mixed bathing) is diminishing. In the large cities, the standard *sentō* (bath house) is divided into two large rooms of equal size with a partition about six-feet high between them.

The person, usually an older man or woman, who takes the money for admission just inside the entrance is seated in a raised chair, something like a pulpit, that permits him or her to not only control the entrances but also oversee both the male and female bathing rooms. With this arrangement, it is often possible for the sharp-eyed bather to cop a quick look into the room of the opposite sex as he or she stands at the pulpit paying the admission fee.

But so much for depraved city life. It is in the rural areas that one is more likely to find the true Japan. Not so many years ago, in June, I visited the Daisetsu-zan National Park in Hokkaidō and arrived one afternoon at a pleasant *ryokan* (inn) where I planned to spend a couple of days.

Two buses had just pulled up in front of the *ryokan* and were unloading about one hundred boys and girls of high-school age. Later I asked my roommaid who they were and learned that they were students from Sapporo on a school-supervised excursion and that the several adults chaperoning them were teachers.

About four-thirty, before my preprandial drink, I changed to *yukata* and wandered down to bathe in the mammoth public bath on the first floor of the inn. As I entered, a tremendous commotion arose from the assembled bathers, but they were not one bit more surprised than I was. All the students—boys and girls—were bathing together, with their chaperons right there among them. Obviously, all were *mappadaka* (buck naked).

Although I have bathed in *konyoku-buro* many, many times without much outward indication of embarrassment, that afternoon in Hokkaidō was too much for me. Gathering my scattered wits and bathing equipment, I beat a fast retreat down the corridor to a smaller *kazoku-buro* (family bath), where I locked the door and washed myself in glorious solitude.

When we were stationed in Kyūshū shortly after the end of World War II, one of my classmates developed a mania for *konyoku-buro*. He fell into the habit of leaving Fukuoka alone on Friday evening to spend the weekend in one of Kyūshū's many *onsen* (hot-spring) resorts. It was his practice to try a different *onsen* every weekend, and he soon became a *tsū* (expert) on this subject.

Since he was a man of lusty appetites, none of us deluded ourselves that he was even vaguely interested in the curative qualities or chemical properties of the natural hot-spring waters. We knew he went to them for one purpose only—to see what there was to be seen.

Nevertheless, there were American women and some purityrannical

American men in our unit, so he thought it advisable to construct an elaborate cover story for his trips. He began to tell anyone who would listen about his several physical ailments and how they responded wonderfully to one or another of the various hot-spring waters. On Monday of every week, he would enthusiastically hold forth on how the waters of the Tsuetate hot spring had worked miracles for his arthritis or how two hours of deep soaking (and intent ogling) in the *onsen* in Hida had completely rejuvenated him.

About Wednesday of every week, however, he would get back the developed film he had taken over the previous weekend, and when I saw that, I had no doubt at all about the true purpose of his trips. And I must admit that he did take some fine photographs of the unadorned female form at unobserved moments.

He was beholden to me for having introduced him to a winsome sixteen-year-old lass whom we affectionately called the Chocolate Kid and so, when I said I wanted to accompany him on his next *onsen* trip and observe his camera technique, he agreed, albeit reluctantly.

After undressing in the "locker room" outside the bath itself, it was his method to drape a large bath towel over his left arm and conceal his ready-to-shoot camera, which he held in his right hand, under the towel. Then he would stroll into the bathing area unconcernedly, while whistling off-tune between his teeth. Choosing a corner and pretending to busy himself with soap, towel, and bath stool, he would wait until the consternation caused by the arrival of a foreigner—a rare event—had died down, and then he would cautiously expose the lens of his camera and fire from the hip, so to speak.

He was seldom caught in the act of taking these pictures, and even when he was, the bathers did nothing but laugh and sink deep into the hot water.

This devotee of the *onsen,* however, had not calculated on one contingency: MacArthur's headquarters in Tōkyō began permitting wives to join their husbands on Occupation duty in Japan before he was fully ready for his to come. (He had visited only fifteen of the twenty-nine well-known *onsen* in Kyūshū.)

When his wife did arrive, he was smart enough to realize that she would hear about his addiction to hot-spring bathing from others and would regard it as extremely suspicious indeed if his need for the curative powers of the *onsen* should cease, miraculously, on the day of her arrival.

There was no help for it. He had to continue going to the hot-spring resorts and to at least offer to take his wife with him. To our amazement, she accepted his offers, weekend after weekend, until she too had toured most of the major *onsen* of Kyūshū.

I had to admire her adaptability, but I suspect that she may have understood the game. Since she and her husband had been married for eight years, she must have had previous hints of his predilections.

We all agreed that it ended in a draw. He had done a lot of ogling of naked Japanese women and had repaid this debt by letting Japanese men have similar undraped views of his wife.

Stage Three: Advanced

CHAPTER 17

Proverbs

Proverbs (*kotowaza*) have been called the "collected wisdom of mankind," "the mirror of the thoughts and sentiment of a nation," and, by Cervantes, "short sentences from long experience." But if "An apple a day keeps the doctor away" is representative of the "collected wisdom of mankind," then we are sailing through perilous straits indeed. Aside from this—or possibly because of it—proverbs have fallen into a state of comparative disuse and disrepute in the U.S., where it is considered impossibly bromidic and even camp to seriously announce that "A bird in the hand is worth two in the bush" or that "The devil finds work for idle hands."

Not so in Japan, where proverbs still enjoy currency and respect. Perhaps this is to be expected in a culture that has been slower than ours to cut its ties with the past and where that old-time religion is still good enough for many. An example of proverb viability is the card game of *iroha-garuta,* played by both children and adults at the New Year. The skill of the players varies with their knowledge of *kotowaza,* and the game both reflects and helps maintain popular acquaintance with proverbs.

I recommend that the student spend additional time on the study of proverbs for several reasons: 1) they provide many excellent guideposts to the study of social psychology in Japan and glimpses into traditional attitudes and beliefs, 2) they are rich in historical reference, 3) they can serve to explain otherwise uncomprehended customs and mores, and 4) as pattern sentences to be memorized and used with suitably substituted words, they are useful language aids.

Further, an aptly used proverb will give your audience a favorable impression of your linguistic ability and general acquaintance with Japanese culture. I call this *kotowaza-otoshi* or proverb-dropping, an effective device in persuading your listeners to believe that you know more Japanese than you actually do. I have watched Americans speak at length in fairly difficult and correct Japanese without causing their Japanese listeners to evince so much as an eyelash flicker—until they

147

dropped a proverb. Then men gasped in amazement and women swooned in admiration.

Estimates of the number of Japanese proverbs and proverbial expressions range as high as twenty and thirty thousand. Most are of native Japanese origin, some are adaptations from the Chinese classics, and a few are direct importations from the West. Two books that I used in my studies can provide you with more proverbs than you will ever need to know or could realistically hope to learn: *A Collection of Japanese Proverbs and Sayings,* by Professor Hitoshi Mizukami, and *Japanese Proverbs,* by Rokuo Okada. The latter is the later publication and, as such, may be easier to obtain.

As is the case with our proverbs, the Japanese have many that are based on mere superstition and old wives' tales—for example, these two: *Tera no jinai de korobu to sannen no uchi ni shinu* (A person who falls inside the precincts of a temple will die within three years), *Hōki wo matagu to nanzan suru* (A woman who straddles a broom will suffer difficult childbirth).

Even in English translation, many proverbs are not even comprehensible to foreigners without specific knowledge of the panel of the Japanese scene they refer to. Take, for instance, *Kariru toki no Jizō-gao, kaesu toki no Emma-gao* (When borrowing, the face of Jizō; when returning, the face of Emma). One look, however, at the smiling countenance of Jizō, the guardian deity of children, and at the absurdly angry features of Emma, the King of Hades, will bring this saying into clear perspective. *Masamune de daikon wo kiru* means to cut a radish with a "Masamune," but this conveys little until one learns that Masamune was the most renowned of Japanese swordsmiths and that samples of his work are now valued in the tens of thousands of dollars.

Uchi ni icha hamaguri-gai, soto e decha shijimi-gai is translated as "A clam at home, a corbicula abroad." The corbicula is a favorite shellfish of the Japanese, who know that it is much smaller than the clam— knowledge which most Americans do not have. This proverb stands in parallel relation to our "A lion at home, a mouse abroad," and is, incidentally, strikingly descriptive of many of today's Japanese businessmen and government officials, who depart from Haneda airport with their claque shouting *Banzai!* and arrive in the U.S. or Europe alone, uneasy, forlorn, and misunderstood.

A proverb from the pages of history is *Odawara hyōjō* or Odawara conference. In the sixteenth century the lord of Odawara castle, when called upon to surrender by Toyotomi Hideyoshi, conferred at great length with his lieutenants but they were unable to decide whether to yield or fight on. Wearied with waiting, Hideyoshi finally destroyed them, and an Odawara conference came to mean a long session at which nothing is decided.

Iza Kamakura is a proverb taken from literature, a source that is not as extensively mined for *kotowaza* as it is in English. In the Nō play *Hachi-no-ki* (The Potted Plants), a poor samurai plays unwitting host to one of the Hōjō family, rulers of the Kamakura *bakufu* (feudal government) and of Japan. He burns his prized potted plants to provide warmth for his disguised guest and tells him that if an emergency should arise in Kamakura, he would speed there to fight in support of the government. This statement has been abbreviated to *Iza Kamakura* and means: "In case of an emergency."

The existence of the proverb *Rusu-mimai wo madō ni seyo* (Don't make frequent visits to a home when the husband is away and the wife is alone) indicates that the fear of such hanky-panky was not a complete stranger to the Japanese hearth. This testimony to the universality of male appetites is supported by *Yoso no hana wa akai* (Other flowers are redder than mine). In this category, my favorite is *Nyōbō wa hito no ga ii, setchin wa uchi no ga ii* (I prefer other's wives, but my own toilet). Note the word *setchin* for toilet: It is written with the characters for snow and shadow, and I like to imagine that the origin may have been a shadow thrown on the snow by a person answering nature's call in the snow on a moonlit night. At least it is a usable mnemonic.

Japanese general indifference to alliteration and rhyme extends to their proverbs, but there are a few exceptions: *Iki jibiki* (A living dictionary), *Umpu tempu* (Trust to chance), and *Moto no Mokuami* (One finishes as one begins) [a historical reference].

As in many other fields of communication, the Japanese do not balk at calling a spade a spade in their proverbs, which make frequent reference to urination, feces, breaking wind, menstruation, and so forth. I will avoid belaboring this subject and mention only two examples: *He wo hitte shiri tsubome* (Closing the anal exit after breaking wind). This refers to the look of assumed innocence on the face of a man who has committed a gross blunder. And *Waga kuso kusaku nai* (My own excrement does not stink).

Reference to an evil practice of the past, fortunately long since abandoned, is made in *Ko wo suteru yabu aredo, oya wo suteru yabu nashi* (There are bamboo groves where you can abandon your children, but none where you can abandon your parents). There were times in Japan's checkered past when *mabiki*—the weeding out of children—was practiced. This proverb emphasizes that duty to parents is greater than duty to offspring. In partial contradiction to proverbial testimony, however, there is the legend of Obasuteyama, the mountain where old women were cast off to die. One such mountain was near Sarashina in the Shinano district and another on Hachijōjima in the Seven Islands of Izu.

People and places are characterized in such proverbs as: *Edokko wa yoigoshi no kane wo motanai* (A true son of Edo does not go to bed with any money left in his pocket) and *Edo wa hito no haki-dame* (Edo is a dumping ground of people).

Traditional attitudes toward women are colorfully and succinctly depicted in these sayings: *Hara wa karimono* (The womb is a thing for hire), *Onna wa mamono* (Women are devils), *Onna-hideri wa nai* (There is never a shortage of women), *Onna sannin yoreba kashimashi* (When three women get together, the noise is deafening), and *Shichinin no ko wo nasu tomo onna ni kokoro wo yurusu na* (Don't confide in a woman, not even one who has borne you seven children).

Cats do not fare much better than women at the hands of Japan's proverbialists: *Neko ni koban* (Gold coins before cats [or, Pearls before swine]) and *Neko yori mashi* (It's better than nothing [lit., It's better than a cat]).

Although far from being fond—as a race—of feline pets, the Japanese did provide them, perhaps inadvertently, with a measure of protection with this *kotowaza: Neko wo koroseba shichidai tataru* (If you kill a cat, your family will be accursed even unto the seventh generation).

The apparent truth of this proverb was dramatically demonstrated in recent years by the Case of the Cat and the Cook. A cook at one of the restaurants in the Tōkyō Kaikan one day caught a stray cat that had been pilfering food and threw it into a hot but empty oven and closed the door. For many months thereafter, wags plagued Tōkyō Kaikan waitresses by trying to order *yaki-neko* (roast cat). Japanese witnesses of this cruel scene, thinking it best to let sleeping dogs lie—or cooking cats die—kept their silence, but a justifiably horrified foreign woman who was there having dinner at the time did enough complaining for all. Thanks to her, the ailurophobic cook was discharged. Several years later, an enterprising reporter tracked the cook down and considerably strengthened the belief of his newspaper's readership in the proverb by printing that the ex-cook's luck had gone from bad to unbearable: he had lost several more jobs, he had lost the sight of one eye in an accident, and he had lost his wife to a *komusō* (a mendicant strolling priest who plays a flute). The ex-cook himself, however, obstinately refused to regard the loss of his wife as a misfortune at all.

Proverbs about other beasts and birds concern mostly dogs, horses, monkeys, crows, sparrows, and tigers. Since tigers are not indigenous to Japan, I assume that most of this last category must be of Chinese provenance.

Popular attitudes, old and new, are proverbially demonstrated in such sayings as *Hito wo mitara dorobō to omoe* (When you see a stranger, assume that you are looking at a thief). This is such a widely held belief even today that I have concluded that the Japanese have an undeserved lack of trust in each other. *Jishin, kaminari, kaji, oyaji* tells us that earthquakes, thunder and lightning, fires, and fathers are the most dreaded things in Japan, in that order. *Tabi no haji wa kakisute* affords a significant insight into Japanese national character and partially explains how the soldiers who raped Nanking could return to a homeland under the domination of a victorious and not-always-so-gentle enemy and change completely to become affable, amenable, and cooperative. A literal translation of *Tabi no haji wa kakisute* would be: "Scratch off shame when you are away on a trip," or more freely, "There is no need to feel any shame when you are away from home." Since the fear of shame is one of Japan's strongest social sanctions, the Japanese tend toward excessive behavior much more while abroad than at home, where the threat of neighborhood or group ridicule is more effective in keeping children—and adults—out of mischief than the rod.

The following two proverbs I like because they are forceful and chromatic ways to express one's point. The first is said of a lovable child: *Me no naka ni irete mo itakunai* (It would not hurt even if he [or she] were put in my eye). The second, *Doku kuwaba sara made* (If you are going to eat a poisoned [but presumably delicious] food, you might as well lick the plate), is comparable to our "As well hanged for a sheep as for a lamb."

I think that my favorite *kotowaza* of them all is: *Hidari-uchiwa de kurasu.* It is refreshingly Japanese in that it leaves much unsaid. The four words mean only "Living with a left fan," but these four evoke a picture of a man taking his ease during the heat of summer and fanning himself with a fan held in his left hand. The reason he holds the fan in his left hand is that this leaves his right hand free to keep a firm grip on his cup of *sake* or glass of *biiru*—or possibly to fondle his *geisha*. It is implicit that he has sold one or more of his daughters into concubinage or to the *karyūkai* (the "flower-and-willow world"—a much friendlier description, I think, than our down-to-earth, no-nonsense-now "red-light district") and is living the good life on the proceeds from the sale.

CHAPTER 18

Dialects

Dialects and Standard Japanese

Students are sometimes tempted to try their wings with dialect *(hōgen)* long before they attain respectable proficiency in correct standard Japanese *(hyōjungo)*. This is ill-advised because these attempts never come off quite right. Mr. Average Japanese is so overwhelmed at hearing any correct modicum of his language from the mouth of a Westerner that to go beyond this into the realms of dialect is like beating a dead horse. If you use a dialect, you will already have exceeded his capacity for reaction. You will, in fact, often retrogress and diminish the initial favorable impression you have made because he may not understand you at all or, if he does, he may assume that you have accidentally uttered a combination of sounds that happens, unbeknownst to you, to mean something also in, for instance, the dialect of Kumamoto.

I remember a Negro sergeant in Fukuoka in 1945: he had learned two or three hundred words in Japanese from his truelove, a girl whose *Hakata-ben* (the local dialect) was as pure as any I have ever heard. To hear him drawl this dialect of southern Japan overlaid (or undermined) by his own deep-dyed Southern Negro accent was indeed a memorable experience.

I remember also a Jewish DP who worked in a sundries house in Ōsaka and spoke the *hōgen* (dialect) of that city with fair fluency. And there was the American girl who came to Ōsaka to marry a puppeteer and who later enjoyed some fame on television; she spoke what Japanese she knew in a reasonable approximation of the Ōsaka dialect. In both cases, these Westerners were speaking the only kind of Japanese they knew. For them, there was no choice.

You may now and then meet Westerners like these who speak a Japanese dialect, but I have never met one who can do it really well. I doubt that such exist, because this approaches being a contradiction in terms. To speak a dialect well, one should have been raised from infancy in the region of the dialect with limited exposure to alien speech. Even those

153

Westerners born and raised in Japan have such considerable exposure, through foreign schools, travel, and cosmopolitan associations, to standard Japanese and other tongues that they learn or retain little of the *hōgen* that may have been spoken where they lived.

Standard Japanese is understood throughout Japan. Although dialectal speech can be reproduced in writing by use of the *kana* syllabary, all publications are written in standard Japanese. And, in this age of advanced media of mass communication, there are very few Japanese who cannot put aside enough of their dialectal mannerisms to make themselves thoroughly understood by persons knowledgeable only of standard Japanese, when the occasion requires.

Characteristics of Japanese Dialects

Just as the cockney dialect of British English is spoken in the same city that saw the development of the King's English, so there is a dialect of Japanese that flourishes almost in the shadow of the Imperial Palace walls. Called *Tōkyō-ben,* it is the fast, clipped speech of the *Edokko,* the true son of Tōkyō, "born in Kanda and raised in Shiba." A characteristic of *Tōkyō-ben* is the change of *ai* to *ei* in certain verbs *(ikanai* becomes *ikanei)* and *ae* to *ei* or *ē* in certain nouns *(omae* becomes *omē).*

The city of Ōsaka has its own distinctive *hōgen,* and, as might be expected of this capital of commerce, a hallmark of its dialect is the greeting *Mōkarimakka?* which derives from *Mōkarimasu ka?* and means "Are you making any profit?" *Bon-bon* is used for a small son, usually of a well-to-do family. *Koisan* and *o-itohan* are both used for *ojōsan* or daughter. A phonetic trait is the substitution of the sound *h* for *s* in verbs, and what we hear is *omahen* or *arimahen* for *arimasen* and *ikaremahen* for *ikaremasen.*

The dialect of Kyōto is associated with the *Kyō-onna,* the women of that ancient capital, and is distinguished by soft, lisping locutions. *Desu* becomes *dosu,* and the final *u* is clearly enunciated. When asking one's pardon, the *Kyō-onna* say *Kitsu-kitsu kannin dosse* instead of *Hontō ni gomen nasai.*

While Kyōto and Ōsaka each have dialectal locutions unique to their own immediate environs, there are also words and phrases used throughout the Kansai district, including Ōsaka and Kyōto, and called, logically enough, *Kansai-ben.* Examples are *onago* for *onna* (woman), *mamushi* for *unagi* (eel), and *murasaki* for *shōyu* (soy sauce).

Zūzū-ben, the dialect of Tōhoku, is characterized by the replacement of the syllable *shi* with *zu,* as in *zumbun* for *shimbun* (newspaper) and *zassu* for *zasshi* (magazine).

The *namari* (another word for dialect) of Kagoshima Prefecture is usually considered to be the most difficult for outsiders to comprehend. Satsuma, the old name for the district that approximates present-day Kagoshima, was the tightly ruled fief of the Shimazu clan, which at times in history was strong enough to ignore imperial edicts from Kyōto and shogunal commands from Edo. The distance from Kyōto and Edo enhanced Satsuma seclusion; being the first fief in Japan to manufacture firearms augmented its power. To facilitate the early detection of Kyōto or Edo *inu* (spies), the Shimazu rulers encouraged the development of a dialect conspicuously distinctive from those spoken in other parts of Nippon. Their efforts bore fruit—bitter, say some—and, as a result, the speech of the inhabitants of modern Kagoshima may cause the first-time visitor to wonder if he took the right airplane. In *Kagoshima-ben,* one says *omansa* for you, *oidon* for I, *yoko ogoisa* for pretty girl, and *yoka nisedon* for handsome man. *An yoka nisedonna omunsu o jirojīro mitondo* means "That handsome man is staring at you."

Around the Usui Tōgc (Usui Pass) of Honshū, when one meets an acquaintance in the evening, he greets him saying, *Kutta ka ya?* (Have you eaten?) instead of *Komban wa* (Good evening). A person in pitiable condition there can be described as *oyake nai* from *oya ga nai,* meaning "to have no parents."

In Wakayama Prefecture there is a small district whose speech is an example of *gyaku-hōgen* or reverse dialect. Its inhabitants use *aru,* the verb "to be" for inanimate objects, in place of *oru,* the verb "to be" for animate objects, and vice versa. In illustration, they would say, *Meitō ga obon ni oru* (The celebrated sword is on the tray) and *Yoidore no samurai ga soko ni aru* (The drunken samurai is over there). They also use the verb *hoeru* (to bark) when they mean to speak in a loud voice.

In *Hakata-ben,* when calling out to someone, a local citizen will use *ano kusa* instead of *ano ne,* and he will substitute *ka* for the final *i* in many adjectives, e.g., *samuka* for *samui, atsuka* for *atsui,* etc.

From the forementioned random examples, the reader can see that Japanese dialects manifest themselves in three forms: 1) characteristic alterations in pronunciation, e.g., *nei* for *nai* in *Tōkyō-ben* and *arimahen* for *arimasen* in *Ōsaka-ben;* 2) substitution of entirely different words for standard words, e.g., *oidon* for *watakushi* in *Kagoshima-ben* and *hokko* for *baka* in *Kagawa-ben;* 3) contraction or elongation of standard words, e.g., *wa* for *watakushi* in the dialect of the Sannohe district of Aomori and *samuka* for *samui* in Fukuoka.

Oddly enough, on the island of Hokkaidō, which many Japanese think of as being about as far from civilization as you can go, you hear speech less marred by dialect than in most other regions of Japan. As the state of Oklahoma has many place names of Indian provenance, so Hokkaidō has many of Ainu origin. The Ainu, however, while leaving the mark of their quaint tongue on rivers, mountains, and towns (e.g., Tokushunbetsu, Fuppushi, Nipesotsu, Furukamappu) in Hokkaidō, did not possess sufficient numbers or influence to leave their stamp on the local speech. This is not so strange. In the United States, aside from proper names, we use very few words of Indian origin. The conquering or admired culture seldom borrows language from the conquered or admiring culture. Furthermore, this northernmost of the four main islands was largely populated by migration, beginning after the Meiji Restoration (1868), from all parts of Japan. In a welter of many dialects, the simple requirements of mutual comprehension forced the newly arrived inhabitants toward standard Japanese.

No discussion of dialects in Japan should end without mention of the Yokohama dialect described in the book *Exercises in the Yokohama Dialect,* written in the early Meiji era by a group of sprightly young Englishmen using the nom de plume of the Bishop of Homoco. (Readers familiar with Yokohama will recognize Homoco as Hommoku, that district of Yokohama which was—at the time the book was written—the largest licensed quarters catering to Westerners in Japan.) This delightful book was republished in 1953 and is, I believe, still available.

This so-called Yokohama dialect was a port-pidgin comprising not only Japanese and pseudo-Japanese locutions but also importations from Chinese, Malayan, and even Anglo-Indian (the word "bobbery," for instance). *Walk allimasu* meant *wakarimasu; coots pon pon otoko* was a *kutsuya* or bootmaker; *okee aboneye pon pon (ōkii abunai pon pon)* was a big, dangerous bang—an earthquake.

Increasing social mobility and television will doubtless diminish the uses and users of *hōgen* in time, but I clearly remember the uproar when Ōita Prefecture was the scene of acrimonious wrangling over the question of whether or not to permit the use of dialect in the several speeches of welcome that were to be made on the occasion of the visit of the crown prince and princess to that prefecture in Kyūshū. The school in favor of the use of dialect held that its suppression would strip the welcoming ceremonies of local flavor. The opposing forces stated in rebuttal simply and effectively that there would be no point to speeches that were not understood by the distinguished guests.

It is not inconceivable that the student will encounter dialect in his work or where he lives or in his travels. Frequent meetings with a particular dialect may inspire in him a desire to learn enough of that speech to understand what he is likely to hear often. He is well advised, in any case, not to make extensive use of dialectal forms, especially not away from the district of the dialect. The Japanese have a deep-rooted admiration for formal learning but near disdain for language casually picked up, as it were, in bars and boudoirs, in the field and in kitchens. In the same manner that usage by a Westerner of the feminine forms of speech causes a Japanese to suspect the behind-the-scenes presence of an "only" or *ne-jibiki* (sleeping dictionary), so dialectal speech will occasion curious suspicions about how it was learned.

CHAPTER 19

Bar Talk

Where the Good Drinking Is

Ah, the wonderful world of Japanese bars! Even if I were a sworn teetotaler, I would visit them often just for the atmosphere. Whenever I return to the U.S., I never really begin to miss Japan until I drop into a bar in a city like Chicago or New York, and then I usually telephone immediately for the first available reservation back to Tōkyō.

One of the first things to know about drinking in Japan is the vocabulary for drinking establishments.

JAPANESE DRINKING ESTABLISHMENTS

sakaba = bar (lit., *sake* place)

izakaya = bar, saloon (lit., a place where one can be with *sake*. A drinking place, often with a long bar, that serves *sake*, beer, and Japanese brands of whiskey. Not exclusive or expensive.)

bā = bar

sutando bā = a stand bar or standing bar, which is usually a small establishment with a bar and only one or two, if any, tables

hoteru bā = a hotel bar

sakagura = a *sake* bar (lit., a *sake* warehouse. Generally *sakagura* specialize in *sake*, although beer and food are usually served as well.)

nomiya = a small, intimate establishment, often in the suburbs, that serves various kinds of food and drink. Inexpensive and non-exclusive.

biya hōru = beer hall

kyabarē = a drinking establishment with hostesses, dancing facilities, and entertainment

gei-bā = a "gay" bar

Differences, slight though they may be, are generally based on the kinds of liquor served, the level of the clientele, and whether there are hostesses or not.

When in the mood for bottled encouragement, we Americans will not boggle at entering the first bar we find. Such whimsical selection is not advisable in Japan, where many bars are outrageously expensive, some are dishonest, and a few are dangerous.

A Japanese man may have one or three or five favorite bars, but the odds are good that he will have investigated each one before his first visit there alone, usually by going as a guest of a regular customer. Before he touches lip to glass for the first time in such a bar, he feels that he should have knowledge of the scale of prices, the clientele, the hostess (if any) charges, the possibility of arranging to pay at the end of the month, whether or not he should buy drinks for the hostesses, their morals, and whether or not he can depend on the bar madam or manager to see that he gets home in safety if he has too much to drink.

In addition to learning the same, you—as a foreigner—should acquaint yourself with basic barmanship in Japan, especially with such matters as how to deal with the madam and bartender, when and how much to tip, the hours and days when the bar will be less crowded and you will be even more welcome and more at ease, and so forth. Once you have staked out your bar(s), be patient and easy in developing a good relationship with them. The Japanese bar is not an automatic liquor-dispensing machine. Many more sensitivities are involved than in an American bar. Do not expect to be fully accepted into this, your home away from home, on the first or second or even third visit, no matter how generously you tip. The bar employees will be slightly uneasy about you—a foreigner—until you have been there several times and demonstrated to their satisfaction that you behave in the manner they expect of you, which does not necessarily mean that you cannot sing or get stone-drunk or pinch the girls.

Once you have selected a few good bars and have established yourself there, the rest is easy sailing—if you can afford it. If you know good Japanese already, your enjoyment should be greatly enhanced. If you are learning Japanese, you will find the bar an excellent place to practice your lessons, sharpen your comprehension, and pick up new vocabulary.

In Japanese bars, you should also bear in mind that the Japanese are not strong drinkers and that much is forgiven a person under the influence of alcohol. It often requires only one highball or a few cups of *sake* to make many Japanese very red in the face. Alcohol brings an immediate infusion of blood to the head, and this embarrassing coloration deters some from further drinking. When, however, they do continue, most become drunk quickly. On the milder drinks such as beer and *sake,* they can often stay on their feet, but highballs and cocktails have a devastating effect.

Then, when tight, Mr. Average Japanese overdoes it. Repression of emotions, individuality, and true opinions while sober is the reason for most wild behavior when under the influence. Evidence of this is found in such oft-heard sentences as, *"Shirafu jā, ienai* (I couldn't say it while sober). The social pattern in Japan imposes such a tight, all-demanding way of life that it needs a safety valve such as drinking. The Japanese are aware of this and consequently tend to overlook many untoward things that are done and said while drinking.

On a number of occasions, drunken Japanese have insulted me or the woman in my company and on one occasion even climbed on top of my parked car and began stamping on the thin metal of the hood. When I rushed to the defense of that which was mine, a friend or friends of the drunkard would intervene with the statement, "He is drunk, so you must forgive him." To the Japanese, no more need be said. The point that he became drunk of his own volition means nothing. Physical and mental harm that may have been caused by a drunken person also seems to mean little. No matter what he did, he must be forgiven. Although there has been little change in drinking habits in recent years, the problem of drunkenness has roused the ire of officials, journalists, educators, and some members of the judiciary, as the following quotations will attest:

"Japan is a paradise for drunken men. Intoxicated behavior is dismissed lightly, even in criminal cases. A man generously forgives another for words said or actions committed under the influence of alcohol." This statement was made by Mrs. Toshiko Tazaki, vice-president of the Tōkyō Metropolitan Federation of Women's Organizations.

"In Japan, the drunkard's Eden, you may drink like a baboon and not loose an iota of respectability in the eyes of the people, be you a Lord Abbot or a Minister of Education." Quoted from an article by Santarō in the *Asahi Evening News.*

"... the ordinary citizen believes that the best policy is to endure everything and do nothing when the other party is a drunkard." Quoted from the English-language *Mainichi Daily News.*

"The public must not yield to drunkards. ... The first step toward the extermination of this nuisance is to train the public to believe that disorderly conduct by drunkards must not be tolerated." From a statement made by Mr. Kondō, Chief of the Crime Prevention Department of the Tōkyō Metropolitan Police Department.

A U.S. marine who loaded up in a bar in Yokosuka and shot a Japanese to death was acquitted by a Japanese court because the marine was drunk when he committed the crime. A Japanese judge in Kyōto became so incensed at the laxity of Japanese law on this point that he let a practically convicted murderer go scot-free (there are no juries in Japan) in order to draw the spotlight of public attention to this sad situation.

Another explanation for this lenient attitude toward drunken actions is to be found in Shintō mythology. The large family of gods who founded Japan were heavy *sake*-drinkers. They were often drunk, and the mythology nowhere implies censure for this drunkenness. If it was good enough for the gods, why not for us? the Japanese ask. Think of what our attitude toward drinking might be if the Bible told us that Christ and his disciples met every afternoon in a Jerusalem cocktail lounge and got glassy-eyed.

It was only after the arrival of many Westerners and the vogue of Western customs and thinking after the Meiji Restoration in 1868 that the idea that rip-roaring, irresponsible drunkenness might not be so proper after all began to even be considered in Japan. Still, to most Japanese, this reeked of Victorian prudery and New England puritanism —and most of them paid it no more heed than they do today. Those few who consorted frequently with foreigners attempted to repress any gay or mischievous feelings arising from *sake,* but most Japanese considered this very poor form and referred to it as "killing the *sake*" *(sake wo korosu).*

Many Japanese women, contrary to the woman quoted above, encourage drinking in their menfolk for their own purposes. They feel that, when sufficiently drunk, the man will reveal all to them—illicit affairs, hidden bank account, and so forth. They gain more and more control over a man each time he gets swopped and unburdens his soul in their company.

Even many of the Japanese who really don't like to drink pretend to be drunk at parties for business purposes. I remember once joining a Japanese party that was well in progress. One acquaintance was particularly boisterous and more than one sheet to the wind. Nevertheless, an important matter had come up that day that I had to communicate to him before the following morning. I called him aside and explained that I had an urgent message for him. In a flash, he became perfectly sober, heard me out, made an intelligent answer, and then quickly went loop-eyed again. He was not drunk but he had to pretend to be so in order to get along with his fellow businessmen.

Put-on drunkenness as a social asset is borne out by the following paragraph, another quotation from the columnist (now deceased) Santarō:

"If a respected foreigner in this country wished to gain the extra good opinion of his native friends, he could do no better than become their willing guest or victim at a typical Japanese dinner and get as drunk as a lord so he had to be shoved into his car and escorted home by two or three pretty but efficient maids. It would elevate his credit in their eyes as nothing else could. It would show his implicit confidence in and his appreciation of their friendly attitude toward him."

There is one other typical Japanese attitude that may explain in part the tolerance of drunkenness, and this is the hesitation to caution, warn, or advise another person, especially in the presence of that person's friends, about his drinking. The experience of an American friend of mine is a good example of this. He was invited to the home of the parents of his Japanese wife for dinner. During dinner, his wife's younger brother, who was fifteen years old, kept partaking freely of the *sake* and toward the end of the evening became so drunk that he passed out and had to be carried to his room. Later, after he and his wife had left, he asked her if it was customary for her parents to allow their fifteen-year-old son to drink at all, let alone pass out, in the company of guests. His wife replied that of course it was not permitted, but that even his parents did not dare shame him in front of guests by denying him *sake* or cautioning him about the amount he should drink.

As a foreigner you may find yourself the victim of bad Japanese drinking habits from time to time. When a drunken Japanese sights a Westerner, one of two things sometimes happens. One possibility is that he will develop a very friendly attitude, shake hands four or five times, perhaps slobber on your lapel, try to give you a drink, practice his broken English on you, pay absolutely no heed to what you say in reply, and then turn around to grin at his friends as if to say, "See, you guys, I can speak English and buddy up with a foreigner, too." This apparent friendliness, however, can turn very quickly to rage if you ignore him and so cause him to lose face in front of his friends. The other possibility is that he will adopt a hostile attitude from the beginning and shove against you and mouth derisive remarks about foreigners in general and Americans in particular.

Drinks, Drinking, and Drinkers

Now that you know what to expect of drunkards in Japan, let's take a look at the fundamental drinking vocabulary:

I. ESSENTIAL INGREDIENTS

biiru = beer

nama-biiru = draft beer

bin-zume no biiru = bottle beer

kan'iri-biiru = canned beer

bin-zume no nama-biiru = bottled "draft" beer

ōbin, kobin = large bottle, small bottle (for beer)

kuro biiru = dark or black beer

sutainii = steinie (small bottle of beer)

jokki = mug

sake (o-sake) = Japanese fermented rice beverage, although this word (with the variant reading of its *kanji, shu*) can be used to describe other kinds of liquor

Nihon-shu = sake (lit., Japanese sake). Use this word to distinguish Japanese *sake* from other kinds of liquor.

tokkyū (shu) = special or top-class *sake*

ikkyū (shu) = first-class *sake*

nikyū (shu) = second-class *sake*

amakuchi = sweet or light (said of *sake* and wine)

karakuchi = dry

sakazuki = *sake* cup

tokkuri, o-chōshi = the porcelain decanter in which *sake* is warmed and from which it is poured

budōshu = wine of the grape variety

yōshu = Western-style liquor (a generic word)

haibōru = highball (usually made with soda)

mizu-wari = whiskey with water (lit., water divided)

sōda-wari = whiskey with soda (lit., soda divided)

o-choko = jigger

shōchū = a strong drink made from the dregs of *sake* brewing

imo-jōchū = a strong drink like *shōchū* but distilled from potatoes. Often brewed in farm homes.

awamori = a strong, inexpensive drink originally made only from millet but now made from rice and sweet potatoes as well

nezake = nightcap

asazake = a morning drink

yakezake = *sake* drunk in anger, jealousy, frustration or desperation.

And the most essential ingredient of all: *nomishiro* or *sakadai* (drinking money).

II. DRINKERS AND DRUNKARDS

karatō = a tippler (lit., the salty party, and by extension a member of that party)

nomi-tomodachi = a drinking pal

geko = teetotaler (lit., the lower door)

hidari-tō = a drinker (lit., party of the left, and by extension a member of that party, although it has no reference to political beliefs)

yopparai = a drunkard

yotte iru; yopparatte iru; yop-

paratta = to be drunk

nomi-nakama = drinking pals

nombē = a drinker; a drunkard

sake-nomi = one who drinks

yoi-dore = a sot

jōgo = a drinker (lit., the upper door)

naki-jōgo = a maudlin drinker. (Can also be used about an excessively sentimental person, such as a girl who often cries while watching movies.)

III. DRINKING

gabu-nomi suru = to chug-a-lug or gulp down a drink

ki de nomu = to drink straight

rappa-nomi wo suru = to drink from the bottle

zombun ni nomu = to drink one's fill

hashigozake wo yaru = to go from bar to bar drinking

sake no mushi ga okoru = to be in the mood for a drink

sake ga mawaru = to feel what one has drunk

bikun wo abiru = to be slightly intoxicated

bā de kibarashi wo suru = to refresh oneself in a bar

kitsuke wo ippai yaru = to have a bracer

iroke-nuki de nomu = to drink without calling in girls

shujin (okusan) wo suppokashite nomi ni iku = to give one's husband (wife) the slip and go out drinking

IV. EXCESSIVE DRINKING

nomisugite abare-kuruu = to run amuck after having too much to drink

tandeki seikatsu = a riotous life

ranchiki-sawagi wo yaru = to go on a spree

yoitsuburete iru = to lie drunk on the floor

tokkuri to shinjū suru = to die from excessive drinking (to commit double suicide with a *sake* bottle)

hebereke ni you = to get falling-down drunk

chidori-ashi de aruku = to walk drunkenly (like a plover)

guden guden ni you = to get blind drunk

Danshu Tomo no Kai = Alcoholics Anonymous

futsukayoi = hangover

mukae-zake = hair of the dog

o-sake ya onna ni kotte iru = to be given to drink and women

haiban rōzeki = a wild drinking party

ōdora, kodora = drunkards, drinkers (lit., big tigers, little tigers)

tora ni naru = to get drunk (lit., to become a tiger. Possibly from the wobbly-headed *tora no hariko*—toy papier-mâché tiger)

V. Drinking Proverbs

Yoidore kega sezu. = Drunkards break no bones.

O-sake wa mambyō no kusuri. Whiskey cures all.

Sake wa hyakudoku no chū, hyakuyaku no chō. = *Sake* is the worst of all poisons and the best of all medicines.

Names and Games and Things

Toilets also being necessary accessories to drinking, they deserve comment in passing. Those in the smaller bars (and even in some large nightclubs) are often communal, and it is refreshing to take first-time visitors to Japan to these places. Not all Japanese are aware that one should sit, not squat, on Western-style toilet seats, so some bars post instructions about how to use them properly—with detailed diagrams— on their toilet walls. In one of my *yukitsuke no bā* (favorite bars) in Tōkyō, the management has installed a five-foot long basin, at appropriate height, with a metal handrail over it. The instructions direct those who have had too many to plant their feet firmly, grasp the handrail with both hands, and empty their stomachs therein. Some words for toilet in a roughly ascending order from vulgar to refined language are: *setchin, kawaya, habakari, benjo, gofujō, kōka, semmenjo, toire,* and *o-tearai.* Instead of rattling the door or barging in on someone, the procedure for entering a toilet or a public toilet stall is to give several light taps to the door. If no return taps are heard, one may assume that the toilet is unoccupied.

When you return to your table from the toilet, one of the hostesses may very well have a hot, wet hand towel *(o-shibori)* waiting for you. If she whispers, *"Shakai no mado ga aite imasu"* (The window of society is open), you should check your fly.

The system of charging for and reimbursing hostesses may differ greatly with the bar. Some bars, like Ginza's famous and exclusive Rat Mort, pay their girls a straight salary so they do not have to push drinks. Others, the clip-joints, have systems that encourage the girls to *segamu* (badger) the customers for more drinks and tips. Some will pour *itama-shii monogatari* (heart-breaking tales) into your ears about their rent being due or the new dress the madam requires that they buy. If you are *jō ni moroi* (tender-hearted), you should memorize several responses that might assist you in fending off such requests:

Moji-dōri ichimon nashi da = I'm literally penniless. (Better use this at a bar where you are known and can pay later.)

Kinsen no koto wo iu yō ni natte wa iro-keshi da. = When you begin to talk about money, you take all the romance out of it.

Ōki wo nozomazaru mono wa kami ni chikashi. = Those who want the least are nearest to God.

Kyoei wa eien ni minoran zōka nari. = Vanity is a flower that never blooms.

Kami yo! Kono aware na shōjo no ue ni sachi wo taresasetamae! = Have mercy on this poor girl, O God!

Japanese names are easy vehicles for puns—and easy ways to arouse laughter among your captive (captor?) audience of hostesses. At first blush, the following names sound like standard, commonplace names of men or women, but all are *double entendre.* Trying to explain them in English seems to remove the flavor from the jest, but I will hazard an explanation of the first two: *Shimizu Mieko* can mean slip-showing girl and *Aiba Noriko* can mean favorite-horse-ride girl. Try them in your favorite bar. Female names: Shimizu Mieko, Aiba Noriko, Honekawa Sujiko, Chino Michiko, Okuyuki Fukako, Fukadani Kusako, Koshi Keiko, Doteno Takako, Maguchi Hiroko, Endō Mameko. Male Names: Nakaashi Tachidōshi, Nemoto Futoshi, Honekawa Sujio, Yoshikita Yattarō.

In the *mizu-shōbai* (entertainment world; lit., water-business), games are definitely in. Japanese bar hostesses have devised countless little games which they use to buoy up a customer's spirits, amuse him, and keep him in a friendly and generous drink-buying mood. There are myriad bar games played with matches, coins, glasses, cigarettes, and napkins. Some of these games are childish, but some require long-practiced dexterity or true wit. Some of the games involve a knowledge of *kanji*. Here are three *kanji* games which will allow you to participate in the merrymaking and which should help to raise your standing.

1. Begin with the *kanji* for day, 日. Ask your hostess if she can write eight more *kanji* by the addition of only one stroke each. Few can. The eight are: 白, 甲, 目, 田, 旧, 且, 申, 由.

2. Write 桝 and ask your hostess how to read it. This is a made-up character, but she may not realize this. The outer two tree radicals together, 林, are read *hayashi* (forest); the inner radical 米 is *kome* (rice), and the reading of the whole character is *hayashi-raisu* (hash rice, a lunch-counter favorite).

3. 櫻 is the old *kanji* for *sakura* (cherry). It can be broken down into these radicals: 木 *(ki)*, two 貝 *(kai)*, and 女 *(onna)*. Taking the sounds but not always the meanings and rearranging them, we can produce a meaning like, *Nikai no onna ga ki ni kakaru* (The girl on the second floor is always in my thoughts).

Some bar bills are so high that when one is asked to pay up, he feels that *shiri no ke made mukareru* (even the hairs on his buttocks are being plucked) and he is tempted to *nomi-taosu* or *nomi-nige wo suru* (to flee without paying his bill). Until recently, when a customer—being either broke or too drunk—left without paying his bill, the bar had someone follow him home and demand payment from his family. The man who followed him was called a *tsuke-uma* (a following or attached horse), and *uma wo hiku* (to lead a horse) meant to be followed home from a bar by such a bill collector.

CHAPTER 20

Slang and the Current Idiom

Most of this chapter will be used to list a selection of Japanese slang words and idiomatic expressions. The list makes no pretense at being comprehensive. Rather, it was prepared to give the student a general concept of what such words in Japanese are like, how they are formed, and at what, if anything, they cast their irreverence.

A new crop of slang and idioms appears every season, and, in the way of the species, a few find a lasting place in the language whereas many just fade away. The life span of these words and expressions is, I feel, often shorter than those in English, and I have knowingly included in this list some examples that are becoming shopworn and battered. Most, however, are still in fairly common use.

anego = a woman, usually tough and wordly wise, who has risen through bars and clubs to an influential position in the "floating world."

bakkushan = an attractive rear view of a woman. From the English back and the German *schön*.

buta-bako = jail (lit., pig box). An older expression but still in common use.

chimpira = a punk. Also called *machi no shirami* (town lice).

chonga = a bachelor.

deka = underworld slang for cop.

dokushin kizoku = the nobility of single persons, referring to those young people who have incomes from their jobs but live with their parents and usually incur no expenses such as rent or board.

gametsui. From the title of a Tōhō movie. It means "stingy in cunning and devious ways" and derives from an old locution of the Ōsaka slums: *Aitsu game ya* ("That guy is tight-fisted").

gei boy = gay boys or young homosexual men. This has been extended to *gei bā* (gay bar) where the host(esse)s (if any) are young men who often disguise themselves as women. Now also called *burū-boizu* (blue boys).

gozen-sama. Lords and nobles in old Japan were called *gozen* or *gozen-sama* (honorable presence in front), but written with different characters, *gozen* can also mean "morning." A man who comes home the morning after an all-night carousal or assignation is sometimes called *gozen-sama.*

H (eitchi) = abbreviation for *hentai-sei* (aberrant sex). An older usage which is nowadays used to mean lewd or sexually risqué.

hajiki = gat, gun. An older example of underworld argot.

himo = a male who is attached to a woman in an influential position, such as the minor toughs who hang around certain female owners of night clubs or *ryokan,* popular entertainers, etc. Also, a man who allows his prostitute girl friend to provide part or all of his livelihood.

hokōsha tengoku = pedestrian's paradise. Some cities block off vehicular traffic on busy shopping streets at certain times so that pedestrians can stroll about causally, without fear of being run down.

ikasu. Used mostly by girls, this verb means "to cause to go" and is similar to the English "It *sends* me." An example of usage is, *Kare wa gutto ikasu wa yo!* (He really sends me!).

Jimmu irai —— = the ——since Jimmu. The economic boom beginning in 1957 was said to be the greatest since the days of Japan's first emperor, Jimmu, or in other words, in the history of Japan. This expression has been extended to include various other ultimates.

jinkō shojo = artificial or man-made virgin. (See "Parts of the Body," pages 138–39.)

Juku = short for Shinjuku, one of the wards of Tōkyō.

kamatoto — a person who pretends ignorance, especially about the basic facts of life.

kamo = a sucker (lit., a duck). An example of its usage is *Ii kamo ga negi wo shotte kita* (A good duck has come bearing an onion *or* A prime sucker, ready for the kill, has appeared). This derives from the practice of cooking onions with a duck, as we would cook pork with beans or corned beef with cabbage.

karaoke bā = a bar where customers take turns singing to entertain (?) the others in the bistro. (Perhaps the management has found that those intending to perform drink more to bolster their courage, while the non-performing patrons imbibe faster to steel themselves for the coming onslaught on their audile sensitivities.)

katai = straight, square (lit., hard).

kinchaku. Literally this is an old-fashioned kind of purse with drawstrings, but the slang usage refers to a similar muscular contraction of the lower parts of a woman so gifted.

kone, kone wo tsukeru = relationship, to establish a relationship with. An abbreviation of the English word "connection." This usually means getting to know an important person with the purpose of employment or profitable business in mind.

madogiwa-zoku = the beside-the-window tribe. Those employees who, lacking qualifications for reasons of advancing age or general ineptitude, are given little work to do and so place their desks beside windows, from where they can fill their time by watching the passing parade.

Narayama-mōde = making a pilgrimage to Mt. Nara. A short story was built around the legend about men and women over seventy being left to die on Mt. Nara to reduce the number of mouths to feed. *Narayama-mōde* is used to refer to parents not entirely welcome in the homes of their children, older employees nearing retirement age, and persons in fear of dismissal from companies planning personnel curtailments.

neta = the material for a hold-the-presses story (often scandalous). *Tane* (seed) with its two syllables reversed.

ochikobore = those pupils who don't do well in school and can't keep up with classmates.

oiraku no koi = the love of a much older man for a young woman.

orei-mairi. This old example of underworld parlance was revivified by the postwar upsurge in gangland activity. Its literal meaning is a courtesy call to express appreciation. Actually, it is a hoodlum's revenge on someone who has informed the authorities of his evil deeds.

pan-pan or *pansuke* = a streetwalker. The former is a postwar word probably brought home by Japanese soldiers returning from Southeast Asia and the latter is its derivative.

Rosuke = a perjorative for Russian, from the *Ro* in *Roshiya* and the *suke* (guy, fellow), in, for instance, *kumosuke* (see p. 177).

S (esu). Taken from sister, this letter is used to describe the very close friendships formed between girls, usually in middle school. Although my informants tell me that these friendships are not overtly lesbian in nature, I wonder how a psychiatrist would analyze the subconscious longings leading to these affairs.

saikō. This word as an adjective means the highest. When used adverbially, *(saikō ni)*, it makes a superlative of the adjective that follows it. Used alone as slang, it is equivalent to the English slang, "It's the most" or "It's the greatest." In this form it is complimentary. *Saitei* (the lowest) is the antonym.

sakasa-kurage = lit., an upside-down jellyfish. *Tsurekomi-ya* (inns catering to short-time or one-night couples without luggage) proliferated in post-1945 Japan. Although few of them had access to natural hot springs, they used the *onsen* mark (♨) on their signs. A wit imagined this mark to resemble a jellyfish turned upside-down. The appellation still sticks.

sarakin = lit., salaryman's financing. Loan companies that specialize in lending money at high interest rates to salaried workers who have little if any collateral to offer.

semmuha = lit., war-no-faction. Those younger persons who were born after the Pacific war or were too young to remember it. Many of them are said to be, comparatively speaking, without the spirit, determination, and fight of the older generations, such as the *yakeato-ha* (the war-ruins faction) or the *Shōwa hitoketa-ha* (the faction born during the first nine years of the Shōwa era).

shimariya = a tight-fisted person.

shirubā māketto = the 'silver market.' The market catering to the needs of those over fifty years of age.

tarento kōho = a 'talent candidate.' Said about those persons who used their TV or movie fame to elevate themselves into the Diet.

warunori suru = to get carried away.

yami no onna = a streetwalker (lit., a woman of the darkness).

yoromeki = philandering (lit., faltering). From the novel *Bitoku no Yoromeki (The Faltering of Virtue)* by Yukio Mishima. Extended to *yoromeki-zoku* and *yoromeki-madamu* (the philandering tribe *and* philandering madams).

yowai = lit., weak. In recent years girls have given this word hard use. The meaning is to have a weakness for, as in *Watashi wa John Foster Dulles-shi ni yowai wa* (I go for John Foster Dulles).

zurakaru. Hoodlum slang meaning to flee, to make one's getaway.

CHAPTER 21

How to Be Insulting in Japanese

The Warui Kotoba Conspiracy

A fellow student of mine once went to great trouble to have his favorite English insults translated into Japanese, only to learn later that they carry little or no force in this language. In illustration, *shiseiji* means illegitimate child, but if you call a Japanese a *shiseiji,* his reaction will likely be one of puzzlement. Illegitimacy does not carry the stigma in Japan that it does in the Western world, which is only as it should be, since the child is in no way at fault. The emperor Taishō, for example, was the illegitimate son of the emperor Meiji, but this knowledge does not seem to perturb the average Japanese. (There being no issue from his marriage to the empress Shoken, the emperor Meiji had taken a *sokushitsu*—a noble concubine.)

Being foiled on this front, my fellow student next asked one of our teachers to prepare a list of the most stunning and forcible insults, pejoratives, and curses in Japanese. When finally ready, the list was short, unimaginative, and seemingly ineffectual. *Baka*—meaning fool and written with the characters for horse and deer—and *chikushō*—meaning beast —were the strongest words the teacher could think of.

For a long time thereafter, I made no special efforts to learn any pejoratives other than the few that occasionally came my way in the course of my regular studies. I was far from being convinced, however, that the Japanese were incapable of insulting each other. Finally I came to realize that our teachers, the authors of our textbooks, and the homeland Japanese themselves were parties—some perhaps unwittingly—to a monstrous conspiracy to prevent us stalwart, red-blooded Americans from learning to insult ourselves—and them—in their language.

Time and time again, after I came to Japan, I would chance to overhear altercations between men who were obviously on the brink of a bare-knuckle fist fight and, from their fast *yari-tori* (give and take), I would manage to pick up part of a phrase here and there that, judging from the reaction, was particularly choice. With this tidbit clutched to my breast, I would hurry off to seek out a Japanese friend and press him or her (preferably the latter) to explain more fully to me the meaning and uses of this wondrous insult.

But here the workings of the sinister conspiracy were exposed. My would-be informant usually pretended ignorance of the insult or simply refused to discuss it, maintaining that it was a *warui kotoba* (a bad word) and one that I shouldn't use. I would protest that I did not really plan to use it, that I only wanted to be able to understand it in the event that it was used against me in the future. This availed me nothing.

So I bided my time. With the passage of years, my comprehension improved to the point that I no longer had to rely on the members of this conspiracy for information. I usually understood what was said and later I checked what I had heard with my dictionaries and sometimes with friends, who became more willing to impart knowledge once it was apparent that I was in possession of the complete word or phrase and determined to carry on from there.

What I can, therefore, offer to the serious student in this chapter is a collection of insults and sharp retorts collected at random and against great odds over a period of thirty-nine years. It is by no means a comprehensive list; it is admittedly spotty. But it should serve as a starter for your own collection.

Insulting with Nonpolite Language

If, as I suspect it will, it is someday proved that the Japanese lag behind us Westerners in the sheer beauty, sustained invention, and gasp-producing force of our native insults, a partial explanation must be that the Japanese can put a person in his place very neatly through the use of the nonpolite forms of their language. The nonpolite pronouns for you, e.g., *kimi, omae, kisama,* are examined in Chapter 15, "Polite and Nonpolite Speech." In addition, one should take note of the verb form *agaru,* which is attached to the base of other verbs to add the meaning of "coming up" or, in other words, of "taking some action in the presence of a superior." Thus, instead of *Itsu kimashita ka?* (When did you come?), one could say, *Itsu ki-agatta ka?* (When did you have the gall to come up into my superior presence?).

This is very rough and strongly insulting, and care, therefore, should be exercised in its use. This *agaru* can, of course, be used with many verbs: *taberu* (to eat) becomes *tabe-agaru, iu* (to say) becomes *ii-agaru,* and *iku* (to go) becomes *iki-agaru*. Please note that in fast speech, the *y* sound sometimes enters before the initial *a* of *agaru*, and *ii-agaru* may then sound more like *ii-yagaru*.

If you are ever called *omae* (which is worse than being called *kimi* but not as bad as being called *kisama*) and want a good, solid comeback, I recommend: *Omae to wa nan da, kisama! Yabanjin no kuse ni* ... (loosely, this might be given as, "What the devil do you mean by calling me '*omae*,' you low-born barbarian!").

Handy Insults and How to Fashion Them

Babā (or *baba*) is Japanese for old woman and is sometimes extended to mean ugly old woman or crone. My notes show that I have collected a comparatively large number of expressions insulting to such crones and hags, and the only explanation that I can offer is that this is a reflection of the frequency of usage. Older Japanese women do tend to go to pot more quickly and more thoroughly than their Western counterparts. Also, in compensation for years of being brow-beaten by husbands and mothers-in-law, they in turn often become tyrannical and sharp-tongued when they themselves have daughters-in-law and maids to boss. Be that as it may, take any of the following words, add *babā,* and you will have a good, sound insult for the likes of them.

shiwakucha = wrinkled	*kōshoku* = lustful
shagaregoe = coarse-voiced	*oibore* = withered up
hihi = baboonlike	*waniguchi* = alligator-mouthed
hanuke = toothless	*tarejichi* = saggy-breasted
samehada = shark-skinned	*sabiana* = rusty-holed
oni = devilish	*umeboshi* = prune-faced
kurumaebi = hunch-backed	*yokubari* = greedy
fugu = globe-fish-faced, i.e.,	*karajishi* = lion-dog-faced, i.e.,
stupid-looking	like the Okinawan stone dogs
yanime = rheumy- or bleary-eyed	

Jijī (or *jiji*), meaning old man, can be substituted for *babā* in the above phrases where distinctions of sex will permit.

References to one's unpleasing physical characteristics arouse ire and ill-will in Japan, of course, just as elsewhere. The following should do the trick:

deme no = popeyed
ganimata no = bowlegged (lit., crab-legged)
sotoashi no = knock-kneed
deppa no = bucktoothed
deppuri-shita = dumpy

nikibi-darake no = pimply
shishi-bana no = pug-nosed (lit., lion-nosed)
kebukai = hairy
tarehoho no = heavy-jowled
zunguri-shita = fat and short

Working with combinations of these and other words, one can confect chromatic and effective insults like: *ganimata no deppa no kusai yabanjin* (bowlegged, stinking barbarian with buckteeth), *tarehoho no sukebege na tsuragamae* (lecherous, heavy-jowled face), *dangobana no kuma-musume* (a hairy girl with a nose like a dumpling), *shōgakkō chūtai no hana-hoji-kurime* (a nose-picking, grade-school dropout).

The following sharp retorts and warnings are frequently heard:

Zama wo miro. = Serves you (him, her) right.
Omae nanka tende aite ni naran zo! = You're no match for me!
Shikaeshi suru zo! = I'll fix you for that!
Myō na ki wo okosu na. = Don't try anything funny.
Yokei na o-sekkai da. = None of your business.
Sono te wa kuwan zo! = None of your tricks!
Omae no taido wa nattoran zo! = Your attitude is intolerable!
Gesu-batta koto wo iu na. = Don't be vulgar.
Nani! Kuru nara, koi! = Let's have at it, then! (Said just before the first blow is struck.)
Mogaite mo shikata ga nai. = It's no use struggling.
Tawakeru na. = Don't play the fool.
Katte na netsu wo fuku na. = None of your lip.
Monoii ni ki wo tsukero. = Watch your language.
Shikujiru na. = Don't screw it up.
Tsumaranu koto ni dada wo koneru na. = Don't fret over trifles.
Hana-kakatta koe de nakigoto wo iu na. = Stop your whining complaints.

Listed next are several choice insults which you would do well to have polished and ready for instant use:

gongo dōdan na usotsuki = an abominable liar
haji-sarashime = a disgraceful hussy

wagamama no gonge = the embodiment of selfishness
seishin no kusatta otoko (onna) = a depraved man (woman)

sukoburu-tsuki no kechimbō = a notorious miser

shōne ga magatta hito = a hopelessly corrupt person

Hicks, Foreigners, Animals, and Such

To many Japanese, country people are inferior and contemptible. In bygone days, the farmer or *o-hyakushō-san* (lit., Honorable Mr. Hundred Names) was ranked above the artisan and the merchant. Nowadays, derision of the rural districts, which is partly a reactionary denunciation of the old ways, continues to be noticeable and perhaps even increases slightly along with the population shift to the cities. Who, after all, is more contemptuous of the poor than the *narikin* (nouveaux riches)? *Inaka-mono* and *inakappei* (or *inakappe*) both mean hick. *O-nobori-san* (the honorific *o* and *san* are sarcastic) is a country fellow just "come up" to the big city. *Yama-dashi* (fresh from the hills) and *yama-zaru* (mountain monkey) can best be given in English as hayseed or country bumpkin.

By extension, foreigners were to the Japanese, as we were to the Chinese, even lower than their own country people and were (and sometimes still are) called *ketō* or *ketōjin*. *Ketō* is written with the characters for "hair" and for "foreign" or "Chinese" (to the early Japanese, all foreigners were Chinese) and can be translated as hairy foreigner or hairy barbarian. The *tōjin* in *ketōjin* is the same as that in Tōjin Okichi, that unfortunate woman who was said to have been the *rashamen* (foreigner's mistress) of Townsend Harris, the first U.S. Consul in Japan. *Yabanjin* is the specific word for barbarian, and *yotsu-ashi no yabanjin* (a four-legged barbarian) is a prime insult.

The derogatory word *sukebei* has been examined elsewhere (p. 128), so I will note here only that it means lecherous.

Invidious comparisons with animals are to be found among Japanese insults, as they are in most other languages. Caution should be exercised, however, in direct translations from English. Calling a Japanese man a *hebi* (snake) may not cause him to swell his chest in pride but neither will it make him crawl away in shame, stunned by the power of the verbal blow. *Kuma* (bear) is not used to describe grumpy old men, and the *tanuki* (badger) is considered far more sly than the *kitsune* (fox). *Dongame* (a slow, stupid turtle) is, however, an insulting word, and *ke-mushi* (caterpillar) will arouse spasms of distaste in the Japanese. The above-mentioned *kuma-musume* (bear-girl) means something like the bearded lady of our circus. Persons who drink much are said to drink like a cow *(gyūin suru)* or python *(uwabami no yō ni nomu)*. Japanese trenchermen don't eat like pigs but like horses *(bashoku suru)*.

Inu-goroshi (lit., dog killer) is the Japanese expression for dogcatcher and is a very pungent insult. It is not, however, because the Japanese honor dogs so much that they use dog slayer as an expression of vilification but rather that the profession of dog catching is near the bottom of the job scale. *Semmitsu-ya* (broker or real-estate agent), *toritate-nin* (bill collector), *oshiuri-ya* (a salesman who pushes in), and *kumosuke-unchan* (a rude and reckless taxi driver) rank only slightly higher. *Kumosuke* has the literal meaning of cloud man or cloud fellow, and it originally meant palanquin bearer. I am not certain of the etymology but I like to recall, when I think of this word, the India-ink drawings of palanquins emerging from the cloudy mists of the Hakone mountains. As to present usage, if you are displeased with a taxi driver's attitude, you can try this shaft: *Nan da! Kumosuke no kuse ni namaiki ja nai ka!* (What's that? You're damned impertinent for a mere *kumosuke!*).

In language school, when we first learned of the *eta* (written with the characters for "dirty" and "much") or pariah class of Japan, another classmate decided to make this word the big gun in his arsenal of insults, and for a considerable time after arriving in Japan, he took to task those who thwarted him by calling them *eta*. He fully anticipated that this Big Bertha of insults would evoke roars of rage, ashen faces, drawn *samurai* swords, and perhaps other equally dire insults in return. Instead, however, the pejorative from which he had expected so much was met with gentle looks of puzzled incomprehension.

In the fullness of time we came to realize that the word *eta* itself is not readily understood in its verbal form by many Japanese. (Unfortunately, those my classmate wished to wound most deeply were usually members of the uncomprehending majority.) More common and readily understood words for *eta* are *shin-heimin* (new citizens, inasmuch as the *eta* were only granted citizenship after the Meiji Restoration), *buraku-min* (people of the hamlet; *buraku* is a shortened form of *tokushu buraku,* meaning special hamlet), and *hashi no mukō no hito* (beyond-the-bridge people, implying those who live along the riverbank, which is where the *eta* gathered when they could not live in the towns). A gesture (see Chapter 5, "Sign Language") of identification is to raise one hand with the fingers outspread and the thumb folded in. The significance is that the person referred to deals in the products of certain four-legged animals. Folding in the thumb brings up another interpretation, namely, that less than the right number (of fingers on a hand) indicates some-ting imperfect.

The *eta* were tribes of outcasts in the days when the Japanese were pushing north against the Ainu. Criminals and deserters may have form-ed the original nucleus of the *eta*. With the onset of imported Buddhist sanctions against the handling of the flesh and hides of four-legged creatures, such work came to be the hereditary professions—slaughter-ing, butchering, tanning, shoe-making—of these people. Thus developed the traditional linking of the *eta* with four-legged animals and the dis-dain in which they were—and unfortunately still are—held. (There is a story, to whose veracity I cannot attest, about the imperial bootmaker, an *eta,* who was given noble rank—lasting from the time he entered the Imperial Palace until the time of his departure—to raise him from his untouchable position to one sufficiently exalted to permit him to touch and measure, without contaminating, the imperial feet.)

For those who find need to upbraid bar girls and serving wenches, I offer the following brief list. The nouns and adjectives can be switched about for greater spice and variety.

atsukamashii surekkarashi = an impudent hussy

zubutoi subeta = a brazen bitch

zūzūshii zubekō = an imperti-nent, delinquent girl

abata-zura no hashita-me = a wench with a pock-marked face

deshabari no abazure = a know-it-all jade

Even though telling a Japanese to go to hell *(Jigoku e itte shimae)* would more puzzle than ire him, you can achieve the effect you desire by saying *Kutabare!* (or *Kutabatte shimae!*) or *Shinde shimae!* (or *Shin-jae!*), all of which mean "Drop dead!"

Although there are plenty of words for whore in Japanese (*jorō, impu, baishumpu,* etc.), calling a Japanese one would be classed as eccentric and would fall short of the mark you are aiming at.

Ahō (fool) is heard nearly as often as *baka,* especially in Kansai. *Teinōji,* written "low-mentality-child," is used to mean a true idiot and not a person whose temporary lapse from good sense has upset you. *Wakar-azuya* is a blockhead or, literally, a not-understanding-person. *Kijirushi* is a nut or oddball. *Tonchiki me* or *tonchiki-yarō* can be translated as "You ass."

Hebo-bunshi is a hack writer; *hebo-shijin* is a poetaster. *Yabu-isha* or *hebo-isha* is a quack doctor.

Of all the people in Japan, I can think of no group which deserves insulting and cursing as much as the taxi drivers do. There are, of course, exceptions. When they are good, they are wonderful—polite, helpful, informative, and not at all greedy. But this minority only serves to emphasize how debased are the majority. One has to deal with them—like New York taxi drivers—as a race apart.

For years I had my ups and downs with them, my little victories and my major defeats. At length, I had the following two cards printed in large quantities and always carried a supply with me.

乗客の皆様

最近運転手不足に付き国語もろくろく話せ
ない無学の雲助を雇わざるを得ません
以後態度をあらためさせますから此の度は
御許し下さいませ

運転手取締局

乗客の皆様

最近タクシー不足につき荒っぽい
運転せざるを得ませんので御乗車
の際は生命保険に入ってからお願
い致します

The card on the left says: *"Jōkyaku no Mina-sama: Saikin untenshu-busoku ni tsuki kokugo mo roku-roku hanasenai mugaku no kumosuke wo yatowazaru wo emasen. Igo taido wo aratamesasemasu kara kono tabi wa o-yurushi kudasai-mase. Untenshu Torishimari-kyoku."* This means: "To All Passengers: Recently, because of the driver shortage, [taxi companies] have been forced to hire uneducated *kumosuke* who cannot even speak our national language correctly. Henceforth we will see to it that they change their attitude, so please forgive us this time. [signed] Driver Control Bureau."

The card on the right reads: *"Jōkyaku no Mina-sama: Saikin takushii-*

busoku ni tsuki arappoi unten sezaru wo emasen no de go-jōsha no sai wa seimei hoken ni haitte kara o-negai itashimasu." This means: "To All Passengers: Because of the present taxi shortage, we cannot avoid driving recklessly. Please be sure that your life insurance is in force before you board this taxi."

When the circumstances indicated, I left one or the other of these two cards in the taxi where it would be in full view of later passengers but invisible from the driver's seat. The ash tray on the back of the front seat was usually so constructed that a corner of the card could be inserted and the card held in place. In case this did not work, I always carried a small roll of Scotch tape in my pocket.

I never really learned what effect these cards—I used hundreds of them—may have had. Obviously each card must have been seen by at least the next passenger in that taxi. I imagine that some of the passengers laughed and mentioned the card to the driver, while others disembarked abruptly when the taxi stopped at the next red light. My pleasure came from visualizing the gnashing of teeth and tearing of hair when the driver himself at last read the card.

Accusing a man of not being manly is a severe rebuke in Japan. (Unmanly is *otoko-rashikunai.*) Note, however, that although this rebuke can be used in reference to a lack of physical courage or strength, it is most often heard when a woman is accusing a man of not conducting himself in the manner she expects him to. She is usually saying, in effect, that he is not providing her with the material goods she expects from him.

As always, the most splendid insults are those based on truth and, for this reason, I am particularly fond of such scathing comments as the one made about a certain Japanese social commentator (of which breed there are far too many): he was accurately called a *fuketsu na dokuzetsuka* (a dirty man with a poison tongue).

And when you really want to hurt a fellow, you might try calling him a *mikaikokujin* (native of an uncivilized country). But, whatever the insult, bear in mind that if you fumble around with your invective or fail to pronounce your barb accurately, you would have been better off if you had treated your foe with only contemptuous silence. Do not get involved in verbal exchanges with a Japanese until you are quite good in the language. Excitement and rage can trip up your tongue and leave you sputtering ineffectually. Remember that you are playing the game in his ball park.

CHAPTER 22

Geisha Talk

One of the three bromidic symbols (with Mt. Fuji and cherry blossoms) of Japan, *geisha* are a uniquely Japanese institution into which wide inroads have been cut by bar and nightclub hostesses. There are still, however, about 60,000 registered *geisha* in Japan, and many others unregistered and often self-styled.

The traditional training of a *geisha* called for her to become a servant to other *geisha* about the age of seven. At this stage she was called a *shikomi-ko* (or *shikomi* or *shitajiko*) At fourteen or fifteen she graduated to the status of *hangyoku* (half a jewel) and continued her training in the *geisha* arts. Next she became an *o-shaku-san* (one who pours), during which period she attended parties and poured *sake* for the guests but did not participate in the conversation or revelry.

When at last it came time for her to become a *geisha,* she chose her *geimei* (professional name; art name—usually one like Little Spring or Flower Willow) and was then escorted around and introduced to the various *ryōtei* (special restaurants) which her *geisha* association served. This was called *o-hirome* (debut). It was followed quickly by the *mizuage-shiki* (defloration ceremony), which was not much of a ceremony, although the customer usually paid dearly to participate in it. After that she was rated as a full *geisha.*

Nowadays all this is changing. Assuming that she is proficient in the various skills expected of a *geisha,* a girl can walk into a *geisha* registry office and register herself for a small amount of money. Most, however, still go through some apprentice training. Those with little training are called *insutanto* (instant) *geisha.* Some other varieties of *geisha* are:

genrō geisha = a very influential, older *geisha*
korobi geisha = a "roll-over" *geisha* (Prostitute would be a more accurate appellation, as it would for the following three.)
shomben geisha = a urine *geisha*
Daruma geisha = a *geisha* who can be rolled over like a Daruma doll
haori geisha. In *geisha*-short postwar Japan, country inkeepers often had

to call in local housewives who could sing and dance a little to entertain guests. When called, the housewife donned her best kimono, put a *haori* (coat) over that, and walked to the inn. (True *geisha* are not supposed to wear *haori* or walk to their assignments.)

meigi = a famous *geisha*

geisha-agari = ex-*geisha*

A *geisha* party has been likened to a church supper with sexy jokes, but I have been to some that did not even offer the sexy jokes. Still, it is true that nothing untoward ever actually occurs at a real *geisha* party, although many of the girls talk a mean fight. (Did I say "girls"? *Geisha* are not supposed to achieve top-notch proficiency in their arts until they reach the age of 50.) Full-fledged *geisha* are not, by definition, virgins. They usually have one or more patrons, but this relationship is entered into with scarcely less care than marriage itself. (And the patron often spends more money on his *geisha* than on his wife.)

The true duty of the *geisha* is to break down the wall of reserve between the hosts and the guests. This she does by telling jokes, keeping the conversation lively, and pouring out thimblefuls of *sake* fast enough to get everyone whiffed. If you do find a *geisha* that appeals to you and you want to see her again in more private surroundings, you should wait until some of the more active games begin and then pass her your wallet, asking her to keep it for you. *(Watakushi no saifu wo azukatte oite kudasai)*. First, she will appreciate your trust in her. Second, this will give you a chance to turn back as you are leaving later to get your wallet from her and exchange a few words in private. Third, it will give her a chance to slip her phone number into your wallet.

You can further impress her by showing familiarity with *geisha* terminology:

akashi senkō = the fee for staying all night with a *geisha*

geiko = *geisha*

geisha ga baishun suru = a *geisha* sells her body. This expression means literally that the *geisha* "sells spring" to her customer. (What a wonderful way to say it!)

geisha ga zashiki ni dete iru = a *geisha* is out at a party

geisha machi = *geisha* quarters, an area in which there are many *kemban,* and *okiya* (for which, see below)

geisha wo ageru = to call in a *geisha*

geisha wo hikaseru = to redeem a *geisha*

geisha wo miuke suru = to take a woman away from the *geisha* business and set her up as a mistress

o-hako wo ireru = to call in a samisen-playing *geisha*

hanadai, senkō-dai, ocha-dai, gyoku-dai = terms for payments to *geisha* (lit., flower money, incense money, tea money, and jewel money)

hōkan = a buffoon; an *otoko-geisha;* a man who performs his specialty (singing? dancing?) at a party alongside the female *geisha*

jimae no geisha = a *geisha* who works independently of an association or *kemban,* one who has paid off all her debts.

kakae-geisha = a *geisha* who is under contract to one *kemban*

kemban = *geisha* assignment facility. A house or office where calls for *geisha* are taken, records are kept, and payments are collected. It is managed by the *geisha* association. *Geisha* are supposed to check in here when their last assignment is finished. These can sometimes be recognized by the *jinrikisha* waiting outside.

kujaku. At the New Year's season, a *geisha* may sit astride her horizontal patron wearing her new, fancy kimono. As the kimono spreads out over their lower regions, it is fancied by some to resemble the tail of a peacock *(kujaku)*.

kuragae wo suru = to change to another *geisha* house (lit., to change saddles)

marukake = a *geisha* whose manager still has financial responsibility for her.

okiya = a *geisha* house, (originally a Kansai word)

o-zashiki = the room in which *geisha* parties are held

zashiki ga kakaru = a client summons a *geisha*

The forementioned locutions are in general use. Those that follow here are used among *geisha* themselves. This is not, however, to imply that they are anything like a code or secret language. Many frequenters of *geisha* parties know them.

o-cha-hiki, o-chappiki = a *geisha* who is free of appointments

o-cha wo hiku = to be free; to have no appointments. (In old Kyōto, *geisha* who had nothing to do were often set to grinding tea, which is what *o-cha wo hiku* means.)

gohiiki = regular customers

hakoya = an agent who arranges a *geisha's* business calls

ippon ni naru = to become a full-fledged *geisha*

kamban wo dasu = a *geisha* operates in her own name, i.e., independently *kobu wo maku* or *kobu-maki wo suru* = the first love act with a patron after the New Year. *Kobu-maki* is a roll of tangle (seaweed) with a dried fish inside.

kuchi ga kakaru = to be called to a party

o-neisan = the term by which *geisha* address each other

o-niisan = the term by which *geisha* address their male guests

shichisan = (lit., "three-sevenths") a *geisha* who buys her own kimono and gives three-sevenths of her earnings to her manager to cover all else

shinneko = a *geisha's* appointment with a patron in private quarters

sotobako = an irregular *hakoya*

o-temoto = the various implements—chopsticks, cups, etc.—that are set before a guest at the dinner table

uchibako = the *hakoya* who usually handles a *geisha's* business

wakame-zake. During *O-Shōgatsu* (when hanky-panky in God's plenty appears to take place), a *geisha* may disrobe for one or more favored clients, lie on her back, and clasp her legs together tightly. A guest will pour sake over her pelvic region, where he then begins to imbibe like a horse at the watering trough. The floating motion of the pubic hairs in the puddle of *sake* is fondly imagined to resemble the motion of the seaweed *wakame* in the ocean.

wake-kamban = operating under someone else's name

o-zashiki wo tsukeru = to start the dancing or other entertainment at a party

Most *geisha* are not attractive to American eyes, but I have seen an old photograph of one who surely must rank as one of the most beautiful women I have ever seen. She was called Kosuzu (Little Bell) of Shimbashi and she later became Mrs. Ryūko Mutsu. Her husband, Count Munemitsu Mutsu, served as Ambassador to the United States from 1888 to 1890 and Minister of Foreign Affairs from 1892 to 1896. I am not certain when they were married, but the period immediately following the restoration of Emperor Meiji witnessed the spectacular rise to power, wealth, and fame of more than a few *geisha*.

In 1905, a Kyōto girl reached what was perhaps the highest peak of wealth ever attained by any *geisha* by marrying George D. Morgan, nephew of John Pierpont Morgan. They lived a reportedly happy life together until his death in 1913. Years later, in 1938, Oyuki Morgan returned to her native Kyōto. Finding herself a cynosure and a constant target for salesmen and confidence men, she withdrew into the seclusion in which she remained until her death at an advanced age.

CHAPTER 23

The Language of Love

The Japanese as Lovers

Consider briefly the following three scenes:

SCENE I. A Japanese business man returns to Tōkyō after spending six months in his company's branch office in New York. His wife and two dozen employees of the home office are waiting at Narita International Airport to meet him. After clearing customs, the man returning from New York begins exchanging *aisatsu* (greetings) with the other employees. His wife waits unnoticed in a corner. When at length the *aisatsu* ritual is over, he walks to the company car, his wife trailing far behind, and gets in. Once they are both inside the car and alone at least, he turns to her impatiently and—asks how the children are.

SCENE II. In a certain magazine article, it was reported that two young movie stars, Yumiko Kokonoe and Yasuo Tanabe, were in love and engaged. Under a large picture of Yasuo was printed what he said to the reporter about Yumiko, his light of love: *"Tonikaku, namaiki na josei desu"* (Anyway, she's an impudent female).

SCENE III. The final scene in a movie shows a *samurai* returning, Ulysses-like, to his home and wife after long years spent a-warring in distant realms. Dismounting from his horse, he wearily sits down on the *engawa* (veranda) of his house and savors in silence the pleasure of being home again. His wife, becoming aware of his presence, comes out on to the *engawa,* bows till her forehead touches the floor, and says, *"O-kaeri-nasai-mase. O-cha wa ikaga de gozaimashō ka?"* (Welcome home. Would you like some tea?). Without looking in her direction, the *samurai* considers this question for a minute and replies, *"Moraō"* (I'll have some). End of movie.

These typical scenes should amply demonstrate that the Japanese are not going to give the Latins much competition for the title of the world's most passionate lovers. Direct statements of affection such as *Kimi wo aishite iru* (I love you) and expressio nsof admiration such as *Kimi wa kirei da* (You are pretty) are, to Japanese men, *kizappoi* (affected). They

185

prefer to demonstrate their affection through actions and attitude, if at all. In letters, they may occasionally let themselves go and write some truly magnificent protestation of undying love like, *Kimi no koto wo tama ni omoi-dasu* (I think of you sometimes).

When they really get serious and begin thinking about marriage, they prefer to have a *nakōdo* (go-between) relay their wishes and emotions to the girl's parents, who will pass them—properly diluted, of course—on to the girl herself. If, however, circumstances are such that the men have to perform this irksome task for themselves, they pop the question in words like these:

Boku ni tsuite kite kuremasu ka? (Will you come along with me?) or *Kimi no mendo ga mitai* (I want to look after you).

A Brief Lexicon of Love

I. KANJI FOUNDATIONS

To aid the student in his comprehension of the Japanese language of love, I will first list seven *kanji* around which it has its foundations. Various derivative terms and their meanings are given under each of the seven.

1. 愛 = *ai, ito* = love, affection, beloved
ai suru = to love
itoshii = darling, pitiful
aiyō suru = to use habitually
aikō = a liking for
aibyō = pet cat
aikokushin = patriotism
aidoku = reading with pleasure

airashii = sweet, lovely
aijin = lover
aisai = beloved wife
aijō = love, affection
aiken = pet dog
aishō = name of endearment
aigo = loving protection

2. 恋 = *koi, ren* = love
koi suru = to be in love
koi-nyōbō = beloved wife
koiwazurai = lovesick
ren'ai = love, passion
koiji = romance
koinagusame = comforting the lovelorn
koishii = beloved

koibito = sweetheart
koijini = dying of love
ren'ai kekkon = love marriage in contrast with a *miai kekkon,* a marriage arranged after one meeting between the couple
koizukare = haggard from love
rembo = love, tender emotion

3. 好 = *kō* = to like; *su(ku)*, *su(ki)* = to be fond of, like, love; *yo(i)*, *i(i)* = good

kōshoku bungaku = pornography   *kōgakuka* = music lover

4. 性 = *sei* = sex, gender; *shō* = nature

sei-seikatsu = sex life   *sei kōi* = sex act
sei-teki = sexual   *sei-teki miryoku* = sex appeal
sei-kyōiku = sex education   *sei mondai* = sex problem
seibyō = venereal disease   *seiyoku* = sexual desire
seiki sūhai = phallicism   *seidōtoku* = sexual morality

5. 情 = *jō* = emotion, passion, affection, human nature; *nasake* = sympathy, compassion

jōfu = paramour   *jōji* = love affair
nasake-bukai = tenderhearted   *jōyoku* = carnal desires
jōnetsu = passion   *jōwa* = lovers' talk, love story

6. 色 = *shoku, shiki* = color; *iro* = color, look, sensual pleasure

iroppoi = amorous   *irozuku* = to be tinged with
irogoto = romance   *irome* = a passionate look
iro-kichigai = sex mania   *shikijō* = sexual passion
shikijōkyō = sex mania   *irobanashi* = love story
shikima = libertine   *irobumi* = love letter
irokezuku = to reach puberty   *irojikake* = pretended love

7. 慕 = *bo; shita(u)* = to yearn for, adore

bojō = longing   *boshin* = yearning
shitai-motomeru = to desire   *shitai-yorokobu* = to hold dear

II. JAPANESE LOVE TERMINOLOGY

The following list consists of words, phrases, sentences, and proverbial expressions that are of general interest and utility to the reader who, like the Student Prince, wishes to study love.

bonnō = carnal desire   *harigata* = a dildo; phallic tool
chijō ni oboreru = to be overcome   *hatsukoi* = first love
   with passion   *hitomebore suru* = to fall in love
dōsei suru = to live in sin together   at first sight

hore-gusuri = a love potion

horeru = to fall in love

iiyoru = to pay court to

itachi no michi-giri wo suru = to stop visiting one's mistress

jiyū-ren'ai = free love

josei-shiiku hō = rules about training women

joshi-inranshō = nymphomania

kakushi-onna wo koshiraeru = to form an illicit liaison with a woman

kampaku-nyōbō = a bossy wife

kamuro = a little girl who is employed in a brothel learning to be a prostitute

kannō wo manzoku saseru = to satisfy one's carnal desires

kanojo ni omoi wo yoseru = to take a fancy to her

Kanojo ni shūshin shite iru. = I'm gone on her.

Kanojo wa kare ni kubittake da. = She is stuck on him.

Kanojo wo netsubō shite iru. = I'm dying for her.

kōbiki = period in heat

kōtō no chimata = red-light district

kudoku = to woo (a girl)

kyūkon suru = to propose marriage

mekake = a kept woman; mistress

mekubase suru = to wink

midara na mōsō ni fukette iru = to be lost in lascivious thoughts

mikkai suru = to meet secretly

mikkaijo = a secret meeting place

mikudari-han = a letter of divorce

misomeru = to fall in love at first sight

netsuppoi metsuki = an amorous or suggestive glance

nikutai shōsetsu = sexy novel

nikuyoku no gonge = embodiment of lust

nyobon = a priest's clandestine romance (rare)

oiraku no koi = love affair between an old man and a young girl

onna-asari wo suru = to search for a woman

onna-deiri = troubles with women

onna wo sosonokasu = to entice a woman

rimbyō = gonorrhea (lit., the lonely disease)

rōraku shudan = measures of enticement

seishin-teki ren'ai = platonic love

seiyoku = sexual desire

shinshitsu no hiketsu = secrets of the boudoir

sukoburu-tsuki no bijin = a spanking-fine woman

teisō-tai = chastity belt

uguisu no tani-watari = a colloquialism meaning one man in bed with two women (lit., a nightingale jumping back and forth over a narrow valley)

yagō suru = to meet in the fields (for lustful purposes)

yuna = a prostitute at a public bathhouse

zakone suru = to sleep together in groups promiscuously (The three *kanji* with which this word is written are: miscellaneous, fish, sleeping.)

Chiwa-genka wa koi no iro-age = Every time lovers quarrel, their love increases.

Eiyū iro wo konomu = Great men are often womanizers.

Hito no koiji ni jama suru yatsu ga uma ni kerarete shinu ga ii = Anyone who interferes in another's love affair should be killed by the kick of a horse.

Sōkō no tsuma wo dō yori orosazu = Don't divorce your wife married in poverty.

Suezen kuwan wa otoko no haji = It is shameful for a man not to accept a woman's favors if they are offered to him.

[Inochi wo kakete] teisō wo mamori-nasai = Guard your chastity [with your life].

Tokaku ukiyo wa iro to sake = Who loves not wine and women remains a fool all his life.

Japanese Romance: Observations and Gleanings

1. Obviously, the male element is still in the ascendancy in Japan, despite inroads made since 1945. The man usually precedes the woman through doors; the girl frequently pays her own share on a date and sometimes the boy's as well; the girl is not escorted home very often and does not expect to be.

2. Being introduced properly is most important. The introducer becomes a go-between, a bearer of welcome and unwelcome messages, an arbiter of disputes, and sometimes the person responsible for arranging the terms of marriage—and of divorce.

3. Public displays of affection are frowned on. However, after dark petting couples can escape censuring looks by hieing off to public parks or to *dōhan-ten* ("companion" coffee shops).

4. If you get to her forty-five-yard line with an American girl, you still have a long, long way to go before you cross the goal. But with a Japanese girl, you have practically scored. In other words, getting a date with a Japanese girl is more than half the battle.

5. In some rural districts, the custom of *yobai* (night crawling) is still practiced. A country gallant wraps a towel around his head and after everyone is asleep, he crawls into the bedroom of one of the unattached women of the household, perhaps a distant cousin or a scullery maid. The towel is only a flimsy pretense at concealing the man's identity. If

the woman rebuffs his advances, she is supposed to pretend not to recognize him, thereby saving his face. Unfortunately, this fine old custom is dying out.

6. Here is another fine old country custom, but one that I hope is not too characteristic. This was reported in *Shūkan Manga Sandē* (Sunday Comic Weekly), and I will quote the magazine verbatim: *Yamanaka-ko no shūhen de wa, o-yome-san ga o-muko-san no uchi ni hairu toki, hi no ue wo tobi-koete iku to iu fūshū ga nokotte imasu. Kore wa amari kyokumō ga kōi to, jōzu ni seikōi ga itonamenai. Da kara kōi ke wo yaku to iu imi desu.* (Around Lake Yamanaka, when the bride enters the bridegroom's home, there is still the custom of having her jump over a fire. If her pubic hair is too thick, she cannot perform the sex act skillfully. Therefore, the purpose of this is to burn off the thick pubic hair).

7. Liaisons between older men and younger women are more common than in the U.S. Obviously, the older men are more likely to have money, and it is they who usually buy geisha from bondage and set up cabaret hostesses as their mistresses.

8. Japanese women are not as devoted to the abstract values of virtue and chastity as American women are—or were before the sexual revolution in the U.S. This is not the same, however, as saying that they are immoral or even amoral. Other social sanctions come into play and tend to accomplish the same ends.

9. The divorce rate, although increasing in the postwar era, is still very low in comparison with that in the U.S.

10. A recent survey taken among women of the *mizu-shōbai* (the world of bars, nightclubs, restaurants, etc.) showed that the men most likely to succeed in romantic adventures had the following qualifications, in this order of importance: *oshi* (push, nerve), *kane* (money), *sugata* (a [fine] figure).

11. In American romance, lovers quarrel, then kiss and make up. The process of kissing and making up follows a pattern: one of the two says something about being sorry and admits that maybe he (or she) might not have been completely right. The other then says about the same thing, and this is repeated until both are "very sorry" and "very wrong." End of fight.

Not so in Japan. It would, in fact, be disastrous for either party in a lovers' quarrel to admit any fault. The other would pounce on this confession and forever hold it like a sword over the opponent's head: "Remember last time? You said you were sorry, didn't you? You admitted you were wrong. Well, that just goes to show that I am usually right, just as I am this time!"

12. After a Japanese man has passed forty and has enough money to be able to afford one, he is often considered *hara ga chiisai* (small-stomached) and unworthy if he does not keep a mistress. Some men may keep *nigō-san* (mistresses) as status symbols while others may do so because they are very fond of their extra-marital sweethearts. In the traditional Japanese view, love and marriage are separate entities. Love is more often found outside than inside the marriage.

13. The weekly magazine *Shūkan Yomiuri* polled 9,500 men and women recently and found that sixty percent of the men wanted to have affairs with other women if they had a chance and that thirty percent more felt that they had to have such affairs, no matter what. Fifty-five percent of the married women polled stated that they would forgive their husbands if these affairs were of a temporary nature.

The preceding comments on mistress-keeping in Japan might cause some American men to want to drop everything and rush off to this best of all possible worlds. They should, however, read on a little further before buying airline tickets.

As Lord Chesterfield said of sexual congress, this business of mistress-keeping can be damnably expensive. Japanese women crave security, and when one does not get the security she desires from legitimate wedlock, she seeks a substitute in the form of a respectable bank balance. Her sometime cynicism is typified by the proverbial expression: *Koi wa koi de mo okane wo motte koi no koi da. Koi* means love and is also the imperative form of the verb *kuru,* to come. Roughly, this expression means, *"Koi"* (love) is all right, but I prefer the *"koi"* in *okane wo motte "koi"* (bring money).

When you break up with a mistress, she uses tears, hysteria, and threats of suicide to bring you to the bargaining table. What she wants, of course, is *isha-ryō* (consolation money) in a quantity large enough that she can buy a restaurant or build an apartment house or lease a tea shop. And, like a seasoned veteran of labor struggles, she thinks nothing of demanding that some poor clown with a monthly salary of $600 pay her $30,000 in *isha-ryō*.

A recent news story told of the president of a medium-sized company who decided to break up housekeeping with his mistress. She demanded ten million yen from him. He counteroffered with two million, but she refused to consider anything less than ten million.

With matters at this impasse, the man cut off all relations with his mistress and began spending more time with his legitimate wife, who lived in an apartment in one of Tōkyō's "mansions." Long before, however, the mistress had taken the key to this apartment from her patron's trousers one night and sent it out to have a duplicate made. Now this duplicate key stood her in good stead. She waited outside the apartment building for several nights until she saw her ex-patron and his wife go out one evening. Then, with the duplicate key, she let herself in, undressed, settled herself in a hot bath, and cut her wrists. Imagine the wife's surprise when she came home that night and found the body of a strange woman taking a blood bath in her bathtub.

One mistress episode that I witnessed concerns a Japanese friend of mine who lived with his legal wife near my house in Tōkyō. I must conceal his identity with the *kamei* (fictitious name) Ikeda. He kept an extremely jealous mistress whose given name was, I believe, Hisako.

Mr. Ikeda was in the habit of staying in his mistress's apartment two nights a week, and she became very upset if he varied at all from this schedule. Once, for some reason, he had not been to see her for a week and she was in a near-hysterical condition. I had a few drinks with Ikeda that Saturday night and he told me how she had been calling him at his office most of the week, urging him to visit her.

The next day was Sunday and I went out for an afternoon stroll. Passing near Ikeda's house, I decided to commit a breach of etiquette and drop in uninvited. Finding four of his relatives from the country there, I started to leave, but he insisted that I join them for a cup of tea. But no sooner was I introduced and seated than another visitor knocked at the door. Mr. Ikeda went to see who it was, and soon we heard a faint commotion and the sounds of a scuffle in the entranceway.

I was on my feet and about to go see if I could be of assistance when the door to the living room was shoved open and Ikeda's mistress burst in. (She had followed him home from the office one night that week to find out where he lived.) Without a word to any of us, she lay down on the floor, face up, and told Ikeda that she would not leave until he consented to come home with her.

The other guests and I began to mutter something about it being late and having to leave. Before we could get up, however, Mrs. Ikeda, who had been out in the kitchen preparing tea and cakes, came into the room with a well-laden tray and began to serve us.

I will always admire Mrs. Ikeda for her composure and *sang-froid* that day. She did not know and had never seen the woman lying on her living-room floor. Indeed, as it later transpired, she did not even know that her husband had a mistress. (He maintained the fiction of all-night *go* games.) But she knelt on the floor beside Hisako, put down the tray, bowed, and said *"Irasshaimase"* (Welcome). Then she placed a cup of tea and a tiny cake on the floor beside her husband's mistress, who was staring stubbornly at the ceiling, and said, *"Dōzo o-agari kudasai"* (Please have some). After that she retreated quietly into the kitchen. (Mr. Ikeda, however, said that she was not so quiet the next time the two were alone together.)

Shortly thereafter, the other guests and I made our exit together, leaving Hisako on the floor with her untasted cup of tea beside her and Mr. Ikeda looking rather forlorn on the other side of the room.

I have before me a clipping from a recent newspaper. It contains a letter submitted by a reader to the newspaper's *minoue sōdan* (consultation about personal affairs) column. This letter, in microcosm, gives, I think, a rather panoramic view of love in Japan. I translate the letter in its entirety:

"I am a twenty-one-year-old woman who was married only two months ago. After the arranged premarriage meeting, we did not see each other socially even once; I thought this was just like the old-fashioned marriages, and I did not feel much inclined to go through with it, but my mother was ailing, so I decided to get married quickly while she was still living. For that reason I did not look well at my husband-to-be's face, so I did not notice it then, but my husband's lips are bigger and thicker than those of ordinary people. He gets angry and tells me that I don't know how to kiss and don't know the pleasure of kissing, but I cannot bring myself to think of living my whole life with him, much less worry about kissing him.

"My husband's elder brother and his wife live near us. My mother became sick suddenly and I went to Nagoya to pay her a sick visit. When I returned, my brother-in-law scolded me, saying, 'You shouldn't go home every time your mother gets sick. You should think only of your husband.' I did not think that my brother-in-law had any right to say that to me, so, at last, I determined to get a divorce. I was two months pregnant and my husband knew it, but I had an abortion without telling him. Since we did not register our marriage, we can get a divorce any time. Now I shudder every time I look at my husband's face."

I don't think that this letter requires any comment except perhaps that I should explain that Japanese men and women, with the full knowledge and approval of their families, often begin living together as if legally married and do not register the marriage at the *kuyakusho* (ward office) until the wife is pregnant or until she is delivered of a normal baby.

The classic case of a malcontent mistress is that of Miss Sada Abe, an attractive woman thirty-one years old, who in 1936 found work as a maid in the Tōkyō *ryokan* of Mr. and Mrs. Kichizō Ishida. In addition to his wife, Mr. Ishida was already supporting a geisha named Koharu but this did not deter him from establishing carnal liaison with Sada (or O-Sada as she was called) within a few days of her arrival at his *ryokan*. Mrs. Ishida, normally a patient and forgiving woman, took a quick, instinctive dislike to our heroine and ran her out.

O-Sada gathered up her scanty belongings and retreated to a *machiai* (house of assignation) called the Masaki in Arakawa Ward, from which she telephoned Kichizō. The lovers were soon reunited, and in their excess of joy they spent the next six days and nights in one long embrace, interrupted only by minimal food, drink, and sleep. One of the Masaki maids was aghast to see that the couple would not break away from each other even when she entered to serve their meals. Another maid expressed her envy at the depth of their mutual and obvious passion.

About eight o'clock on the morning of the eighteenth of May, O-Sada told the maids that she was going out for a short while and that they should let Kichizō sleep late. At noon, however, O-Sada had not returned, and there was still no sign of life in the room where she and Kichizō had performed their sex marathon.

One of the maids finally decided to ask Kichizō if he wanted lunch. A minute later she came tumbling down the stairs screaming. When the police arrived, they found that Kichizō Ishida had been strangled to death with a woman's sash of pink crepe.

But what shocked the hardened policemen of the tough Arakawa Ward was the mutilation visited on Kichizō's body by the passionate O-Sada. On his left thigh, she had written in blood four *kanji* reading *Sada Kichi futari* (O-Sada and Kichizō, we two). Into his left arm she had carved the character for *Sada*. Then, dipping again into the blood flowing from Kichizō, she had written on the sheet in large, bold strokes, *Sada Kichi futari-kiri* (O-Sada and Kichizō, we two alone).

The source of the blood? She had cut off his penis with a butcher knife.

Her crime captured the interest of the nation. It was, in fact, not entirely unwelcome because it contributed largely to relieving the oppressive tension of the three months following the *Ni-ni-roku Jiken* (the assassinations of February 26, 1936).

Three days later the police found O-Sada staying in the Shinagawa-kan, an inn in Takanawa, under the name of Owada Nao. The police had glanced through the *ryokan* register during a routine inspection and had been on the point of leaving when the attention of Detective Andō was drawn to the alias O-Sada had chosen. Nao is an unusual given name, one of the few that could be taken either by a man or a woman.

A sixth sense instructed Andō to check. He knocked at O-Sada's door and said, *"Keisatsu no mono da ga ..."* (I'm from the police ...).

As he entered, O-Sada, after the fashion of so many Japanese criminals, attempted no further evasion and told him openly: *"Ara, keijisan? Go-kurōsama desu. Watashi wa O-Sada desu. O-tesū wo kakemashite sumimasen deshita"* (Oh, Mr. Detective! Thank you for your efforts. I am O-Sada. I'm really sorry to have caused you trouble).

When the detective opened O-Sada's *furoshiki-tsutsumi* (a bundle wrapped in a cloth), he found Kichizō's underwear and personal belongings but not the one object without which Kichizō could not go to his grave a complete corpse. When asked its whereabouts, O-Sada withdrew it, wrapped in paper, from her bosom, where she had carried and cherished it for the three days since her heinous deed. Asked why she had decided to take such a memento, she answered without blush or hesitation that it was the thing that held for her the fondest memories.

Back at headquarters, O-Sada gave the police complete cooperation and told her story in fine detail. She made no attempt to spare herself. If anything, she seemed pleased with what she had done. Her motive? She simply did not want to share Kichizō with any other woman.

One of the detectives wanted to know how O-Sada, a slight, willowy woman, could have strangled Kichizō Ishida, a man with a strong physique. She explained that in the throes of their lovemaking she and Kichizō had discovered that if she applied a brief pressure around his throat and then suddenly released her grip, the resurgence of the temporarily obstructed blood through his body increased the size of his phallic weapon and enhanced their pleasure. She had done this to him so many times that he was not at all suspicious when she substituted the pink sash for her hands. O-Sada had assumed the *chausu* (female-on-top) position and, with the moment of supreme bliss imminent, she twined the pink sash around his neck. Then, instead of releasing the pressure at the right time, she pulled the sash tighter with all her strength. Kichizō may have died of surprise, if not of pleasure.*

In addition to the crimes of murder and corpse mutilation, the prosecution charged O-Sada with sexual perversion. Upon hearing this, she became incensed and immediately demanded legal counsel—about which she had been indifferent until then—to defend her from this cruel accusation. At length the court called in a psychiatrist, who examined O-Sada and concluded that she was not a *hentai seiyokusha* (a sex pervert) but only an *ijō seiyokusha* (an oversexed person). She appeared satisfied with this vindication.

Throughout her trial, O-Sada maintained that, although she did not ask Kichizō this question specifically, there was no doubt in her mind that he would have been thoroughly pleased to meet his fate in that manner. Whether or not the judges placed any credence in her avowal is difficult to determine, but they did hand down a mild sentence of only six years in prison.

One day not long after World War II, a Japanese friend and I were strolling down a street in Atami when she broke into giggles and then pointed out to me the *ryokan* in which O-Sada was then working. I hurried off down the street, casting nervous glances over my shoulder.

Japanese wives still use the *Abe Sada Jiken* (Sada Abe Affair) to frighten errant husbands with. During the Occupation, there was one Japanese girl who, resentful of the pending arrival of her American lover's wife, performed the same amputation on him that O-Sada did on Kichizō. Still another, somewhat more merciful, waited till her American boyfriend fell asleep on their last night together and, instead of cutting it off, painted it with red fingernail polish. (If not a manicure or a pedicure, then a phallicure?) The next morning the boyfriend, still groggy from excessive sex and whiskey and bleary eyed from lack of sleep, bade his mistress a hurried farewell and rushed off to the airport at Haneda to meet the plane his American wife was due to arrive on. From there he took his wife directly to a downtown hotel, where he felt obliged to pretend that he had been without sexual release since their last time together, long months before. When I heard him tell this story later, he said he was just as surprised as she was when they got down to bare facts. He was so surprised that he could not think of a

*Evidence from observers' accounts of executions by hanging supports the idea that choking does indeed produce such startling erotic effects. Kichizō's fate, however, probably deterred seekers of unusual thrills from attempting this particular form of gratification, at least with a jealous mistress in the role of playful garroter.

plausible explanation or, indeed, of any explanation. His wife flew back to the U.S. that evening and he was soon reunited with his Japanese mistress.

CHAPTER 24

Is the Game Worth the Candle?

"Fluent in Japanese"

I have heard it said that we Americans are the world's worst linguists—
and this makes me angry. I don't think that we are the world's worst at
all. The Australian bushmen (many of whom still have not recognized
the cause-and-effect relationship between coition and pregnancy) and
the Hottentots of Africa are worse than we are.

In Japan, however, we may very well deserve the title of the world's
worst, there being no bushmen or Hottentots around to give us competition. I have found that most Americans in Japan can be characterized
by one of the following attitudes:

"If the Japanese want to talk to me, they'll have to learn English."

"Why learn Japanese when I can always hire an interpreter?"

"I'm not going to be here that long."

"Our kids can speak perfect Japanese, so they can talk to the maid
for us."

"I took Japanese lessons for six months, two nights a week, and I
can speak the language fluently."

I remember once sitting for long hours aboard a Japan-bound airplane
next to an Englishman who had lived in Japan for twenty-one years. After
much dialogue about things Japanese, it became apparent that he did
not know the language at all. My involuntary look of surprise prompted
him to explain: "When I came to Japan, learning Japanese just wasn't
considered the thing to do."

Whereas the British may be suspicious of linguistic ability, associating
it, according to Anthony Burgess, with spies, impresarios, waiters, and
Jewish refugees, I believe that we Americans have a genuine admiration
for it but that we, like small children, simply have no concept of what
is actually involved. To us, a foreign language is still basically something
that we dabble in while in high school and college, something that may
help us read a menu in Paris or buy a trinket in Acapulco, or bargain
for a piece of the True Cross in Rome (if only we could think of the

Italian words for "true" and "cross"!). We are steeped in a body of adventure stories, fables, and legends that tell us of Yankee Clipper captains who picked up Cantonese—chop-chop—while in a Chinese port for repairs, and of American businessmen who learn enough Arabic in three months of night school in New York to run rings around the shrewd traders of the Middle East, and of one woman I have always admired in particular, Phoebe, the adult heroine of Clarence Buddington Kelland's *Arizona*—whose Spanish "just came to her" after a few months in Arizona Territory.

As a people, we have not been able to face up to the grim realization that the learning of a foreign language—especially one of the twenty-nine "hard languages" designated by the State Department—is a project that will most probably take years of solid study in school and more years of frequent daily usage in various theaters of experience in the country where the language is spoken.

But, whatever the attitudes and causes, the incontrovertible fact remains that although hundreds of thousands of Americans have actually lived in Japan since the close of World War II in 1945 (these, together with tourists, total well over one million!), I know of less than ten who are fluent—truly fluent—in Japanese. And, even granting that all my years of residence (in Fukuoka, Kōbe, Ōsaka, Yokosuka, Kamakura, and Tōkyō) and my special interest in the subject of Japan experts and linguists may not have uncovered all such Americans, I doubt that there are more than fifteen or twenty who could have escaped my notice. Altogether, I would guess that there are no more than twenty adult Caucasian Americans now in Japan who could accurately be called fluent in spoken and written Japanese.

And yet to hear some persons tell it, every third American you meet in Japan is "fluent in Japanese." Even reputable publications are guilty of perpetuating this false impression. In my files, I find fourteen newspaper reports, casually clipped in recent years for various reasons, each of which describes a particular American in Japan as being fluent in Japanese. I happen to know nine of these fourteen—only one is even close to being fluent in Japanese. Three of the nine have vocabularies of less, I am sure, than one hundred words.

Like "damnyankee" in the old South, fluent in Japanese has become a *kimari-monku* (cliché) and does a serious disservice to the deserving few when used—as it usually is—promiscuously. (Like Coleridge, I hold that "Praises of the unworthy are felt by ardent minds as robberies of the deserving.")

We seldom ever come across descriptions like: "fairly good in Japanese," "She speaks good Japanese but cannot read the *kanji*," "His Japanese is not good enough for technical discussions," etc., etc. It's either "fluent in Japanese" or no mention at all.

The reasons for this situation are readily apparent. Fellow Americans who make or bruit about such judgments are seldom qualified to do so. The same persons would not consider grading the qualifications of a specialist in cybernetics or eutelegenesis, but they hesitate not an instant in making sweeping determinations about the Japanese language ability of other foreigners. (I wish I had ten yen for every American parent who has told me about his child who speaks Japanese "just like a native." I have met many of those children and I would return all those ten-yen coins one hundredfold the day I meet one who is even one tenth as good as his advance publicity proclaims.)

Testing Linguistic Ability

To be accurately judged fluent in Japanese, I believe that a foreigner should have the following qualifications:

1) He should be able to conduct all his daily affairs (business, visits to the doctor, TV-ing, bar-hopping, lovemaking, etc.) completely in Japanese without strain.

2) His accent may not be perfect, but it should occasion no confusion or merriment among his listeners.

3) He should be able to read Japanese (newspapers, weekly magazines, and letters in the semicursive *gyōsho* style), with only an occasional reference to a dictionary.

But then who is to judge? On the professional level, what is needed is a test, conducted perhaps under the auspices of a reputable language school or, for U.S. citizens, the U.S. embassy, or the Mombushō (Ministry of Education), to accurately judge the ability of anyone who seriously wishes to acquire a reputation as a Japanese linguist. The test results should be made public or, at least, be placed on open file. The test should be given yearly. A committee of Japanese and foreign educators and linguists could devise the test and the grading system. Offhand, I would say that the test, which might take from eight to sixteen hours, should require the person being examined to:

1. Translate a newspaper article.

2. Speak in Japanese on the telephone, as a test of accent.

3. Write a letter in Japanese.

4. Interpret a taped conversation between two Japanese.

5. Comprehend a newscast.

6. Identify five major dialects.

7. Read a letter written in *gyōsho*.

8. Take a dictation test involving the writing of fifty *kanji* from among the *Tōyō Kanji* and give the principal readings of each.

9. Give the meanings of one hundred technical words or phrases (twenty each from the fields of medicine, law, economy, science, and the arts), to be selected by the testing committee as being readily understood by the average Japanese college graduate.

10. Walk down the street and read the first twenty signs to be sighted.

11. Give a ten-minute, impromptu talk about an everyday topic of conversation (sports, politics, travel, traffic, etc.), the topic to be selected by lottery.

The results of the test could be graded alphabetically, e.g., AAA would be the rating of persons scoring 95 or better, on a 100-point basis, followed by AA, A, B, C, D, E, F, FF, and FFF.

As the scores became known, we might begin to enjoy a degree of accuracy in reports about linguistic ability. One newspaper might report: "W.K. Nichoson, an AAA Japanese linguist, returned yesterday from a trip to Ishigakijima ..." A friend might say: "You remember Mrs. Karbonkle, the correspondent's wife, don't you? The one who they say is so good in Japanese? Well, she got an FF rating on last month's language test." And we might see an advertisement like this: "Leading American manufacturer seeks mature American for job as Japan Representative. Must have A or better language rating. Knowledge of dildo market also desirable."

Aside from the casual satisfaction (or disappointment) you might receive from learning that you are better than (or not as good as) so-and-so, such a system would provide vital data to would-be employers in all fields, many of whom have been painfully stung in the past after hiring foreigners whose actual ability in Japanese turned out to be many notches below their self-stated ability.

A classmate of mine, Jerry Worth, was once Personnel Officer at the Oppama Ordnance Depot, south of Yokohama. In this position, he often interviewed Americans (mostly ex-servicemen) who wanted jobs at the depot so that they could remain in Japan to be near their trueloves or Mt. Fuji or whatever it was they were hooked on. Worth, who is a famed raconteur, relates the language part of a typical interview as follows:

WORTH: Now, Mr. Jovet, tell me about your knowledge of the Japanese language. You realize, don't you, that it's important in this job? You would have a lot of Japanese working for you in the paint shed.

APPLICANT: Yessir. Well, I'll tell you, I've been stationed out here for three years and I got pretty good in Japanese, if I do say so myself.

WORTH: I'm glad to hear it. I suppose that means you can read *kanji.* How many do you know?

APPLICANT: How many what, sir?

WORTH: How many *kanji?*

APPLICANT: *Kan*-uh-*ji?*

WORTH: That's right.

APPLICANT: Uh, what are *kanji,* sir?

WORTH: The ideographs.

APPLICANT: Huh?

WORTH: Come now, Mr. Jovet. You know what I mean—the *kanji,* the characters. What the Japanese write.

APPLICANT: Oh, them.

WORTH (aside): Amazing.

APPLICANT: Well, I'll tell you, sir. I don't exactly know how to write them *kanji.*

WORTH: I see. All right, never mind that. I suppose that what you meant was that you can speak Japanese.

APPLICANT (brightening): Yessir. I think I can handle their lingo pretty good.

WORTH: Fine. Now say for me, "A bird was singing in my garden at two o'clock this morning."

APPLICANT: "A bird was singing in my ..."

WORTH: No, no, no! Say it in Japanese.

APPLICANT: Huh? Oh, yeah, I see. O.K. Hmn ... *Yūbe sanji,* no, *niji ... niwatori?* uh ... *hanashita.*

WORTH: What you have just said, Mr. Jovet, is that a chicken spoke at two o'clock last evening.

APPLICANT: Heh, heh, heh. Yeah, maybe I ... Say, you sure do know this lingo, don't you, Mr. Worth? How did you ever ...

WORTH: Never mind that. We're discussing *your* ability in Japanese.

And so on.

Japan Area-and-Language Specialists

If we accept as reasonably accurate my postulate that there are extremely few Americans in Japan who can speak and read Japanese fluently, then it should follow that there is a strong and steady demand for their services. Unfortunately, this is not so. There is little demand at all. To examine the reasons behind this anomaly would require probing in depth certain basic American attitudes, which is outside the scope of this book. Suffice it to say here that we have a repetitive cause-effect-cause cycle in operation: there are so few Japan area-and-language specialists that no one tries to utilize the few who exist, either having never heard of such creatures or believing that the breed is so scarce that their efforts would be futile in any case. Since they do not try, there is no demand. There being no demand, few feel justified in undertaking to enter or pursue the profession.

Another powerful influence militating against the development and utilization of these specialists is the refusal on the part of many influential Americans in Japan to admit their value. In most cases, such admissions would be tantamount to confessions of inadequacy in their own jobs. Self-preservation is a strong instinct, indeed.

The indisputable fact is that a thorough knowledge of the Japanese language and culture is important to most jobs in Japan, whether the job holder sells or buys, teaches or preaches, interprets or entertains. Of those Americans in Japan without this knowledge, some have failed utterly, whatever their jobs, while others have done only tolerable work. But even those who are believed to have done good jobs could most likely have done better—much better—with sound area-and-language knowledge.

As discussed in the opening chapter, language frustration is a very real problem for foreigners in Japan. An abyss of incomprehension separates the Japanese and American people—and it is deeper on our side. Language is the only possible bridge over this abyss, the one essential tool we must have to dig out the other necessary knowledge. Crossing over the abyss is like coming out of a deep, dark cavern into the light of high noon. The difference between living in Japan with a knowledge of Japanese and without this knowledge is like, as the Japanese would say, the difference between the moon and a terrapin *(tsuki to suppon hodo chigau)*; it is like being in another world. Explaining this difference to the unknowing is akin to describing color to a person born blind.

Even an AAA language rating in Japanese would not, by any means, guarantee that a man hired for a job in Japan would perform well. He should have a broad knowledge of other facets of Japan, beginning with those that have direct bearing on his work. We should recognize, however, that much general knowledge often accompanies sound linguistic knowledge. The process of acquiring the language usually entails various other knowledge-productive experiences. Obviously, this man should also have those qualities you would expect in any responsible manager, such as intelligence, honesty, and drive. And he should have something else which is very important—a capacity for tolerance and understanding, an empathy, a willingness to at least consider causes of dissension from the Japanese viewpoint as well as from our own.

For those who decide to become Japan area-and-language specialists, there are a number of fields of endeavor where they might put their training and knowledge to income-producing use, e.g., the diplomatic service, missionary work, entertainment, writing, interpreting and translation, newspaper jobs, representing American companies in Japan, working for Japanese companies, and U.S. government and military jobs.

I have worked in a Japanese company (not a joint venture, which is somewhat different) and I would advise against taking this route. To begin with, there are few such jobs. Occasionally a foreigner will become an adviser or *shokutaku* to a Japanese company and spend a few hours there each week, writing English letters or teaching the staff members English, but I refer to full-time, regular employment. I was kindly treated during the years I worked for a Japanese company, but I nevertheless advise against such employment because it is difficult for a foreigner, especially an American, to adjust himself to certain basic Japanese attitudes about the company-employee relationship. It is one thing to understand these attitudes; it is quite another to live with them permanently.

Teaching in Japan could be a fruitful experience, depending on the conditions and location of the school, but only for two or three years. The chances for advancement are restricted, and the job security does not usually extend beyond a short-term contract.

Many American and other foreign entertainers come to Japan these days, but nearly all of them are engaged for brief periods only. These persons do not, of course, need to know any Japanese. I can think of only a very few American entertainers who have been active in Japan for longer periods: two or three women who have occasionally played small parts in movies or TV plays, a part-time band leader, a Eurasian MC who sings, and perhaps one or two others. Their reception is not encouraging. Someday a Japanese-speaking American with a certain appeal or physical comeliness will come along and make his or her fortune in Japanese movies or TV, as Sessue Hayakawa made his in the Hollywood of several decades ago. But the right combination of talent, appearance, and language ability has not yet appeared.

Jobs with the American newspapers and wire services in Japan should be a field worth exploring. The work should be interesting, and it is definitely of vital importance. A knowledge of Japanese would seem to be essential, but of the twelve or fifteen correspondents I have met in the Tōkyō Press Club, only one (a grade B linguist) could do much work in Japanese. Also, I have observed that the correspondents come and go with disturbing frequency. One of them explained to me that a correspondent's low wages and Tōkyō's outrageously high costs do not make for a long and happy relationship.

Writing—free-lance writing of novels, stories, articles, etc.—is a field in which there is a desperate need for persons really familiar with the Japanese scene. That happy combination of an ability to write well and a knowledge of Japan has not come along in the postwar years. Some successful books have been written by authors who know very little about Japan, and some unsuccessful books have been written by authors who know a lot about Japan. But the successful book and the knowledgeable author are still groping about in the dark trying to find each other.

Some Americans have gone into business for themselves in Japan, in such fields as import-export, advertising, travel services, and so forth. A few manage restaurants, shops, and bars. The restaurant managers appear to have been financially successful. And I have often wondered about a chain of small, semi-Japanese-style hotels, away from the population centers, and managed by American couples. But unless the business is one that earns foreign exchange or contributes to Japan's technological or intellectual advance, getting a visa would be a problem.

The missionaries are a group that I admire—linguistically, at least. Most of them appear to get at least one year of intensive language training, which is more than people get in any of the other professions under examination. One point in favor of this work is that the churches allow them to remain in Japan for many years, so that they at least have the opportunity to become expert in things Japanese. Entry into this field, obviously, requires a certain personal conviction and inclination.

For years after the close of World War II, jobs with the U.S. government, including the military establishment, were the best—indeed, almost the only—way to live in Japan. But, with the passing years, such jobs have become fewer in number and smaller in importance. To begin now to prepare for a career in this field (aside from the State Department) would not be wise.

A few years back I knew of two ex-classmates of mine who were working in Japan as interpreter-translators. I have since lost track of them— and know of no others, although there may be a few. The profession is not sufficiently rewarding monetarily, particularly in view of the arduous study and broad knowledge these people are required to possess. Additionally, for most chores, Japanese competition is available at fairly reasonable rates of compensation, but simultaneous interpreters are expensive—and scarce. (The position of the verb at the end of a Japanese sentence makes simultaneous interpretation from Japanese to English practically an impossibility.)

Sometimes we see the names of American translators on the dust jackets of translations of Japanese novels and stories, but I wonder how many of these make their living entirely from this work. I suspect that it is mostly a labor of love. Edward Seidensticker, a well-known and capable translator, is now a U.S. college professor—and I believe he was engaged in other income-producing activities even while he was translating in Japan. One technique employed in such translations (not Seidensticker's, of course) is that a Japanese first translates the work in question into rough English and then has an American polish it. The two share the translator's royalties. Sometimes the Japanese takes the lion's share of the fee but lets the name of his American assistant appear on the cover as sole translator.

The diplomatic service is the field where there should be room for dozens—even hundreds—of Japan area-and-language specialists since it has the responsibility for most of our official relations with Japan. But, unfortunately, the U.S. Department of State does not employ many such specialists and, what is worse, it does not even appear to be at all eager to acquire any more. Its antiquated system of personnel selection, development, and management is the cause of this regrettable situation. The specific policies at fault are: 1) the State Department will not permit its Foreign Service Officers to remain in any one country long enough to become expert in the affairs and conditions of that country for fear of "localism"; 2) except for rare lateral-entry appointees, it will not hire persons over thirty-one years of age as FSO's; 3) it is concerned almost entirely with the projection of its own image of America in foreign countries instead of the absorption, interpretation, and transmission home of foreign events, trends, and intelligence on which to base reasonable, realistic foreign policy; and 4) it will not permit its diplomatic personnel to marry citizens of Japan.

This last policy takes us dangerously close to the brink of madness. I suspect that the authorities responsible for this massive fatuity are guilty of what former Senator Fulbright has called the "arrogance of power"—and what I like to think of as a monolithic body of self-assumed racial superiority so deep-dyed and so misguided as to be incapable of comprehending, much less acting in proper accordance with, what is really a very simple—yet very true—proposition: to wit, that an important portion of the duties of most American diplomats in Japan requires a knowledge and understanding of the country, the culture, and the language—and that marriage to a Japanese is a legitimate means of acquiring such knowledge and deepening such understanding. To deliberately place out of the reach of our diplomats one of the most efficacious methods of area-and-language familiarization is a ludicrously irrational act that probably stems from both the above-mentioned presumption of racial superiority and a semiconscious yearning to emulate the Victorian concept of a pukka sahib.

In fact, I believe that those responsible for these policies are actually guilty of a lack of faith and confidence in our country. In their overweening and evident efforts to set up barriers that separate our diplomats from meaningful contacts with foreign peoples and cultures, they are, I believe, unwittingly revealing their own doubts about the fundamental worth of the American way of life. In effect, they seem to be telling our Foreign Service Officers: "Don't get too close to those foreigners, boys. You might find that you like their ways better than ours—and we don't want that to happen."

In American annals, the case of ex-Ambassador to Japan Edwin Reischauer was a rare exception. First of all, he was not a career diplomat; he did not rise through the ranks of the FSO's. Second, he was appointed to his post long after his Japanese wife had acquired her U.S. citizenship. Even so, for the U.S. to send a Japanese-speaking (Grade AAA, I believe) ambassador to Japan was so revolutionary that the Japanese were dumbfounded. "Who ever heard of such a thing! The Americans must have something sinister in mind! Just imagine sending a Japanese-speaking diplomat to Japan," the incredulous Japanese might well have thought. But after the initial shock wore off, they became immensely pleased. The nation was wreathed in figurative smiles. Reischauer could have knifed a farm boy on the streets in broad daylight (instead of vice versa, as was the actual case) and the Japanese public would have found a way to interpret the affair in their hero's favor. (Perhaps as a well-intentioned demonstration of American-style street fighting and knifemanship for the edification of Japanese youth?)

Anyway, if you are under thirty-one and can resign yourself to not spending much of your career in Japan and never marrying a Japanese citizen—or even ever getting very close to one—then perhaps you should consider the diplomatic service.

The field with the greatest potential for Japanese-speaking Americans is that of representing U.S. companies in Japan. Many hundreds of such companies now require the services of Japan representatives, and this number should increase as the Japanese remove the lingering restrictions on the free entry of American investment capital and technology. Although employment conditions vary with the company, the average emoluments are the highest of those under scrutiny here. A few companies may be hampered by hidebound tradition or myopic management, but most are willing to make policy decisions or changes quickly to adjust to new markets or business conditions. There is no nonsense among these companies about transferring employees periodically so that they will not lose their American point of view or not letting their employees marry Japanese citizens.

But even here, all is not light and laughter. The principal fault to be found with such companies is that when they decide to establish a Japan branch, they tend to select their Japan managers from within their own ranks, without trying to add any Japan area-and-language specialists to the payroll. Many operate on the humorous principle that a man who can sell soap in Hoboken can sell soap in Japan too. Others appear to regard the Japan branch as pre-retirement pasture—a good place to send old Jim Brown, who still has three years remaining before retirement and who is beginning to get in their hair around the home office.

It is, however, difficult to assign much blame to these companies, many of whom have never operated in the Orient. Many may feel a vague uneasiness when they decide to transfer the manager of their Chicago office to Japan, but what choice do they have? They may never have heard of Japan area-and-language specialists or, if they have, they might not know how to go about finding one. Admittedly, this is a difficult task, there being so few.

What happens with tragic frequency is that the company interested in doing business in Japan sends a vice-president there on an exploratory mission and then he returns to the U.S. to delight his cronies with tales about "Ginza secretaries" and Turkish baths, but with little data of value to the establishment of the branch or proposed joint venture in Japan. Then the company decides to send Joe Mucklehead from their San Diego office out to Japan to actually start the business. The next two years witness a steady parade of comic errors, costly mistakes, incredible confusion, and skull-binding frustrations. But God must look after drunkards, little children, and American innocents abroad, because Joe's kind sometimes manage to muddle through—after a fashion.

Although Joe is still countless light-years away from being a Japan specialist, he may have learned a few ground rules that will help him survive until more significant apperception begins to seep through. But at this point, Joe's wife decides that she can't take it any longer, being away from real supermarkets and corner drugstores and other such wonderful places, so she tearfully pleads with Joe to return to the U.S. Joe sends an SOS to the home office, who beat their breasts and cry a lot, but finally they write for him to return to San Diego. The next time the company sends the manager of their Charleston office to Japan, and the sideshow is repeated—with new performers but the same script.

Disadvantages and Future Hopes

Before bringing this book to a close, I feel that I must make mention of one disadvantage in becoming really fluent in Japanese. Although I still believe that the advantages far outweigh this disadvantage, I would not have been completely candid with you if I did not bring it to your attention. First, an illustrative incident:

One day long ago, I rode from Tōkyō to Ōsaka in the *tembōsha* (observation car) of one of the limited-express trains. The *tembōsha* of that time was like a living room, with wall-to-wall carpeting and easy chairs that could be moved about. On that particular day, I was seated in the middle of the car with four American tourists and one Japanese man in front of me and with two Japanese men behind me. The American tourists were two couples who were making their first visit to Japan and the Japanese man seated near them was soon telling them in English about the places we were passing and answering their questions about Japan. Since I was seated next to these two couples, this Japanese man evidently assumed that I was either a member of their party or another American tourist traveling alone, because he addressed his remarks to me as well and I was soon drawn into the general conversation.

He introduced himself to us as, let us say, Mr. Dōmen, the president of a large company that makes a kind of food seasoning. He told us that he graduated from an American university—and that he had crossed the Pacific twenty-eight times. (This latter bit of incidental intelligence wrung oohs and aahs from the tourists.) He spoke English very well, of course, and he was most friendly and charming. Well before we were halfway to Ōsaka, he had issued a blanket invitation for all of us to visit him at his home in Tōkyō when we returned there from the Ōsaka-Kyōto area.

In preparation for this trip, I had packed a book I wanted very much to read, and I had boarded the train hoping to be able to finish it on the way to Ōsaka. I was not, therefore, at all eager to enter into this conversation between Mr. Dōmen and the tourists but, once drawn in, I was content to listen and nod and reply amicably when spoken to.

Even so, I must admit that Mr. Dōmen addressed at least half of his remarks to me. He had been so busy telling us about Japan that he had asked us little more than our names and where we came from in the U.S. Seeing that I was traveling alone, he also asked me if I was married. When I answered that I was not, he seemed more eager than ever for me to visit his Tōkyō home. He said that his niece, who lived with him and his wife, was leaving soon to study in the U.S. and he asked what college I had attended. I told him, and then he said that he very much wanted a younger American like myself (the two couples were in their fifties) to tell his niece about present-day American college life, that his own experiences in an American university were too dated to be of much value now.

Shortly before we sighted Nagoya Castle from the train window, coffee was served and our conversation came to a temporary halt. During this interval, one of the Japanese men behind me tapped me on the shoulder. When I turned toward him, he gestured to me that he needed a match. I had an extra pack, which I gave him, saying, *"Mada arimasu kara dōzo o-mochi kudasai"* (I have more, so please keep these). This gentleman appeared quite surprised at finding that I could speak Japanese. He brightened and immediately struck up an animated conversation with me.

Mr. Dōmen must have seen us talking because he came walking back from his chair opposite the two couples, evidently thinking that we were having trouble understanding each other and intending to lend us a helping hand. Then, when he was near enough to hear me speaking Japanese, an angry expression came over his face and he turned abruptly and stalked back to his seat.

Throughout the rest of the trip, Mr. Dōmen never addressed another word to me. He continued his English explanation of Japan to the four tourists and, toward the end of the trip, he repeated his invitation for them to visit him in Tōkyō. He was giving them his address and instructions for finding his home as I walked past them to get off at Ōsaka. He did not even glance at me.

I was quite busy for the next few days in Ōsaka and gave no thought to the incident, but on the train back to Tōkyō I rode in the same observation car, which brought it to mind. I had obviously offended Mr. Dōmen somehow and I wondered if I had suddenly developed bad breath.

Back in Tōkyō, I happened to visit my Japanese landlady on other business the next day and I asked her for her interpretation of Mr. Dōmen's abrupt *volte-face*. (She was an apperceptive woman whose family was one of Japan's five major *zaibatsu* [financial combines] and I had often sought her counsel.) She was quite definite in her analysis of this case. Mr. Dōmen, she said, was obviously one of those many Japanese who understandably want to show foreign visitors only the best side of Japan. When he heard me speaking Japanese, he knew that I was not a tourist, that I must already be familiar with what she called the *abata* (pockmarks) on the face of Japan. Inviting me to visit his home with four tourists might undermine his efforts. I might question some of his statements in front of them, or I might later tell them a somewhat modified version of his account of Japan's wonders and glories.

Incidents like this have prompted the formulation of Seward's Third Law: *The more fluent a foreigner becomes in the Japanese language (1) the more he will tend to be avoided by many Westernized Japanese and (2) the more ordinary Japanese will expect him to abide by their customs and conduct himself, in general, as a Japanese would.*

Article 2 of Seward's Third Law is suggested by what happened to Lafcadio Hearn while he was teaching school in Matsue, where, as a foreign teacher, his salary was considerably larger than that of comparable Japanese teachers. Hearn was still in the passionate throes of his romance with Japan and had some time before applied for Japanese citizenship. Finally, one grand day, his request was granted and his citizenship papers arrived. A week later, however, he received notification from the Ministry of Education that, in consideration of the change in his citizenship status, his salary henceforth would be reduced to the level of that of native teachers.... Some hold that Hearn's disenchantment with Japan began that day.

But we don't have to dig that far into the past to discover evidences of the workings of Article 2 of Seward's Third Law. Look around you. Watch the policeman wave a non-Japanese-speaking foreigner on when the same violation would have got one fluent in Japanese hauled into the station. Observe how an office clerk or a shopgirl will walk a city block in a heavy downpour to set a bewildered tourist on the right road but barely condescend to tell a foreigner fluent in Japanese the time of day. Notice how the American whose Japanese vocabulary is limited to *sukoshi, takusan,* and *dame* has magnificent success in his romances with Japanese girls while one fluent in Japanese is thwarted at every turn by carping insistence that he show proper respect for the concepts of *giri, on,* and *ninjō,* that he demonstrate an *otoko-rashii sekinin-kan,* which is really nothing more than another way of saying, "You should do what I say you should." I could mention more, but emotion overcomes me.

To return to the question asked in the title of this chapter: Is the game worth the candle?

At times I seriously wonder. But I have fond hopes for the future— at least, for your future. I believe that the day will come when there will be a widespread realization of the value—indeed, of the necessity—for many well-trained Japan area-and-language specialists, when training programs for their development will exist in adequate size and number, when most American organizations in Japan—whether private or official, whether commercial or religious—will have a place for at least one such specialist among their top management, and when they will be adequately compensated for their long, arduous training. I hope—for the sake of those who are serious students of Japan—that this day will soon come.

But in terms of personal satisfaction, I can answer my question in the affirmative. The pleasure has been in the learning, in the dawning of comprehension, in viewing the same scene through new and clearer eyes, in being able to live in and enjoy two worlds instead of one.

The decision, of course, is yours. You should know that the path will not be easy—but things of genuine value are seldom acquired easily. If you determine to become truly fluent in Japanese, may good fortune attend you. May you have the stamina to sustain you across the plateaus of tedium and seemingly little progress, and through the swamps of indifference and misunderstanding. May you reap material rewards aplenty. May you enjoy the game, despite its frustrations, as much as I have.

Index

The "weathermark"
identifies this book as a production of
John Weatherhill, Inc.
publishers of fine books on Asia and the Pacific
Book design by Ronald V. Bell
Composition by Korea Textbook Company, Seoul
Printing by Kenkyusha Printing Company, Tokyo
Binding by Makoto Binderies, Tokyo
The typeface used is Monotype Times New Roman